RETURN TO ZION

University of Nebraska Press

LINCOLN

RETURN TO ZION
THE HISTORY OF MODERN ISRAEL

-ERIC GARTMAN-

The Jewish Publication Society

PHILADELPHIA

All rights reserved. Published by the University of Nebraska Press
as a Jewish Publication Society book.
Manufactured in the United States of America.

Library of Congress Cataloging-in-Publication Data

Gartman, Eric, 1975–, author.
Return to Zion: the history of modern Israel / Eric Gartman.
pages   cm
"Published by the University of Nebraska Press as a Jewish Publication Society book."
Includes bibliographical references and index.
ISBN 978-0-8276-1253-2 (cloth: alk. paper)
ISBN 978-0-8276-1245-7 (epub)
ISBN 978-0-8276-1246-4 (mobi)
ISBN 978-0-8276-1247-1 (pdf)
1. Israel—History. 2. Arab-Israeli conflict. I. Title.
DS126.5.G358 2015
956.9405—dc23
2015017633

Set in Scala OT by M. Scheer.

For my father

Contents

Illustrations

MAPS

Preface

It is often said that truth is stranger than fiction. This maxim is perhaps nowhere more evident than as it relates to the history of Israel, which is the unlikely tale of how a scattered, stateless— and in many ways powerless—people reconstituted itself in its traditional homeland, only to face the threat of annihilation by those who, during the many years of dispersion, had come to regard the land as their home. I have set out to write a narrative that captures this story in a lively manner, focusing on what I see as the two main themes of modern Israel: reconstitution and survival. The reader will not find any discussion of the structure of the government of Israel, nor exhaustive lists of political parties and their representatives in Parliament, nor a bevy of economic data. Instead, this history attempts to place the reader in the time and place of the major development of the Jewish state, re-creating a sense of what it was like for those whose lives formed the tapestry of the saga of Israel. In addressing the conflict with the Arabs, my approach has been to let the two sides speak for themselves through documents from the times. As this is a history of Israel and not of the Arab-Israeli conflict, there are, by necessity, more Israeli sources. Still, the Arab perspective is hardly underrepresented; I wrote this book not to take sides or to persuade, but rather to educate those who may not be familiar with the subject matter and to do so in a readable style.

The world's only Jewish state, Israel is home to six million Jews and a million non-Jews. Israel's influence extends far beyond its borders, however. It is a source of pride and concern for the fourteen million Jews spread across the globe as well as the millions of Christians who view the Jewish state as a validation of their own religious beliefs. Conversely, the presence of a non-Arab state in the heart of the Middle East is a source of friction for Palestinian Arabs in particular and for other Arabs as well. This friction forms the majority of the history presented here. Additionally, the conflict with the Arabs has had far-reaching effects. During the Cold War the superpowers vied for influence in the region by heavily arming both sides. Other outsider nations such as Iran continue to use this conflict to expand their influence to this day. Israel therefore is crucial in today's world. It is my hope that by explaining the Jewish state's history, the reader will better understand the present situation in the Middle East.

Military intelligence played and still plays a large role in these events. Recently declassified documents shed light on the role of U.S. intelligence during the 1967 and 1973 wars and explain why U.S. leaders acted as they did during these two monumental upheavals. As these reports show, the United States predicted that Israel would easily win in 1967, leading President Lyndon Johnson to try to attempt a diplomatic solution. Conversely, U.S. intelligence predicted there would be no war in October 1973. As a result, U.S. and Israeli leaders were caught unprepared when the war began, and they paid a high price for their error. Two Central Intelligence Agency reports on the incident involving the uss *Liberty* during the 1967 war explain that the Israeli attack was indeed a tragic mistake.

History is not boring, and those tasked with writing it should take pains to make sure that it is not presented as a dry and unemotional recounting of events. Rather, it is a living and moving chronicle of those whose struggles have shaped our world. Yet all too often history books fail to do just that, turning magnificent sagas into dull, tiresome tomes. For millions of people the story of Israel is more than interesting: it encompasses the very lives of the people of the Holy Land, Jew and Arab. I set out to tell this tale in a way that conveys not only facts but emotions. For it is emotions that animate the people of the Holy Land. Indeed, a visitor to the region cannot help but be caught up by the passions of those for whom the Jewish state is the embodiment of all their dreams and aspirations, of those who will fight to the end to preserve it, and of those for whom the Jewish state is a foreign invader who took their lands and homes and who will fight to destroy it with all their might.

As a young man I experienced all these emotions firsthand. Although I was born in Israel to an American family and came to the United States when I was quite young, when I later visited Israel I was overwhelmed by the cacophony of sights that confronted me. In the Holy City of Jerusalem, the site of the Jewish Temple in ancient times, Arab merchants crowded the marketplaces. I wondered, If this is the Jewish state, why are there so many Arabs? Why are there so many soldiers carrying automatic weapons? Why is there so much tension? What does it all mean? After returning to the tranquility of suburban Maryland, I began to delve into the history of modern Israel in the hope that I could begin to understand what I had seen. That journey has never ended. The history of Israel is rich, complicated, and fascinating, and I have not stopped reading about it.

Yet in the dozens of books and articles I have read over the years something has been missing: the human element. Most histories do not convey the human element, nor even attempt to do so. This is what I would like to change. I wish to tell the history of Israel in a way that explains why the existence of the Jewish state raises the passions that it does and to tell it in an engaging manner. If I have explained the history of Israel and conveyed the dreams and aspirations of its inhabitants, I will have fulfilled my goal.

Acknowledgments

A first book is always a challenge, particularly in an age when fewer books are being traditionally published. Fortunately, I had help from several people, without whose aid this publication would never have happened. Tom Ambrosio was crucial in reading early versions of the draft and convincing me to expand it. Likewise, Mark Pietryzk also convinced me to expand the early draft; he continued to provide help and guidance throughout the process, encouraging me throughout. More than any single person I relied on him the most. Kenneth Pollack was critical in helping me write the conclusion. Barry Schwartz took the chance on a first-time author, and for that I am eternally grateful. Carol Hupping provided excellent feedback that greatly improved the quality of the book. Erin Greb is responsible for the high-quality maps that are found here. Bernard Reich showed me where to find photographs. Elizabeth Balster, Herta Feely, and Mark Cugini all provided important professional services.

Of course, my family was with me every step of the way. Only they know how important they were to seeing this book completed.

RETURN TO ZION

Introduction

No Master but God

In southern Israel's Judean Desert lies the mountain of Masada. Set slightly off from the rest of the Judean Mountains, Masada aligns to an almost perfect north–south orientation. The land drops off abruptly on three sides to the unforgiving brown and barren desert floor, interrupted only by the sparking blue water of the Dead Sea. The top of the mountain is almost uniformly flat, and it was on this site that the Roman Jewish governor of Judea, Herod the Great, built a citadel designed to serve as a safe haven in the event of a revolt. With its isolated desert location, sharp cliffs, and level plateau, it was an ideal choice for a fort.

The ruins of the fortress are still visible today. On the plateau's summit are the remains of storehouses that were once filled with grain, olives, dates, and other foods—enough to keep a Roman garrison well provisioned. On the side of the mountain are the canals and cisterns the Romans built to channel the rainwater that falls only sporadically in the desert into underground storage to keep the fortress supplied with the most important resource in this parched, sunbaked land. Perhaps most impressive of all is Herod's palace, a splendid three-story structure built by the Roman Jewish governor of Judea, to house himself in luxury. Herod spared no expense for his palace: it included a bathhouse, and the spectacular frescoes that adorned the walls can still be seen. From his tiered palace Herod could enjoy the magnificent view of the region that Masada affords. A stone wall surrounds the fort, protecting against any possible invaders. Behind these walls and protected by Roman soldiers, Herod must have felt safe from any rebellious subjects.

In an ironic twist of fate, however, it was not the Romans who were attacked and besieged on Masada. For in 66 CE Judea rose up against the masters of the ancient world in a rebellion known as the Great Revolt. They succeeded at first, driving back the Romans and temporarily gaining their independence. One of the rebels' first victories was the capture of Masada in a surprise attack. More victories followed and Jewish self-rule seemed near, but it was not to be. The mighty war machine that was Rome came back stronger than ever and relentlessly crushed the rebellion, leaving death and destruction in its wake. The legions made their way to the heart of the rebellion and the heart of Judea, the ancient Jewish capital of Jerusalem with the Holy Temple at its center. The Jewish rebels held off the Romans with their last bit of strength, but they could not keep the mighty empire off forever. The legionaries finally broke through the walls. The Jewish historian Flavius Josephus described the ensuing carnage as the Roman soldiers entered the city:

> They poured into the streets sword in hand, cut down without mercy all that came within reach, and burnt the houses of any who took refuge indoors, occupants and all. Many they raided, and as they entered in search of plunder they found whole families dead and the rooms full of the victims of starvation: horrified by the sight, they emerged empty-handed. Pity for those who had died in this way was matched by no such feeling for the living— they ran every man through whom they met and blocked the narrow streets with corpses, deluging the whole City with gore so that many of the fires were quenched by the blood of the slain.[1]

As the streets ran red with Jewish blood, the Romans burned down the Holy Temple—the very symbol of the Jewish people. The emperor had had enough of the troublesome Jews. He decreed the Jews would no longer run their own affairs. There would be no more Jewish governors of the province.

Yet one Jewish stronghold held out against the might of Rome: the fortress of Masada, home to 963 men, women, and children. An entire legion was dispatched to crush the zealots stationed there in open defiance of the Roman Empire. Using Jewish slaves, they piled rocks onto a natural ridge leading to the mountain. When the ramp was ready, the Romans rolled a giant siege tower and began to batter the walls with a mighty ram. Inside the redoubt, the defenders knew they were about to be overrun. Their leader, Eleazar Ben-Yair, spoke to them on the eve of the final assault. His words, as recorded by Josephus, would become a legendary statement of Jewish independence:

> Since we, long ago, my generous friends, resolved never to be servants to the Romans, nor to any other than God himself, the time is now come that obliges us to make that resolution true in practice. We were the very first that revolted against them, and we are the last that fight against them; and I cannot but esteem it as a favor that God hath granted us, that it is still in our power to die bravely, and in a state of freedom. It is very plain that we shall be taken within a day's time; but it is still in our power to die bravely, and in a state of freedom. Let our wives die before they are abused, and our children before they have tasted slavery; and after we have slain them, let us bestow that glorious benefit upon one another mutually, and preserve our freedom, as an excellent funeral monument to us. For, according to our original resolution, we have preferred death over slavery.[2]

And so it was. Each man retired to his house to slay his family. According to Josephus, the remaining rebels "chose ten men by lot out of them to slay all the rest. And when those had, without fear, slain them all, they made the same rule for casting lots themselves, that he whose lot it was to first kill the other nine, and after all, should kill himself." Upon entering the fortress, the Romans did not find resistance, but the evidence of a mass suicide: "Here encountering the mass of the slain, instead of exulting as over enemies, they admired the nobility of their resolve and the contempt of death displayed by so many in carrying it, unwavering, into execution."[3]

For two thousand years Masada remained the last time the Jews had controlled their own affairs. The Jews had wandered since then, scattering among the nations, unwelcome strangers in strange lands who were viewed as dangerous outsiders.

Until the return to Israel. Two millennia after the destruction of the Temple—on the very same summit where Ben-Yair and his followers had chosen not to be slaves—the Israel Defense Forces (IDF) hold a solemn ceremony at dawn, as their armored corps cadets' pledge: "Masada shall not fall again! Masada shall not fall again! Masada shall not fall again!" It has not been an easy promise to keep. Several times in the new age, Masada's fall seemed imminent. Even when the threat was not immediate, it was always present, never far from any Israeli's mind. This is the story of how close Masada came to falling again and how it was it was averted. This is the story of the return to Zion. This is the story of Israel.

-1-

A Pillar of Fire on the Road to Zion

Beginning of the Return, 1881–1896

The World of the Shtetl

On the afternoon of March 13, 1881, Czar Alexander II of Russia rode with his entourage through the narrow streets of St. Petersburg. It was a Sunday, and as was his custom for many years, the czar was headed to view a military roll call. He was an impressive-looking man: sixty-three years, tall and immaculately dressed, wearing a red cap, a red-lined overcoat with a beaver collar, and gold epaulets with his family crest. Snow still covered the ground; the long Russian winter was not yet over. The czar was accompanied by six horsemen and two sleighs, carrying the chief of police and the chief of the emperor's guard. Policemen lined the street, guarding the route.

The czar himself rode in a closed coach. The coach was bullet-proof—a gift from Napoleon III of France to cement their relationship. The security measures were more than mere precautions. They were quite necessary. Alexander II had survived three assassination attempts in the two years prior. In one attempt an assassin fired five times at the fleeing czar, but Alexander II fled in a zigzag pattern to avoid the bullets and escaped unharmed. Another time the "People's Will" revolutionary group set an explosion on a rail line, but the attack missed the czar's train. The bloodiest incident occurred the year before: a People's Will agent set off a massive charge beneath the dining room of the Winter Palace in St. Petersburg, killing eleven people and wounding thirty. The czar himself escaped harm only because he was late for dinner.

Alexander II was by no means a reactionary ruler. The twenty-six years of his rule were the greatest period of restructuring since Peter the Great had first attempted to modernize Russia. Like his illustrious forebearer, Alexander II had initiated a series of reforms intended to modernize the vast but backward empire. By far his most important act had been to emancipate the serfs twenty years earlier. Forty million peasants were freed of their legal obligations to their landlords in one sweeping gesture. With this move the czar hoped that Russia might catch up with the West. But the emperor had to be cautious: he could not move too fast. Russians might have envied the wealth and power of their Western neighbors, but they still looked upon their freedoms with suspicion. Democracy would mean the end of the old order and the historic union of the Orthodox Church, the military, and the aristocracy. To the old order, the czar was moving too fast. But to the liberals—and especially the radicals—he was moving too slowly, and they meant to start a social revolution with the czar out of the way.

The entourage followed the same route it always did, via the Catherine Canal and over the Pevchensky Bridge. It would be the czar's undoing. For on that Sunday afternoon no fewer than three People's Will revolutionaries waited as the procession made its usual trip. As Alexander rode in his secure coach, a young man carrying a small white package wrapped in a handkerchief stood on the narrow sidewalk. He went unnoticed by the policemen. As the imperial procession arrived, he threw the package under the czar's horses. The bomb inside exploded, killing one rider and knocking the would-be assassin into a fence. The energetic czar emerged from his coach unharmed, and he began to survey the scene. He approached the assassin, who was already being held down by no fewer than four soldiers. His men begged him to return to the safety of the coach, but the czar insisted on viewing the site of the explosion. As they moved toward it, another bomb landed at his feet. This time there was no escape: the explosion rocked the street, knocking the czar and his men to the ground as a cloud of white smoke covered the street. The police chief described the ghastly scene:

> I was deafened by the new explosion, burned, wounded and thrown to the ground. Suddenly, amid the smoke and snowy fog, I heard His Majesty's weak voice cry, "Help!" Gathering what strength I had, I jumped up and rushed to the emperor. His Majesty was half-lying, half-sitting, leaning on his right arm. Thinking he was merely wounded heavily, I tried to lift him but the Czar's legs were shattered, and the blood poured from them. Twenty people, with wounds of varying degree, lay on the sidewalk and on the street. Some managed to stand, others to crawl, still others tried to get out beneath bodies that had fallen on them. Through the snow, debris, and blood you could see fragments of clothing, sabers, and bloody chunks of human flesh.[1]

The czar's attendants took him back to the palace, where he died a few hours later. Had the reform movement died with him? It was the question that consumed all of Russia. It was not clear how his son, Alexander III, would rule. Perhaps no group within the vast, multiethnic realm was more affected by this question than the Jews. Roughly five million Jews—the vast majority of world Jewry—lived hemmed into the "Pale of Settlement," the area where they were legally allowed to reside, which ran from the Baltic Sea to the Black Sea in western Russia. Theirs was a world vastly different from modern America. Their language was Yiddish, a combination of Hebrew and German. Their home was the shtetl (the Yiddish word for "town"), where almost all of them lived, having been barred from owning land or living in the cities. A contemporary vividly described the shtetl as

> a jumble of wooden houses clustered higgledy-piggledy about a market-place . . . as crowded as a slum. . . . The streets are . . . as tortuous as a Talmudic argument. They are bent into question marks and folded into parentheses. They run into culs-de-sac

like a theory arrested by a fact; they ooze off into lanes, alleys, back yards. . . . [At the center] is the market-place, with its shops, booths, tables, stands, butchers' blocks. Hither come daily, except during the winter, the peasants and peasant women from many miles around, bringing their livestock and vegetables, their fish and hides, their wagonloads of grain, melons, parsley, radishes, and garlic. They buy, in exchange, the city produce which the Jews import, dry goods, hats, shoes, boots, lamps, oil, spades, mattocks, and shirts.[2]

From this clever depiction we also gain an insight into the Jews' economic role. With farming and the professions barred to them, they became merchants or artisans, peddlers, blacksmiths, tailors, butchers, shoemakers, bakers, and the like. According to historian Dan Kurzman, "In his tiny shop or factory, or in a candle-lit nook of his dismal house, a bearded figure with side curls might weave fiber into rope, hammer tin into utensils, tan a cowhide that would be transformed into shoes and gloves, stitch by hand the traditional caftan that was worn by most Jews, or distill brandy or brew beer."[3]

Plonsk, another typical shtetl town, is described by Kurzman:

Branching out from the huge market square in the heart of town was a web of alleys paved with pink, red, and blue cobblestones that were often blackened with the slime of open, overflowing sewers. Along the alleys were lines of rickety two-story wooden houses that seemed almost to hold each other up. Inside, wobbly, creaking staircases led to dark rooms with smoky stoves, iron beds, and shelves laden with patched clothing—reeking dungeons, totally cut off from sunlight by the houses on the other side of the narrow street. The poorest Jews lived here: the market women and their pale Talmud-studying husbands, the seamstresses, the food peddlers who sold hot beans to schoolboys.[4]

Other poor Jews were known as luftmenschen (Yiddish for "flying men"), who moved from town to town, looking for regular work and gathering in the market or other public places in search of even the lowliest job.

The Jews of the shtetl practiced a highly ritualized way of life. They followed the 613 commandments of piety that dictated the everyday rites of life, from eating to working to clothing. This is the "tradition" that Tevye the Milkman so lovingly sings of in *Fiddler on the Roof*. And while Tevye admitted that he did not know how or why the traditions came into being, they were in fact adaptations for a group living on the fringes of society, a way of instilling law into a region pervaded by lawlessness, chaos, and fear. If the Jews of the shtetl could not have security in their external life, they would impose order on their internal life, for it was in religion that the Jews of the shtetl found their only solace. Life revolved around religion and around God. Luftmenschen would crowd into their wooden synagogues, where they could come closest to God through the chanting of the Torah and Talmud. One memoir of this time read: "Carried away by the mellow, melting chant of Talmud-reading, one's mind soared high in the pure realm of thought, away from this world of facts and worries, away from the boundaries of here and now, to a region where the Divine Presence listens to what Jews create in the study of His word."[5]

In a society where religion was so highly valued, the schools that taught the word of God were very important. Boys began religious study at an early age and continued for many years. The day when a son began his religious lessons was one of immense significance to his parents. A nineteenth-century Jewish writer vividly captured one such scene:

> Soon a poorly clad couple entered, the man carrying in his arms a young boy of about six, wrapped in a *talit* [prayer shawl]. Both father and mother were weeping with joy, grateful to God who had preserved them that they might witness this beautiful moment. Having extended a cordial welcome to the newcomers, the *melamed* [teacher] took the hero of the celebration into his arms and stood him upon a table. Afterwards the boy was seated on a bench and was the first to receive cake, nuts, raisins and dainties of which the happy mother had brought along an apron-full. The leader then sat down near the youngster, placed a card with the printed

alphabet before him and, taking a long pointer, began the first lesson by blessing his newly-initiated pupil that he may be raised for the study of Torah, marriage, and good deeds.[6]

The boys' parents' zeal notwithstanding, the conditions of these schools were quite shabby. A turn-of-the-century report called them "filthy rooms, crowded from nine in the morning until nine in the evening, with pale, starved children. These remain in this contaminated atmosphere for twelve hours at a time and see only their bent, exhausted teachers. . . . Their faces are pale and sickly, and their bodies evidently not strong."[7]

Events in the outside world rarely gave the denizens of the shtetl cause for hope. The nadir of their fortunes came during the thirty-year reign of Alexander II's father, Nicholas I. Calling the Jews "regular leeches,"[8] Nicholas attempted to cleanse Judaism from the land. According to one of his secret edicts, "The purpose in educating Jews is to bring about their gradual merging with the Christian nationalities and to uproot those superstitious and harmful prejudices which are instilled by the teachings of the Talmud."[9] Consequently Nicholas issued over six hundred anti-Jewish decrees designed to disrupt Jewish life. These included censoring Yiddish and Hebrew books, stifling religious education, mass expulsions, and the conscription of young boys into the army for periods of up to twenty-five years. Jews remained barred from the professions, barred from holding land, barred from living outside the Pale of Settlement. His son, the reformer Alexander I, reduced compulsory military service to five years, allowed Jews into some universities, and allowed Jewish businessman to travel to parts of Russia that had been off-limits. They were still not allowed to own land, enter the professions, or live outside the Pale. Nonetheless, the winds of change were blowing, even into the deepest recesses of the backward empire.

This was the situation the Jews faced when Alexander II was assassinated. Would his son continue the reforms, including possible emancipation, as had been bestowed on their Jewish brethren in Western Europe? The answer came within weeks—it was a resounding "No." Alexander III ended all reforms, including leniency for the Jews. The Jews had no place in the new czar's plans. He would restore the old order. As a wave of pogroms (violent riots) spread from rumors that the Jews had killed the beloved czar, the regime did little to quell the unrest. All across the country, drunken peasant mobs formed and attacked Jewish settlements, killing, maiming, and raping in an orgy of unbridled violence. A Jewish man in Odessa recorded a chilling description of the pogrom as he and his family hid in a cellar: "The situation is terrible and frightening! We are virtually under siege. The courtyards are barred up, and we keep peering through the grillwork to see if the mob is coming down on us. . . . We all sleep in our clothes and without bedding . . . so that if we are attacked we immediately will be able to take the small children . . . and flee. But will they let us flee? . . . Will they have mercy on the youngsters? . . . How long, O God of Israel?" Two days later: "The rioters approached the house I am staying in. The women shrieked and wailed, hugging the children to their breasts, and didn't know where to turn. The men are dumbfounded. We all imagined that in a few moments it would be all over with us."[10] The police held back the mobs in Odessa, but Jews elsewhere were not so fortunate. Hundreds were attacked and maimed.

The attacks continued on and off for the next year. A Jewish man in Vilna recorded:

If someone gets into an argument with a Christian the latter immediately says: "Just wait, soon we'll settle all the scores," or something similar or even worse. What kind of life is this? If I had the courage I would kill all those close to me and then myself, and the farce would be over. If I do not, some drunken riffraff will come along, ravish my wife and daughter and throw my infant Sonia from the third-floor window. Would it not be better for me to kill everyone? What a miserable creature is the Jew! Even when the advantage is clear to him he cannot summon the courage to do a good thing. Death awaits us in any case, so why should we wait?[11]

The following spring the czar passed the May Laws, further

restricting where Jews could live and sending them even deeper into poverty. But that was what the government wanted. The czar's top adviser declared, "One-third will die out, one-third will leave the country, and one-third will be completely dissolved in the surrounding population."[12]

It was a cold, hard slap in the face to the Jews, who had been so hopeful that emancipation was on the way. Now it seemed like a distant dream, shattered in the blood and fire of the pogroms. One Jewish writer described the situation starkly: "The Russian peasant, poor as he may be, is the proprietor of a small piece of land. And his condition is not hopeless—one feels that sooner or later it will improve. But Jewish poverty is utterly without a cure; the Jew has no available means for improving his condition, which will remain abject as long as he lives among alien peoples."[13] With crisis gripping the Jewish community, a conference convened in St. Petersburg to debate emigration from Russia. Many spoke out against it. Emigration would appear unpatriotic and might undermine the struggle for emancipation.

But to others, the situation was quite clear: "Either we get civil rights or we emigrate. Our human dignity is being trampled upon, our wives and daughters and being dishonored, we are looted and pillaged; either we get decent human rights or else let us go wherever our eyes may lead us."[14] As for appearing unpatriotic, one writer scoffed at the very idea: "Sympathy for Russia? How ironical it sounds! Am I not despised? Am I not urged to leave? Do I not hear the word *zhid* constantly? Can I even think that someone considers me a human being capable of thinking and feeling like others? Do I not rise daily with the fear lest the hungry mob attack me? . . . It is impossible . . . that a Jew should regret leaving Russia."[15]

And leave they did. Over the next thirty-three years, some 2.5 million souls (roughly one-third of the Jews of the Pale) departed in one of the largest voluntary migrations in history. The modern reader, appalled by the horrible circumstances the Jews endured, may wonder why still more did not emigrate. But it is always difficult for people to leave what is familiar, especially for a distant, unknown land. Those who did leave mostly made their way to the New World, where America welcomed the new immigrants to help fill their factories and settle the large country. Others found homes in Canada, Argentina, and Britain, where they established new communities whose vibrant Jewish traditions continue to flourish today.

"O House of Jacob, Come and Let Us Go!": The First Aliyah

But there was another choice. The Jews always viewed the Land of Israel as their home, a notion reinforced through their devotion to biblical study and daily prayer. According to one historian:

> Multitudes of Jews, wherever they lived, saw their spiritual home as rooted in a remote land which none of them had ever seen and which few ever expected to behold with their eyes. They lived in a permanent nostalgia, sustained by ways of life which, though often poor and sometimes squalid, nevertheless had the dignity of self-knowledge and self-assertion. This talent for corporate existence was especially conspicuous in the shtetl, the Jewish village within the Pale of Settlement of the Russian Empire. The lives of Jews, however miserable, went forward there in an atmosphere of autonomy. Most of the Jews of Russia and Poland lived under oppression, but they did not feel rootless. Their lives were bound up with religious observance, and their minds and hearts were filled with images of Jewish history and faith. Even when they bowed their heads to secular subservience to gentile empires, they secretly saw themselves as the descendants of prophets and kings temporarily cut off from their own inheritance.[16]

A memoir from the time explained, "Half of the time, the shtetl just wasn't there; it was in the Holy Land, and it was in the remote past or the remote future, in the company of the Patriarchs and Prophets or of the Messiah. Its festivals were geared to the Palestinian climate and calendar; it celebrated regularly the harvests its forefathers had gathered in a hundred generations ago; it prayed for the subtropical rains, indifferent to the needs of its neighbors, whose prayers had a practical, local schedule in view."[17]

Europe was gripped by nationalist movements in the late nineteenth century, and the intellectual ferment inevitably affected the Jews. Soon a number of writers and intellectuals were advocating the re-creation of the Jewish state in the Land of Israel. Two groups formed to bring Jews back to Palestine, one called the "Lovers of Zion" and the other the Bilu, a Hebrew acronym from the biblical verse "O House of Jacob, come and let us go!" With Jews leaving Mother Russia in droves, these movements now had their recruits. They would send young Jews to Palestine, buy land, and have them settle it. They had high hopes, as the Bilu manifesto made clear. This striking document begins by recounting Jewish history: "Nearly two thousand years have passed since, in an evil hour, after a heroic struggle, the glory of our Temple vanished in fire and our kings and chieftains changed their crowns and diadems for the chains of exile. We lost our country where dwelt our beloved sires. Into exile we took with us, of all our glories, only a spark of fire by which our Temple, the abode of our Great One, was engirdled, and this little spark kept us alive."[18] Moving into the modern era, the manifesto declares, "this spark is again kindling and will shine for us, a true pillar of fire going before us on the road to Zion, while behind us is a pillar of cloud, the pillar of oppression, threatening to destroy us."

The biblical Hebrews had followed the Lord's pillar of fire through the Sinai back to the Promised Land. Now the Bilu saw another pillar leading them back to the land of their ancestors, away from oppression: "Sleepest thou, O our nation? What hast thou been doing until 1882? Sleeping, and dreaming the false dream of Assimilation. Now, thank God, thou art awakening from thy slothful slumber. The Pogroms have awakened thee from thy charmed sleep." The manifesto exhorted the European Jews to return to Zion: "Hopeless is your situation in the West; the star of your future is gleaming in the East." As for their goals, they were quite explicit: "We want a home in our country. It was given to us by the mercy of God, it is ours as registered in the archives of history." By the end of 1882 nearly seven thousand

Jews had emigrated from Russia to Palestine, hoping to rekindle the spark of Zion.

To say it didn't turn out to be as easy as the Lovers of Zion and Bilu had imagined would be a gross understatement, particularly in light of the new immigrants' expectations. "It is hard to describe the romance—the hope, light, and joy—that filled their hearts," one of the early pilgrims recounted, "as they set sail for the land of their fathers to be pioneers of Jewish agriculture. Each man painted in the brightest colors a picture of his farm-to-be in the Land of Israel. . . . Each man would have his own wheat field, vegetable garden, and chicken run. . . . In the land flowing with milk and honey, of course, all this would be supplemented by olives, almonds, figs, dates, and other delicacies."[19]

This idealized version of what their lives would be like was quickly dashed. The biblical land "flowing with milk and honey" was, in fact, no paradise. Quite to the contrary—the privations they suffered in the new land were innumerable. The plight of the migrants began with the arrival at the port of Jaffa. Without a deep-water harbor, the ships dropped anchor while sturdy Arab oarsmen rowed the passengers to land. In stormy weather, the waves would bob the rowboats up and down, so that the passengers had to be loaded quickly as the waves elevated the boats. Once on land the immigrants would be forced to wait in the rain or under the beating sun while the Turkish officials decided whether or not to admit them. If they were allowed in, the immigrants would climb aboard donkeys and ride off to their new homes—ramshackle mud huts, with shared, crowded rooms. They were eaten alive by all manner of pests, including insects, vermin, rodents, scorpions, and snakes. There was no running water or even furniture, save a few old packing cases and tins. They could count on only one hot meal per day of the barest ingredients, perhaps pita bread with canned fish and olives. Since the Lovers of Zion scarcely had any funds, the land they managed to acquire tended to be rocky, marshy, teeming with flies, and invested with malaria. The new immigrants were from the shtetl, where Jews were not permitted to hold land. Therefore they had little idea how to farm and were not used to the hours of backbreaking physical labor and daily toil in the fields that agriculture demanded.

One pioneer recorded what it was like for the new immigrants as they tried manual labor for the first time in their lives. In an entry from 1882, the new farmer wrote:

> When I first started work, I tended to swing my hoe and to strike sideways, in every direction. But after a short while, my hands would blister. Blood would flow and I would experience horrific pain which would compel me to cast down my hoe. Then I would immediately be stricken by the weakness of my resolve and would admonish myself, saying "Is that how you intend to demonstrate that Jews are capable of physical labor?" An inner voice tauntingly cried out, "You will not stand this decisive test!" Then with all my resolve and despite the pain, I resumed hoeing. I worked frantically for two full hours and when my strength finally gave in, I collapsed and was immobilized for the rest of the day. My back pain was unbearable, my hands full of wounds, those four morning hours seemed like an eternity.[20]

In addition to the backbreaking labor, bouts of dysentery, typhus, and malaria limited their work and health. Before long, disease, poor sanitation, and the lack of medical facilities took their toll on the lives of the settlers. Roving bands of Bedouins raided the tiny villages. In the twenty years after the death of Alexander II, several thousand Jews made aliyah—that is, "ascended" to the Holy Land—but most returned to Russia, unable to cope with the harsh new life. The movement teetered on the brink of collapse. Only financial assistance from the French baron Edmond de Rothschild saved the Lovers of Zion from an early demise. But dependence on overseas Jews was not the goal of the pioneers— they were supposed to be self-sufficient. By the turn of the century, only about five thousand Jews lived in the rural settlements, surviving on Rothschild's largesse. The future of Zionism was very much in doubt. But events in Western Europe, where the Jews had been emancipated and supposedly assimilated, would forever change the destiny of the Zionist movement.

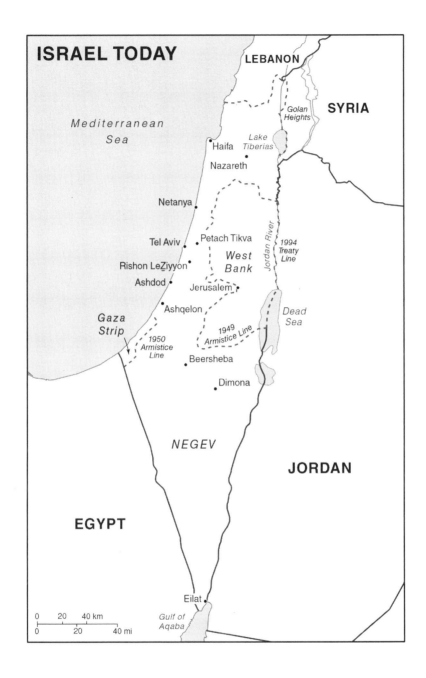

ISRAEL TODAY

LEBANON

SYRIA

Golan
Heights

Mediterranean
Sea

Lake
Tiberias

Haifa

Nazareth

Netanya

Tel Aviv

Petach Tikva

Jordan River

1994
Treaty
Line

West
Bank

Rishon LeZiyyon

Ashdod

Jerusalem

Ashqelon

Dead
Sea

Gaza
Strip

1950
Armistice
Line

1949
Armistice Line

Beersheba

Dimona

NEGEV

JORDAN

EGYPT

Eilat

0   20   40 km

0   20   40 mi

Gulf of
Aqaba

1. Israel Today. © Erin Greb Cartography.

-2-

An Eye toward Zion

The Zionist Movement Ascendant, 1896–1918

"A Marvelous and Exalted Splendid Figure": Theodor Herzl and Zionism

On the morning of January 5, 1896, a Viennese journalist named Theodor Herzl arrived in Paris to cover the degradation ceremony of Alfred Dreyfus, a French Jewish army captain found guilty of spying for Germany. The charges were false, the evidence used against him forged. In time Dreyfus would be exonerated and cleared of all charges. But the mood was quite different on that cold morning. Herzl was an assimilated Jew, well educated and well regarded in his profession. Like many of his compatriots, he had believed that Jews could live comfortably in Europe, in the spirit of the Enlightenment and the emancipation granted by the French Revolution. But things had changed. In his hometown of Vienna, the anti-Semitic Karl Lueger had been elected mayor. Incidents of anti-Semitism were on the rise in France, as well. What Herzl witnessed that morning changed his life, and with it the future of a Jewish state.

Herzl's chilling description of the event appeared in his newspaper later that day:

> On this dismal winter's day the degradation of Captain Dreyfus, which was carried out on the grounds of the Military Academy, drew large numbers of the curious to the vicinity. Many officers

were present, not a few of them accompanied by ladies. Entry into the grounds of the *Ecole Militaire* was permitted only to army officers and some journalists. Outside the grounds swarmed the morbid crowds which are always attracted by executions. A considerable number of police were on duty. At nine o'clock the great open court was filled with a detachment of troops in square formation; five thousand men in all. In the center a general sat on horseback. A few minutes after nine Dreyfus was led forth. He was dressed in his captain's uniform. Four men conducted him before the general. The latter said: "Alfred Dreyfus, you are unworthy to bear arms. In the name of the French Republic I degrade you from your rank. Let the sentence be carried out." Here, Dreyfus lifted his right arm and called out: "I declare and solemnly swear that you are degrading an innocent man. *Viva la France!*" At that instant the drums were beaten. The officer in charge began to tear from the condemned man's uniform the buttons and cords, which had already been loosened. Dreyfus retained his calm bearing. Within a few minutes, this part of the ceremony was over.

Then began the parade of the condemned before the troops. Dreyfus marched along the sides of the square like a man who knows himself to be innocent. He passed by a group of officers, who cried, "Judas! Traitor!" Dreyfus cried back, "I forbid you to insult me!" At twenty minutes past the parade was over. Dreyfus was then handcuffed and given into the custody of the gendarmes. From that point on he was to be considered a civilian prisoner and treated as such. When he had been led away the troops defiled off the grounds. But the crowd surged toward the gates to watch the condemned man being led away. There were passionate shouts. "Bring him out here, and we'll tear him to pieces!" But the crowd waited in vain. There was a curious excitement among those who had been able to witness the ceremony of the degradation. The strange, firm bearing of the prisoner had made a profound impression on some of them.

As Dreyfus was being paraded before troops, among whom were a number of recruits, he kept calling out, "I am innocent!" When he passed near a group of journalists he stopped for a moment and said, "Tell all France that I am innocent!" Some of the journalists retorted with insults. Part of the crowd outside, which was able to catch a glimpse of the ceremony, shouted again and again, "Death to the traitor!"[1]

Writing on the Dreyfus Affair, Herzl remarked:

> Death to the Jews? The Dreyfus case embodies more than a judicial error; it embodies the desire of the vast majority of the French to condemn a Jew, and to condemn all Jews in this one Jew. "Death to the Jews" howled the mob, as the decorations were being ripped from the captain's coat. Where? In France. In republican, modern, civilized France, a hundred years after the Declaration of the Rights of Man. The French people, or at any rate the greater part of the French people, does not want to extend the rights of man to Jews. The edict of the great Revolution has been revoked.[2]

Moreover Herzl could not believe that Dreyfus was guilty: "A Jew who, as an officer on the general staff, has before him an honorable career, cannot commit such a crime. The Jews, who have so long been condemned to a state of civic dishonor, have, as a result, developed an almost pathological hunger for honor."[3]

The degradation of Dreyfus put Herzl over the edge. No longer could Jews expect to live as a minority; they must have their own state. A few months after the degradation ceremony, Herzl published *The Jewish State*, a pamphlet calling for Jews to leave Europe and create a country of their own. In his treatise, Herzl declared assimilation was a false dream:

> We have honestly endeavored everywhere to merge ourselves in the social life of surrounding communities and to preserve the faith of our fathers. We are not permitted to do so. In vain are we loyal patriots, our loyalty in some places running to extremes; in vain do we make the same sacrifices of life and property as our fellow-citizens; in vain do we strive to increase the fame of our native land in science and art, or her wealth by trade and commerce. In countries where we have lived for centuries we are still cried down as strangers, and often by those whose ancestors were

not yet domiciles in the land where Jews had already had experience of suffering.

Herzl lamented, "If only we could be left in peace . . . but I think we shall not be left in peace." His solution was plain: "Let the sovereignty be granted to us over a portion of the globe large enough to satisfy the rightful requirements of a nation; the rest we shall manage for ourselves."[4] In the new state Herzl envisioned, Jews would not live in isolated ghettos but in a modern, secular, and scientific society.

Herzl concluded the pamphlet with a powerful emotional flourish on the promise of the Zionist ideal:

> The idea must radiate out until it reaches the last wretched nests of our people. They will awaken out of their dull brooding. Then a new content will come into the lives of all of us. Each one of us need only think of himself, and the procession becomes tremendous. And what glory awaits the selfless fighters for the idea! That is why I believe that a race of wonderful Jews will grow out of the earth. The Maccabees will rise again! Let the word be repeated here which was given at the beginning; the Jews who will it shall have their state. We shall at last live as free men on our own soil and die peacefully in our own homeland. The world will be liberated by our liberation, enriched with our wealth, made greater by our greatness. And that which we seek there for our own use will stream out mightily and beneficently upon all mankind.[5]

The Jewish State struck like a thunderbolt on European Jewry. "When I had read it to the end, I felt that I had become another man," one Zionist wrote Herzl. "The broad perspectives, and the faith, strong as a vision, which speaks from every line of *The Jewish State*, has opened before me a new world, whose existence I had indeed long suspected, but which I had never beheld."[6] Herzl's biographer described its effect on Zionist youth:

> A door had been flung open for them, light streamed in. Clarity, dignity, strong faith and a prophetic, appealing pathos lifted them out of the dreariness of the daily reality. That flutter of eagles' wings

which, as Herzl told later, he felt above his head when he wrote *The Jewish State*, became audible now to these of his readers. Now they suddenly saw before them a goal, a great and attainable goal, and the steps which led to it. And all this from a Viennese litterateur, an editor on one of the greatest German newspapers, who until now had worried little about Jewish matters—a man who lived in the world of writers, who had moved in the circles of the great, and who had suddenly turned back to his despised people."[7]

Theodor Herzl was the leader the Zionists so desperately needed. Under Herzl the Zionist movement exploded onto the world scene as a force to be reckoned with. With his articulate manner, elegant dress, and regal demeanor, Herzl cut an impressive figure, charismatic and radiant. He was also tireless, working relentlessly to achieve his dream. He met with the grand vizier of the Ottoman Empire as early as 1896. Upon his return from Constantinople and arrival at the rail station in Sofia, Bulgaria, a mob of several hundred jubilant Jews engulfed the Viennese messiah. For surely he was the man who would finally deliver them a state of their own! They carried him off the train to a synagogue, where people insisted on kissing his hand.

At the synagogue, he stood at the altar platform. He was not sure how to face the congregation without turning his back to the Holy of Holies, and then someone cried out, "It's all right for you to turn your back on the Ark, you are holier than the Torah!"[8] They were quite evidently in awe of him in Sofia—they would not be the last to express an idealized view of the man from Vienna.

On August 29, 1897, the first World Zionist Congress gathered in Basel, Switzerland. Assembling the two hundred delegates from across Europe was not an easy endeavor. But with his relentless work ethic and charm, Herzl managed to bring the disparate and far-flung branches of Zionism together. The first speaker was Herzl himself. All eyes focused on him as he rose and walked upright to the lectern. The delegates were transfixed: "It was extraordinary!" one delegate wrote.

What had happened? This was not the Dr. Herzl I had been with hitherto, and with whom I was in discussion as recently as last night. Before us rose a marvelous and exalted splendid figure, kingly in bearing and stature, with deep eyes in which could be read quiet majesty and unfettered sorrow. It was no longer the elegant Dr. Herzl of Vienna; it is a royal scion of the House of David raised from among the dead, clothed in legend and fantasy and beauty. Everyone sat breathless, as if in the presence of a miracle. And in truth, was it not a miracle which we beheld? The dream of two thousand years was on the point of realization; it was as if the Messiah, the son of David, confronted us; and I was seized by an overpowering desire, in the midst of this, to cry out, loudly, for all to hear "*Yehi hamelech*"—Hail to the King![9]

Realizing the importance of the moment, Herzl remained outwardly calm, even as he trembled from excitement within. "We are here to lay the foundation stone of the house which is to shelter the Jewish nation," he declared in a firm voice. "It is the duty of this Congress to see to it that when its sessions have come to an end, we do not relapse into our previous condition of disorganization. We must create here and now an organ, a permanent organ, which the Jewish people has lacked till now."[10] Herzl was good to his word: the World Zionist Organization was founded at the Congress. The next speaker declared anti-Semitism was on the rise in Europe, and Jews—an alien among hostile peoples— needed a state of their own: "After a slumber of more than thirty to sixty years, anti-Semitism broke out once more from the innermost depth of the nations, and his real situation was revealed to the mortified Jew. He has lost the house of the ghetto, but the land of his birth is denied to him as his home."[11] Several of the delegates cried.

At the conclusion the Congress released the Basel Declaration, stating, "The aim of Zionism is to create for the Jewish people a home in Palestine secured by public law"[12]—in other words, a charter. Such a charter would provide the legal basis for a Jewish state. With the magnificent Herzl at its head, the Congress was a success. Herzl realized it, writing in his diary, "At Basel

I founded the Jewish State." Then he added prophetically, "Perhaps in five years, but certainly in fifty, everyone will know it."[13] In fact fifty years later the United Nations would declare the birth of the Jewish state.

But in 1897 a Jewish state was still a long way off. The Zionists did not have much leverage to acquire such a charter. They had little money, few members, and modest notoriety. But the Zionists did have a big diplomatic card: Herzl himself. His fame preceded him, and he managed to acquire meetings with world leaders through "personal subsidies" of key advisers. Once such meeting was with the German kaiser in Palestine, when Herzl unsuccessfully sought German backing for a Jewish charter. Undeterred, Herzl sought out contacts in other countries—including the Ottoman Empire, which held the land of Palestine.

His efforts paid off. In May 1901 Herzl was summoned to a royal banquet in Constantinople to meet with the sultan himself. One can only imagine Herzl's excitement as he rode the train to the Ottoman capital. This was his chance. The sultan, Abdul Hamid II, had in his powers to grant a Jewish charter, and Herzl had in his powers considerable financial backing. They were an odd pair: the sultan a small, shabby man, wearing a fez that was too large for him; and Herzl, tall, magnificent, and immaculately dressed in a suit. The sultan spoke first, presenting Herzl with a medal, and repeatedly emphasized his friendship with the Jews. Herzl responded by quoting the old fable of Androcles, who removed the thorn from a lion: "His majesty is the lion, perhaps. I am Androcles, and perhaps there is a thorn which I could withdraw. I consider the Ottoman public debt the thorn. If this debt could be removed then the life strength of Turkey could unfold anew."[14]

Herzl explained that his associates would supply the funds in return for a charter for the Jews. The sultan was delighted by the proposal and again spoke favorably of the Jews. The next day Herzl met with the grand vizier and the minister of finance to discuss the details. Herzl proposed that the Jews buy up the public debt over a period of three years in exchange for a charter for a land settlement company in Palestine. Herzl then returned to Vienna, sure he had convinced the sultan and his advisers of the benefits of a deal. A Jewish charter seemed imminent to him and his followers.

Herzl returned triumphantly, news of his meeting with the sultan enhancing his standing among the Zionists. He had met with the sultan—now all he needed was 1.5 million pounds. Surely he had the leverage to raise the money. But it would not be so easy: the only Jews who had that kind of wealth were the Rothschilds and the Montefiores, and neither family was interested.

There was no tangible benefit in the enterprise for the two great families. Edmond de Rothschild had subsidized the first settlers, with their enterprises under his control. There was no such arrangement in Herzl's plan. Other Jews remained skeptical of the sultan's professed friendship with the Jews. Lacking the funds, Herzl sought to buy time with the sultan, but it was all for naught. When he returned to Constantinople, he found the Ottomans had merely been using the Zionists as a bargaining chip for gaining a loan from the French.

Herzl was not done; he would meet with leaders of Britain, Italy, and even the pope himself. When Herzl died suddenly of a heart condition in 1904, one historian wrote, "It was as if the Jewish people had lost its father. Among the masses of East European Jewry the dread announcement had something of the effect of a new destruction of the temple."[15] A huge funeral procession accompanied Herzl to his grave. While he never gained the national charter he had fought so hard for, his organizational skills and showmanship brought the Zionist movement together, boosting their profile and funding. It was a monumental achievement, and he would go down in history as the father of Israel.

"My New Heaven": The Jews of the Second Aliyah

The Zionists now had a well-run, well-funded international organization, but the number of Jewish settlers in Palestine remained tiny. Events in Russia would once again prove decisive. In the spring of 1903 rumors spread that the Jews had killed a Christian as part of a blood ritual for the Passover holiday. That Easter Sunday riots rocked the empire. A newspaper account from the time ran:

In Kishineff, all was quiet until Easter Sunday, when at noon the crowd on Chuplinksy place, where amusement and other booths had been erected, became excited. Several Jews, who came to watch the Christians enjoying themselves, were attacked. They ran away. The cry "Kill the Jews!" was raised, and the mob, which swelled instantly followed in hot pursuit, where a fearful riot took place.

It is impossible to account the amount of goods destroyed in a few hours. The "hurrahs" and the pitiful cries of the victims filled the air—wherever a Jew was met he was savagely beaten into insensibility. One Jew was dragged from a street car and beaten until the mob thought he was dead. The air was filled with feathers from torn bedding. About 3 o'clock in the afternoon the rioters were signaling and whistling in the principal streets. The miscreants began there by breaking windows.

At nightfall quiet was restored, at least in the center of the city, and it was presumed that the disturbance was at an end. Police, troops, and mounted gendarmes patrolled the streets, but the real assault only began on Monday morning, when armed with axes and crowbars, the mob set upon its work of destruction, damaging the best houses and shops, clothing themselves in pillaged clothing and carrying away huge bundles of loot.

The mob ignored the order of the patrols and the police to disperse, and continued to rob, destroy and kill. Every Jewish household was broken into and the unfortunate Jews in their terror endeavored to hide in cellars and under roofs. The mob entered the synagogues, desecrated the biggest house of worship, and defiled the scrolls of the law.

The conduct of the intelligent Christians was disgraceful. They made no attempt to check the rioting. They simply walked around enjoying the frightful "sport."

On Tuesday, the third day, when it became known that the troops had received orders to shoot, the rioting ceased. The Jews then came out of their houses. The streets were piled up with the debris and they presented a horrible appearance. The big Jewish Hospital is filled with dead and wounded. Some bodies are mutilated beyond identification. From a distance there could be heard heart-rending groans and pitiable wailings of widows and orphans. The misery of the Jews is indescribable. There is an actual famine. The prices of all living commodities have gone up.[16]

Eighty-five Jews died in the attacks. The Kishinev pogrom sent more Jews fleeing Russia. This time those who made aliyah were better funded, better organized, and better prepared. But most of all they were ideologically committed. Their goal was not only to build a new Jewish state, but to build a new Jewish people. No longer would they be the city-dwelling shopkeepers or students of the Eastern European shtetl; they would be new Jews, pioneers and laborers, working the land—"to build and be rebuilt," as their slogan went. Instead of being "huge heads on chicken's feet," meek and unhealthy, they would till the soil like other people. To achieve this vision they demanded the "conquest of labor"— that is, they would only hire Jews to work their land. They would be self-reliant, owning, working, and defending the land. Socialism was a key component of their ideal, as they would share the work and help their fellow Jews. All of these ideals came together as they created new two types of shared agricultural communities: moshavim, where each farmer owned land but cooperated in marketing and production; and kibbutzim, where everything was shared and decisions were undertaken communally. The kibbutzim would become the very symbol of the new immigrants, a collective where everyone worked hard to contribute to the common good.

The task before them was quite formidable. "The hard truth is that when the early Zionists arrived, the country was a neglected estate," a Zionist author wrote.

History had done the worst of which men are capable. Invading armies, improvident farmers and the ubiquitous goat had destroyed the forests. Orchards had given way to scrub and cactus, the old terraces had fallen into disuse and the sand encroached and invaded everything like a yellow plague. The total effect was of a land that seemed to reject human settlement. Seldom was there shade from the sun or shelter from the driving winter rains. In many areas stagnant pools of water hissed and buzzed with the fever of malaria.[17]

But the pioneers met the challenge: working hard, buying land, draining swamps, and planting trees to create the bones of a new state. Through their efforts, the land began to turn green again.

A new immigrant named David Green captured his generation's idealized view of the land upon his arrival at the settlement of Petach Tikva ("Gates of Hope"):

> The howling of jackals in the vineyards; the braying of donkeys in the stables; the croaking of frogs in the ponds; the scent of blossoming acacia; the murmur of the distant sea; the darkening shadows of the groves; the enchantment of stars in the deep blue; the faraway skies, drowsily bright—everything intoxicated me. I was rapturously happy, yet all was strange and bewildering, as though I were errant in a legendary kingdom. Could it be? Joy turned to exaltation. My soul was in tumult, one emotion drowned my very being: Lo, I am in *Eretz Yisrael?* And *Eretz Yisrael* was here, wherever I turned or trod. All night long I sat and communed with my new heaven.[18]

Things would not always been easy for David Green, however. He would suffer from bouts of malaria, poverty, unemployment, and melancholy. But he stayed on, propelling himself forward with an iron will. It was fortunate for the Jewish community in Palestine that he did; he would later Hebraize his name to David Ben-Gurion, Israel's first prime minister.

Upon the founding of one of the first agricultural villages, another new immigrant read a poem:

> As long as deep in the heart
> The soul of a Jew yearns
> And toward the East
> An eye looks to Zion

Our hope is not yet lost
The hope of two thousand years,
To be a free people in our land
The land of Zion and Jerusalem

The poem was called "Hatikvah" ("The Hope"). It captured the essence of the movement and quickly became an important Zionist hymn.

Not all of the new immigrants worked in agriculture, however. In 1909 a group of sixty Jews living in the Arab town of Jaffa purchased land north of the city. Their goal was to build no less than a new, modern city with wide streets, running water, electricity, and sanitation—a model for the Jewish community. From this small start Tel Aviv arose. A few years later the poet Chaim Nachman Bialik wrote of Tel Aviv in glowing terms:

> I see a Hebrew creation such as Tel Aviv as decisive, as against the creations of hundreds of years in the Exile. I wonder whether there is a corner like this for Israel anywhere in the entire world. Such house-building, purely and solely by Jews, from top to bottom, this is a spectacular sight. The creation of an entire Hebrew city is sufficient to till the hearts of the skeptics and doubters with faith that Israel's renaissance is an undeniable fact. Here in Tel Aviv, with all my senses I feel that I have not, nor could I have any other homeland but this place. And blessed be all the builders who have embarked on our eternal building in this corner, the only one in the world.[19]

The Jewish community as a whole began to feel a growing sense of identity and called themselves the Yishuv (the Settlement).

The new settlers revived their own language: Modern Hebrew. The key figure in the revival of Hebrew was Eliezer Ben-Yehuda, a young European immigrant. "In order to have our own land and political life, it is also necessary that we have a language to hold us together," he declared. "That language is Hebrew, but not the Hebrew of the rabbis and scholars. We must have a Hebrew language in which we can conduct the business of life."[20] Upon arriving in Jerusalem he and his wife vowed to speak only Hebrew for the rest of their days, a pledge they kept. Ben-Yehuda immediately set out to revive the language of the Bible, which had not been used in everyday life for nearly two thousand years. He printed a Hebrew-language newspaper, which had only a couple of hundred readers for most of the 1880s. He spoke only Hebrew to his family and eventually published a multivolume Hebrew dictionary.

Most of all, Ben-Yehuda sought out young pioneers to teach the revived language. He found recruits among the idealistic men and women of the new aliyah. It could not have been easy for the Yiddish and Russian speakers, after hours and hours of toil in the field, to use a new tongue for daily interactions. But speak it they did! For the first and only time in history, a dead language was revived, much as the pioneers sought to revive the Jewish people on their ancestral homeland. It was an epic achievement, one of the founding myths of Zionism, a testament to the idealism and hard work of the pioneers. And although the national charter that Herzl had so desperately sought remained elusive, international upheaval would soon intervene on the Zionists' behalf. The capriciousness of war has always changed the destinies of peoples and nations in unexpected ways; the Zionist enterprise would be no exception.

"The Third Temple of Jewish Freedom": The Balfour Declaration

The First World War erupted in the summer of 1914, engulfing all the major European powers in a protracted struggle. Although it was not a main front in the war, the people in Palestine—Arabs and Jews alike—suffered greatly, and the population of both communities declined. But out of the fire of the Great War, an opportunity presented itself to the Zionists. The leader of the English Zionists was Dr. Chaim Weizmann, a chemist who created a synthetic (acetone) to compensate for Britain's lack of cordite during the war. His work for the British brought him into contact with officials in the highest level of the cabinet, and he did his utmost to support the creation of a Jewish home in Palestine. He found a receptive audience among British policymakers because a Jewish state had the potential to aid the British war effort on two important fronts. By the summer of 1917 British needs dictated keeping Russia from leaving the war and bringing the United States into it. Support for a Jewish state would potentially rally Jews in both countries to the Allied cause. Moreover, Britain feared Germany might release its own statement of support for a Jewish state. The stage was set for the biggest diplomatic triumph in Zionist history.

The cabinet member who pushed the hardest for such a statement was Lord Arthur Balfour. Balfour realized that Britain could gain the support of Jews in Russian and America for the war by making a statement declaring a stance in favor of Zionism. With Russia teetering on the brink of leaving the war, keeping Russia engaged in the fight was crucial. The United States, long on the sidelines, was leaning toward war, and Balfour hoped that the support of American Jews would tilt the balance in favor of the pro-war sentiment in the United States. The rest of the cabinet agreed with him. On November 2, 1917, Britain issued the Balfour Declaration, stating, "His Majesty's Government views with favour the establishment in Palestine of a national home for the Jews, and will use their best endeavors to facilitate the achievement of this object, it being clearly understood that nothing shall be done which may prejudice the civil and religious rights of existing non-Jewish communities in Palestine."

The legal charter the Zionists had fought so hard was finally a reality. Newspapers realized its importance, trumpeting "A State for the Jews" and "Palestine for the Jews." Weizmann himself was ecstatic: "Mid storm and fire the people and the land seemed to be born again. The great events of the time of Zerubabel, Ezra, and Nehemiah repeated themselves. The Third Temple of Jewish freedom is rising before us!"[21] He was hailed as a hero and the Yishuv celebrated. The London bureau of the World Zionist Organization declared, "The Declaration puts in the hands of the Jewish people the key to a new happiness and freedom. All depends on you, the Jewish people, and on you only. The Declaration is the threshold, from which you can place your feet upon holy ground. After eighteen hundred years of suffering your recompense is offered to you."[22]

A mere five weeks later British forces captured Palestine from the Ottoman Empire. When the war finally ended in 1918 Britain set up military rule in Palestine. It was a time of high hopes in the Yishuv and among Zionists worldwide. A Jewish state seemed in the offing. Herzl's dream was coming true.

-3-

It Is Good to Die for Our Country

Tension under the British Mandate, 1918–1933

The First Martyr

On March 1, 1920, about a hundred Bedouins gathered outside the tiny Jewish settlement of Tel Hai, in the far north of Palestine. The area around Tel Hai had been abandoned by the British in deference to their postwar treaty with the French. But when French forces arrived they were routed by Bedouins, who sought the territory for their own. The presence of the large band of Arabs outside their settlement disturbed the settlers at first. However, when five heavily armed men stepped forward, the settlers recognized one of them as their neighbor. The Arabs asked to search Tel Hai to ensure that no French soldiers were present. This did not raise any alarm, since it was a common practice. The commander of Tel Hai, Joseph Trumpeldor, accepted the request and led them into the stockade, past the fortified walls, and into a yard. They then entered a small house.

Trumpeldor himself had arrived in Tel Hai only a few months earlier. He had made a name for himself fighting for Russia against the Japanese in 1904, when he had lost an arm. Later he made aliyah to the Holy Land, where he successfully lobbied the British for the creation of a Jewish legion composed of Jews from Palestine. They had seen action in the waning days of World War I. Upon his arrival at Tel Hai, Trumpeldor began drilling the settlers for an attack and worked on improving the settlement's fortification. As a result the little compound was well defended against an outside attack.

As Trumpeldor led the Arabs into the small house, a settler who understood Arabic rushed up to him and explained that the Bedouins were not looking for French soldiers at all. Instead they were planning to seize the Jews' weapons. Trumpeldor raced out of the house and into the yard, where he fired his pistol in the air. His training paid off, as everyone realized it was the signal to open fire immediately. The settlers quickly gunned down a Bedouin carrying a machine gun.

But then Trumpeldor was shot in the stomach and lay writhing on the ground. Inside the house, the Arabs tossed a grenade into the attic, killing Tel Hai's only two women, along with two men. The Arabs opened fire, killing an American volunteer with a clean shot to the head. Hearing the gunfire, the Bedouins massed outside the village attacked. Tel Hai was now besieged from outside and from within, but the settlement's fortified windows provided the Jews with excellent protection. Several Arabs fell to the defenders' guns. The Bedouins' initial assault failed, but the Bedouins regrouped. Meanwhile two other pioneers raced into the yard under a screen of fire and lifted Trumpeldor off the ground and into the safety of the living quarters.

Trumpeldor's stomach wound was horrible, his entrails clearly exposed. He told an orderly to reinsert them, but the orderly did not know how. Trumpeldor had no choice but to guide the poor orderly himself. With the first-aid equipment in the attic and out of reach, the orderly dressed the wound with a towel. Despite his grievous wound, Trumpeldor said, "These are my last moments. Tell everyone that they must stand firm until the very end for the sake of the people of Israel's honor."

They did not fail him. The shooting continued for three hours. While the Arabs fled from inside the compound, the settlers held firm. The machine gun from the dead Arab proved to be quite helpful. By the time it was over, fourteen Bedouins lay dead in front of Tel Hai, and many more were wounded. When the firing ceased, a doctor arrived at Tel Hei and went to Trumpeldor's side. When asked how he felt, he replied, "It is no matter—it is good to die for our country." Trumpeldor succumbed to his wounds a short time later, the first martyr for the new Jewish state.

The battle of Tel Hai vividly illustrated the fact that to the local Arab population, the Jews were not welcome—at least not in large numbers. As long as they had been confined to small groups of isolated farmers and city dwellers, there were no major problems with the Arabs. But in large numbers, the Jews would supersede the Arab population of Palestine, changing the character of the region. And this the Arabs would not tolerate. Although the local inhabitants did not think of themselves as a distinct group of people separate from the rest of the Arab nation, they certainly *did* think the land was theirs. No matter how well-intentioned the Jewish pioneers may have been, this was a problem they had not foreseen. And it would ultimately come to define the very nature of life in the Holy Land.

The issue was foreshadowed as early as 1899, when a leading Arab notable, Yusuf Khalidi, wrote in a letter to the Zionists that "the world is vast enough—there are still uninhabited countries where one could settle millions of poor Jews, who may perhaps become happy there and one day constitute a nation. That would perhaps be the best, the most rational solution to the Jewish question. But in the name of God, let Palestine be in peace."[1]

Theodor Herzl himself wrote back. "Do you really think that an Arab who has a house or land in Palestine whose value is three or four thousand francs will greatly regret seeing the price of his land rise five or tenfold? For that is what necessarily will happen as the Jews come; and this is what must be explained to the inhabitants of the country. They will acquire excellent brothers . . . who will cause the region, their historic motherland, to flourish."[2]

Here we see the debate framed in terms that would continue for decades. For the Arabs, the Jewish question was essentially a European one. The Jews might have previously lived in the Holy Land, but that was thousands of years ago, and a new group of people had moved in and now called Palestine their home. Thus the Jews must look elsewhere. For the Jews, Palestine was their home—they were not moving in, they were moving back. As for the Arabs, they would benefit materially from the Jews' return.

Over the years the two narratives would be modified, but not greatly. The Jews became another wave of European imperialists in the Arabs' minds, foreigners who stole land to which they had no claim. The solution was for the Jews to leave Palestine. A leading Palestinian scholar explained, "The Palestinians and other Arabs did not see the emerging conflict as one between two rights. They could not accept that after a hiatus of two millennia contemporary Jews had a political title to Palestine that overrode the rights of contemporary Palestinians. The Palestinians saw themselves as the descendants of the aboriginal inhabitants of the land, including the pre-Hebraic and post-Hebraic ethnic strands."[3] Conversely, the Jews claimed that the land had been theirs since time immemorial, and they were only reclaiming what was rightfully theirs. The Arabs were intransigent, rejecting the Jews' right to be there. The Jews claimed they had pioneered the land and, through their heroic efforts, made it bloom.

An early example of the conflicting narratives came in the form of a large purchase of land by the Zionists in 1919, in the Valley of Harod in northern Palestine. Two years later a group of seventy-five determined youngsters of the Labor Brigade made their way into the desolate, swamp-infested valley. At first they lived in tents, slept on metal beds, and had no electricity or running water. The work was terribly hard. There were rows of fields to be cleared, planted, and sown. All this had to be done under a searing sun, with mosquitoes constantly biting them, with few modern tools, and with no amenities. Malaria laid low many a young pioneer. During the winter, winds tore through the valley, and rain knocked down their flimsy tents. Yet their spirits remained high. At night they sang, danced, laughed, and spoke in grand terms of the new world they were creating.

One youngster explained what they were trying to achieve:

We were on our own. We left the past behind. We have cut ourselves off from all we were. We have distanced ourselves from
our previous identity and from those dearest to us. Overnight we
were uprooted from the rich soil of our parents' culture that was
enriched with thousands of years of history. Then, after being
uprooted were thrown forcefully by a supreme hand onto this barren land. In parched, sun-struck field we are now face with naked
rocks, exposed to the fire above. Face to face with the elements,
face to face with brutal existence, no protection at all. And here,
in this desolate valley, we must sculpt our lives. From these rocks
we must carve our new foundations. In the Ein Harod valley we
must dig, dig deep, to find the hidden spring that will nourish-
and inspire- our lives.[4]

The outpost, now known as the kibbutz of Ein Harod, grew as
more young pioneers arrived, and more barley and tomato fields
were planted. They set up shops for carpentry, shoemaking, and
welding. A clinic was established, alleviating the woes inflicted
by the ubiquitous malaria they almost all suffered from. They
also brought in cows and chickens to supplement their meager
diet. Cultural life was not neglected either; they set up a library
and even brought in a piano. Their crowning achievement was
the draining of the malarial swamps, achieved by digging well-
lined canals and clay pipes. It was slow, backbreaking work. The
pioneers had to shovel into the hard soil and line the channels
with gravel, gravel that had to broken by hand with chisels. But
the swamps slowly turned into fields, capable of feeding many
more people than lived in the remote kibbutz.

To the pioneers, it was more than a successful agricultural
project. They were building a new type of Jew to inhabit the new
country they were creating. A young poet spoke to the youth of
Ein Harod, telling them:

From the nation's valley of death rose a new generation. This
generation finds life's meaning in toiling our ancestor's land and
reviving our ancient tongue. The draining of the Harod swamps,
which only covered the land after our people were forced to go

into exile, is a true wonder. But this wonder also symbolizes the draining of the swamp our nation was bogged down in during two millennia of exile. You, the pioneers of Harod, are the heroes of the new generation. What you are doing is healing the land and healing the nation.[5]

Another account called it "one of the signal achievements of Zionism: a romantic enterprise, as a malarial wasteland was transformed into one of the glories of Jewish Palestine."[6]

To the local Arab inhabitants, however, it was anything but glorious. The owners of the land who had sold it to the Jews were absentee landlords from Beirut who had made good money from the sale of the land. But the Arabs who lived and worked on the land were forced to leave, as the Jews hired only their own workers, in keeping with their ideology of the conquest of labor. Several thousand peasants were evicted, not only creating tension as a result of one large land sale, but also raising Arab awareness that the same fate may befall the inhabitants of all of Palestine. Anti-Zionist sentiment gripped the Arabs of the land. They began to organize against the invaders. The battle of Tel Hai was only the first encounter.

The British Honor Their Pledge

Caught between the two groups were the British. The Balfour Declaration of 1917 stated, "His Majesty's Government view with favour the establishment in Palestine of a national home for the Jewish people, and will use their best endeavours to facilitate the achievement of this object, it being clearly understood that nothing shall be done which may prejudice the civil and religious rights of existing non-Jewish communities in Palestine." Here was the crux of the matter: the Arabs felt the establishment of such a home in Palestine did indeed prejudice their rights, and before long they made their sentiments known.

On the morning of April 4, 1920, six hundred Arab Christian and Muslim pilgrims gathered in Jerusalem's Old City. It hardly seemed like an unusual event. Large numbers of pilgrims congregated in Jerusalem regularly for religious ceremonies. This gathering, however, was political as well as spiritual. The leaders and followers called for Arab independence and an end to the Zionist enterprise in Palestine. A cry of "Kill the Jews!" went out. Violence erupted as the crowd went on a rampage and began stoning and looting Jewish shops. Khalil al-Sakakini, one of the Arabs' leading intellectuals, described the chaos:

> A riot broke out. The people began to run about and stones were thrown at the Jews. The shops were closed and there were screams. Afterwards, I saw one Hebronite approach a Jewish shoeshine boy, who hid behind a sack in the wall's corners next to Jaffa Gate, and take his box and beat him over the head. He screamed and began to run, his head bleeding and the Hebronite left him and returned to the procession. The riot reached its zenith. All shouted, "Muhammed's religion was born with the sword."[7]

The violence continued for three days until the British restored order. In all, six Jews were killed, two hundred were wounded, and many shops were looted or destroyed. As a result, the Jews established a defense force, known as the Haganah. The following year, larger-scale violence rocked the Mandate, as Arab rioters attacked Jewish shops and stores. This time the Jews, with the Haganah behind them, fought back. Fifty Arabs and fifty Jews had been killed by the time the riots were over.

The Arabs did not restrict their efforts to mere physical violence, however. In 1921 an Arab delegation in London pressed new colonial secretary Winston Churchill to limit Jewish immigration and land purchases. Churchill assured them that "the Jews will not be allowed to come into the country, except insofar as they build up the means for their livelihood." Moreover, "they cannot take any man's lands. They cannot dispossess any man of his rights or his property."[8] But support within Britain for the Zionist enterprise was waning, as Arab objections became more apparent and the cost of maintaining Palestine rose. The House of Lords voted against accepting the Mandate, but Palestine's fate would be decided by the House of Commons.

Churchill told the House of Commons that it was important for Britain to honor her pledges. He also claimed the costs of maintaining Palestine would drop in the next few years. Churchill viewed a Jewish home as morally right as well as in Britain's interest: "It is manifestly right that the scattered Jews should have a national center and a national home to be reunited and where else, but Palestine with which for 3,000 years they have been intimately and profoundly associated? We think it will be good for the world, good for the Jews, good for the British Empire, but also good for the Arabs who dwell in Palestine, and we intend it to be so."[9]

As proof of how they would benefit, Churchill told the House of Commons about a Zionist hydroelectic project that would provide power and irrigation: "I am told that the Arabs would have done it for themselves. Who is going to believe that? Left to themselves, the Arabs of Palestine would not in a thousand years have taken effective steps toward the irrigation and electrification of Palestine. They would have been quite content to dwell—a handful of philosophic people—in the wasted sun-scored plains, letting the waters of the Jordan continue to flow unbridled and unharnessed into the Dead Sea."[10] Churchill may have hoped that British rule in the Middle East would have been easier if there were a developed area next to British holdings in Egypt—the Suez Canal— and along the British oil pipeline that ran from Iraq to Haifa. And he felt the Jews were more capable of developing Palestine than were the Arabs. Whatever his motives, Churchill convinced the House of Commons, who voted overwhelmingly to accept the British Mandate from the League of Nations.

Nonetheless, the terms of the Mandate would be far less favorable to the Zionists than they had envisioned. Palestine would be restricted to the land west of the Jordan River. In a White Paper issued in 1922, Churchill tried to allay Arab fears, stating that His Majesty's Government had not "at any time contemplated, as appears to be feared by the Arab Delegation, the disappearance or the subordination of the Arab population, language or culture in Palestine." As for the Balfour Declaration, it did not "contemplate that Palestine as a whole should be converted into a Jewish National Home, but that such a Home should be founded *in Palestine*."[11]

It was far less than the Zionists had hoped for after the Balfour Declaration's strong statement of support for a Jewish home, but nations do what they must in wartime. There was no reason to assume that Britain would honor its pledge to "facilitate the achievement" of a Jewish home if its interests after the war did not dictate such a course. Indeed, there were many in Britain who would have turned their backs on the wartime pledge. It was the Jews' good fortune that the colonial secretary favored their cause. Moreover, while the Balfour Declaration was seen as the legal mandate for a Jewish home, it was at the time of its issue merely a promise. It was the 1922 White Paper that delivered the promise. Over the next few years, the Jewish home would become a reality.

With the Mandate firmly established, more Jewish immigrants flooded into Palestine. Unlike previous waves, the migrations of the 1920s built up the urban centers of the Yishuv. With the urban centers came the institutions of a modern state: banks, schools, industry, newspapers, the Histadrut (a trade union), and eventually an administrative arm of the World Zionist Organization known as the Jewish Agency. The Haganah expanded. More land was purchased, and more settlements arose. In 1925 the first Jewish institute of higher education—the Hebrew University on Mount Scopus in Jerusalem—was established.

The poet Chaim Nachman Bialik captured its meaning for the Zionists:

Thousands of our young sons, responding to the call of their heart, stream to this land from all corners of the earth to redeem it from its desolation and ruin. They are ready to spill out their longing and strength into the bosom of this dry land in order to bring it to life. They plough through rocks, drain swamps, pave roads, singing with joy. These youngsters elevate crude physical labor to the level of supreme holiness, to the status of a religion. We must now light this holy flame within the walls of the buildings, which is now being opened on Mount Scopus. Let these youngsters build with fire the lower Jerusalem while we build the higher Jerusalem. Our existence will be recreated and made secure by means of both ways together.[12]

Jewish attachment to the land was growing stronger. In December 1928 members of kibbutz Beit Alpha in northern Palestine were digging an irrigation channel when they uncovered a brilliantly colored mosaic floor. They were stunned to see Hebrew writing on the stones. Realizing that they had made an important find, they quickly summoned the only Zionist archaeologist they knew: Eliezer Sukenik, from Jerusalem, who had been preaching for years that pioneers needed to report any archaeological finds they might come across. Sukenik hurried from Jerusalem with his eleven-year-old son, Yigael, and quickly began expanding the excavation site. What they found as they pushed back more and more soil was an ancient synagogue, adorned with splendid mosaics, the first intact ancient Jewish mosaics discovered. On one end was a vivid depiction of the story of the sacrifice of Isaac. Abraham appeared with a beard and a halo, along with other characters from the story. On the other end of the floor was a depiction of the Ark of the Covenant, flanked by two menorahs and guarded by great lions.

The beautiful, well-preserved artwork was reason enough for the find to be important. But it was vastly more than aesthetically pleasing. Sukenik described what it meant: "Suddenly these people saw things that were never so tangible before. There was suddenly a feeling that this parcel of land—for which they had suffered so much—wasn't just any piece of land but the place where their fathers and grandfathers had lived and died fifteen hundred or two thousand years before. All their work now had a different significance. Their history had been uncovered, and they could see it with their own eyes."[13] The synagogue and mosaic at Beit Alpha became a sensation in Palestine. It even made it into the *New York Times*. Pilgrims from all over Jewish Palestine came to see it, for it was evidence that the Jews had been here and that they were simply returning home.

It was exactly what Sukenik had been trying to achieve for his entire professional career. His goal was to create "Jewish archaeology" as a tool of national rebirth in Palestine. Sukenik was the first to demonstrate the power of archaeology, and it was a lesson that greatly impressed his young son. Beit Alpha was not the only archaeological site young Yigael visited. In 1927 an immigrant wrote a poem about Masada, largely unknown to Jews until that time. In the poem, Jewish pioneers dance atop the fortress while singing, "Masada shall not fall again!" It was the first time the phrase was introduced. The story struck a chord with the settlers, who felt they were surrounded by enemies, and Masada became a destination for many young Zionists, including young Yigael Sukenik. But unlike Beit Alpha, there had been no systematic excavation at Masada. It was too remote and too large. Yigael Sukenik would one day change that.

"A Natural Conflict": Zionism and the Arabs

The Zionist dream was becoming more and more of a reality as a quasi-state arose in Palestine under British protection. But how would they deal with the Arabs? That was the issue that divided the Zionists. The Labor Zionists of the Mapai Party, the mainstream of the Zionist movement, hoped an accommodation could be reached. Led by David Ben-Gurion, they believed they could work with the Arabs to reach a deal: "If the Arabs agree to our return to our land, we would help them with our political, financial, and moral support to bring about the rebirth and unity of the Arab people." Furthermore, he explained,

> we were neither desirous nor capable of building our future in Palestine at the expense of the Arabs. The Arabs of Palestine would remain where they were, their lot would improve, and even politically they would not be dependent on us, even after we came to constitute the vast majority of the population, for there was a basic difference between our relation to Palestine and that of the Arabs. For us, the Land was everything and there was nothing else. For the Arabs, Palestine was only a small portion of the large numer-

ous Arab countries. Even when the Arabs became a minority in Palestine they would not be a minority in their territory, which extended from the Mediterranean coast to the Persian Gulf, and from the Taurus Mountains to the Atlantic Ocean.[14]

Others Zionists were not as sanguine. Led by the fiery Vladimir Jabotinsky, they were called the Revisionists, because they sought to revise the Mandate to include a Jewish state on both sides of the Jordan River. The Arabs had to be made to realize that the Jews would not be driven off by force. Only once the Arabs realized the Jews were there to stay would peace be possible. "The tragedy here lies in the fact that there is a collision between two truths," Jabotinsky explained, referring to both sides' rights to the land. "But our justice is greater."[15] He rejected the Mapai line that a deal could be reached: "But the Arabs loved their country as much as the Jews did. Instinctively they understood Zionist aspirations very well, and their decision to resist them was only natural. Every people fought immigration and settlement by foreigners, however high-minded their motives for settling. There was no misunderstanding but a natural conflict."[16] No agreement was possible with the Palestinian Arabs; they would accept Zionism only when they found themselves against an "iron wall," when they realized they had no alternative but to accept Jewish settlement. There were other differences between Mapai and Revisionism. The former was dedicated to socialism; the latter preferred free enterprise. Mapai sought accommodation with the British; the Revisionists sought to drive them out. But most of all, it was the Arab issue that divided them, with the Revisionists calling for a more active defense against the Arabs. These dual visions of Zionism remain with the Jewish state today.

On Friday, August 23, 1929, an unusually large number of worshippers gathered in the Old City of Jerusalem. This was not a typical Friday prayer crowd. Men had been brought in from the countryside. A crisis had been brewing for several months. At issue was the critical spot in the Old City in Jerusalem—known to Muslims as the Haram al-Sharif, the site where Muhammad ascended to heaven, marked by the spectacular Dome of the Rock and the Al-Aqsa Mosque, and to Jews as the Temple Mount, where the sacred Temple had stood in ancient times. Below the Muslim shrine on the mount, Jews gather to pray at the Wailing Wall, the only remnant of the Temple. There is no better symbol of the conflict than the two religious sites only a stone's throw apart. Over the years it would become a source of conflict many times; 1929 was only the first encounter over Palestine's holy sites. Instigating the Arabs was the senior cleric of Palestine—the mufti of Jerusalem, Hajj Amin al-Husseini. Declaring that the Arab people in Palestine and the Al-Aqsa Mosque were in danger from the Jews, the mufti's men urged the crowd to protect Palestine from the invaders. The crowd dispersed from the Haram al-Sharif (the Temple Mount) into the Jewish neighborhoods, crying, "*Itbah al Yahud!*"—"Kill the Jews!" They fell upon defenseless Jews, attacking, stabbing, and killing as they went. British police seemed impotent; instead Haganah members rushed from their homes and work. Armed with guns and grenades, they stood atop roofs, inside windows, and astride alleyways. They stopped the riots where they were deployed, but they could not cover all of Jerusalem.

The worst violence, however, was in Hebron. The old Jewish community there had no Haganah members and was virtually defenseless. A Jewish resident recorded the events as an Arab mob attacked a group in the middle of prayers:

Here come the Arabs! We went to reinforce the door and ran around the room like madmen. The shrieks of the women and the babies' wailing filled the house. With ten other people I put boxes and tables in front of the door, but the intruders broke it with hatches and were about to force their way in. So we left the door and began running from room to room, but wherever we went we were hit by a torrent of stones. The situation was horrible; I can't describe the wailing and screaming.

In one room my mother was standing by the window shouting for help. I looked out and saw a wild Arab mob laughing and throwing stones. I was afraid my mother would be hit, so I don't know how, but I grabbed her and shoved her behind a bookcase in the corner. I hid another young woman there, as well as a twelve-year-old boy and a yeshiva student. Finally, I went behind the bookcase myself.

Suffocating, we lay on top of one another and heard the sound of the Arabs singing as they broke into the room and the shouting and groaning of the people being beaten. After about ten minutes the house grew still except for some stifled groans. Then there was loud gunfire, apparently from the police.

I barely managed to get out of my hiding place. It was difficult to move the bookcase because of the bodies that lay piled up against it. My eyes were dark from the sight of the dead and the wounded. I could find no place to put my foot. In the sea of blood I saw Eliezer Dan and his wife, my friend Dubnikov, a teacher from Tel Aviv and many more. . . . Almost all had knife and hatchet wounds in their heads. Some had broken ribs. A few bodies had been slashed and their entrails had come out. I cannot describe the look in the eyes of the dying. I saw the same scene everywhere. In one room I recognized my brother's wife, who lay there half-naked, barely alive. The entire house had been looted, it was full of feathers and there were blood stains on the walls. . . .

I approached the window and saw policemen. I asked them to send a doctor. That same moment some Arabs passed by carrying a dead man on a stretcher. When they saw me they threatened me with their fists. I returned to my hiding place. A moment later I heard voices. They were the voices of the wounded who had gotten up and also of people who had been miraculously saved by hiding in the shower room behind the toilet. Apparently the Arabs had gotten as far as the toilet and killed one of the people there.

I recognized my brother among the injured. He had a hatchet wound on his head and a large bruise on his forehead, probably from a rock. I threw water on him and he stood up, but died of his wounds a few hours later. Dubnikov had apparently died of suffocation. His murdered wife lay next to him. I again approached the window and asked for doctors, because many people could have been saved with prompt medical help. One of the policemen outside answered me in Hebrew—soon, he said. About a quarter of an hour later, some cars came to take us to the police. We began taking care of the wounded.[17]

Nearly seventy Jews were killed in Hebron. Most were saved by Arabs, who hid them in their homes. The survivors fled. The second holiest city in Judaism, the site of King David's coronation and the Cave of the Patriarchs, had no Jews whatsoever. In all, over a hundred Jews and a hundred Arabs were killed in the riots. Most of the Arabs were killed by British police in the later stages of the riots. The violence was the worst Palestine had suffered. In contrast to the disturbances of 1920 and 1921, both sides were better organized, better equipped, and clearer in their goals. The outlines of the conflict were becoming apparent for all to see. In this atmosphere of tension, David Ben-Gurion decided to see for himself if peace with the Arabs were possible. He met with a high-ranking Arab attorney in the British administration, Musa Alami, who was also a relative of Hajj Amin al-Husseini. Although they got along well as they sipped their tea, Alami told the Jewish leader that it would be better for the land to remain poor and desolate for another hundred years than to let more Jews enter Palestine. Ben-Gurion was surprised: Prior to that meeting he had accepted the idea prevalent among the Zionists that the Jewish presence would greatly benefit the Arabs. Ben-Gurion later explained that the meeting shattered his assumption that the Arabs had no reason to oppose the Zionist enterprise.

Ben-Gurion did not give up, though. He proposed various schemes for coexistence with the Arabs. But they all made one demand Ben-Gurion could not accept: a Jewish minority in Palestine. The failure of the peace proposals cast a dark cloud over the Jewish enterprise in Eretz Yisrael. But troubled as the Jewish situation in Palestine may have been, a new threat arose that challenged the very existence of the Jews in the European heartland, where the vast majority of world Jewry still lived.

-4-

The Great Catastrophe

Jews Flee Nazi Germany while Palestine Erupts, 1933–1939

January 30, 1933, stands as one of the blackest days in the long list of black days in Jewish history. It was on that day that the leader of the National Socialist Party—"Nazi," for short—became chancellor of Germany. Adolf Hitler came to power promising to rid Germany of the Jews. It became apparent very quickly that he meant to keep his word. The new government expelled Jews from the professions and barred them from universities, and a few were even attacked.

The world responded. In countries across the globe, Jews and non-Jews alike rallied and announced a boycott of German goods. Hitler had promised to revive Germany's moribund economy, and the boycott would undermine that promise. And the boycott began to bite. The German fur, diamond, and shipping industries were particularly hard hit. But the Nazis never considered backing down to the Jewish conspirators, who they believed were bent on destroying the "Aryan" race. Instead, they announced their own boycott of Jewish goods within Germany, set for April 1. As the deadline approached many inside and outside of Germany doubted if the Nazis would actually carry it out. On the announced date the world waited with bated breath. German Jews began the day with their usual routine, only to encounter a terrifying spectacle. Jewish merchants were met with hordes of brown-shirted Nazi youth camped out in front of their stores, chasing away their customers. The Brownshirts painted yellow Jewish stars on the windowpanes and wrote "Juden!" in large letters. They yelled, "Buy German. Don't buy from Jewish stores!" at passersby. When brave German citizens tried to enter stores and buy whatever they could lay their hands on, the Brownshirts grabbed them, held them down, and stamped the word "traitor" on their foreheads in front of cameramen. The intimidation worked. Most Germans stayed away from the Jewish stores. Other Jewish shops were vandalized, their windows shattered, their merchandise destroyed. Stink bombs were rolled into the larger Jewish-owned department stores. The terror was not limited to just these. Nazi hooligans chased clients away from Jewish doctors and lawyers; they hauled judges off their benches. Many were beaten, a few were even killed. Such incidents took place throughout all of Germany.

In this manner, the Nazi era formally began. The Jewish economy in Germany was crippled, even as the German economy suffered under the global boycott. Leaders of the anti-German boycott, like the American rabbi Stephen Wise, hoped their measures would crack Hitler's Germany, forcing the Nazis to relent on the Jewish issue.

The Transfer Agreement

But there was another solution. On March 16, 1933, four prominent German Zionist émigrés gathered in Jerusalem to discuss the plight of their brethren. It would be great if the German Jews would come to Palestine, they all agreed. Unlike most Jewish immigrants, they could afford the entry fee of 1,000 pounds required by the British. But German law prevented them from taking currency out the country. One of the Zionists suggested the German government might allow a 1,000-pound exemption if the Jews immigrated to Palestine. The others were incredulous. Negotiate with the Nazis? Even if the Nazis agreed to negotiate with Jews, what would the Nazis gain from it? The departure of thousands of Jews, he responded. After all, wasn't that what the Nazis wanted?

It seemed far-fetched, but it was at least worth a try. To negotiate with the Nazis, the Zionists chose Sam Cohen, a German Jewish businessman with dealings in Palestine.

Cohen proved to be a fortuitous choice. For the deal Cohen put together was nothing short of genius. Cohen met with two high-ranking German officials, proposing a 1,000-pound currency exemption in order to pay the entry fee. It wasn't good enough for the Germans. They proposed the Jews be allowed to leave with 1,000 pounds as long as the rest of their money and property was forfeit to the German state. Cohen knew there was no way the German Jews or Zionists could accept this. Therefore he worked out an elaborate plan that would enrich all parties involved.

Under his plan, the Anglo-Palestine Bank would buy the German goods the Yishuv needed—farm equipment, fertilizers, coal, iron, cement, and the like. The German manufacturers would then be paid from the émigrés accounts. The émigrés, upon arriving in Palestine with 1,000 pounds, would be compensated by the Anglo-Palestine Bank for the use of their funds to buy the equipment. In this roundabout manner, Germany would gain the money it badly needed, the Yishuv gained the materials necessary to build a state, and the German Jews gained a safe haven along with compensation. It was an elegant solution to a dire situation that threatened the very existence of Jews in Europe.

Nazi approval of the plan came swiftly—Jewish emigration from Germany was exactly what they wanted. Zionist approval, however, was a different story. In August 1933 Zionist leaders gathered at the Eighteenth World Zionist Congress in Prague. It was here that the fate of the so-called Transfer Agreement would be decided, along with the fate of German Jewry and perhaps even a Jewish state itself. David Ben-Gurion prophetically explained why he favored the agreement. "Hitler's rule places the entire Jewish people in jeopardy," he had told the Histadrut Council earlier that year. "What will be our strength and weight in Palestine on the awful judgment day, when the great catastrophe bursts upon the world? Who knows—perhaps only four or five years stand before us and that terrible day. During this period we must double our numbers, for the size of the Jewish community then may determine our fate in that decisive hour."[1]

Opposition to the agreement was led by none other than Vladimir Jabotinsky, founder of the Revisionist Party and a skilled orator. "We sympathize with the position of our German brethren. But Hitlerism is a danger to the sixteen million Jews all over the world and German Jews cannot influence us not to fight our enemy. Our enemy must be destroyed!"[2] The Transfer Agreement was humiliating. Jews in Palestine would not abandon the boycott and would never purchase German goods through the agreement. He called on Jews to unite and take their rightful places fighting Hitler. Jabotinksy and the Revisionists were not alone in their opposition to the deal. A Polish delegate claimed that the Jews in nearby countries were also threatened by Hitler and that the Transfer Agreement was a betrayal of the Jews of Eastern Europe.

Mapai members retorted that the German crisis was secondary to the establishment of Palestine, for whereas Hitlerism was a temporary phenomenon, a Jewish home would be permanent. Therefore, all efforts must be made to transfer the Jews to Palestine to build the national home: "The anti-Hitler boycott is a means to a goal—not a goal itself."[3] That goal was a state for the Jews: "If it is impossible to restore the refugees to their country, or to receive them in another country, then the country of their ancestors must be given back to them. Nothing is more straightforward or just. The idea of Zionism as the solution of the Jewish question must now again rise before the world like a new daylight!"[4]

But Rabbi Stephen Wise, the American leader of the anti-German boycott, still held hope that his measures would break Germany. He warned that the Transfer Agreement would divide the anti-Hitler front. He rejected the Zionists' claim that the settlement of Palestine took priority over everything else: "As long as the Jews in Germany have not received their former legal rights again, and as long as the German government does not enable Jews the right of free emancipation with all their property, it is inadmissible that any agreement of any kind may be signed with the present German government."[5]

Supporters of the plan noted that it did not end the anti-German boycott. Moreover, rejecting the plan was dangerous: "If the Congress does revoke the agreement, it will be assuming a very heavy responsibility; it will endanger the existence of many German Jews. The Transfer Agreement in no way interferes with the boycott movement, since no new currency would be flowing into Germany as a result of the agreement."[6]

The debate went into the early hours of the morning. In the end, Mapai remained the largest voting bloc. Along with other delegates who realized that the Transfer Agreement would not only save German Jews but also create a Jewish state, they gained the necessary votes. The plan was adopted, and with it, a huge step forward to creating a homeland was taken. Those present realized it, for they adopted two monumental motions: one calling for the blue and white Star of David to be adopted as the official flag of the Jewish state; the other declaring the Zionist hymn "Hatikvah" as the national anthem. Seventeen hours after the session began, the delegates left, singing "Hatikvah" in the halls of Prague. They had agreed to a deal with the devil, but its dividends would be enormous.

Over sixty thousand Jews and $100 million (roughly $2 billion in 2015 dollars) came into Palestine over the course of the Transfer Agreement. The total number of Jewish immigrants fleeing from Germany, Austria, and Eastern European countries under the threat of Fascism was even larger—roughly two hundred thousand from 1933 to 1939. English writer Christopher Sykes recorded what was like as the exiles arrived in Palestine:

> There was no more moving sight in those days than the arrival at Haifa or Jaffa of a Mediterranean ship carrying Jews from Europe: the spontaneous cries of joy at the first sight of the shore, the mass chanting of Hebrew hymns or Yiddish songs usually beginning raggedly over all the boat and sometimes swelling into a single harmony; the uncontrolled joy of these returning exiles (for so they thought of themselves); a man seizing hold of a stranger and pointing with tears of joy to the approaching land crying "Zion!

Zion!" and "Jerusalem!" Such scenes made many of those who saw them recognize as never before that the human spirit cannot be destroyed, and the Jewish inspiration is among the sublimest expressions of the unconquerable soul. Zionism showed itself at its very finest in those years. Enthusiasm went hand in hand with practical sense. The Zionists remember how the mass-migrations of the mid-twenties had endangered their purpose, and they succeeded in settling the thousands of newcomers with extraordinary skill. Unemployment crises inevitably arose on several occasions, but they were always kept under control, and the control was largely Jewish. Palestine was the answer to Hitler![7]

The immigrants who came to Palestine in these years were by far the most economically productive wave to enter the Holy Land, bringing their knowledge and expertise in many fields. New industries sprang up, the cities blossomed, and the economy boomed. More land was purchased, and more land was cultivated. By 1939 there were nearly half a million Jews living in Eretz Yisrael, roughly thirty percent of the population. And herein lay the problem: the Arabs of Palestine saw the land as theirs, the Zionists as invaders, and the British as enablers. Sykes noted, "The Arabs looked on with dismay. Seen through Arab eyes, this great work of rescue and redemption had nothing beautiful about it and seemed on the contrary to be a stark act of oppression against themselves."[8] By the mid-1930s, Palestine was powder keg waiting to explode.

An Irrepressible Conflict: The Arab Revolt

The lid blew off in May 1936. Arab leaders met in Jerusalem and demanded an end to Jewish immigration and land purchases, as well as an Arab majority government. When their demands were not met, they declared a general strike, which lasted six months. More significantly, violence erupted across the country. Jewish orchards and farms were destroyed, and twenty-one Jews were killed in the first month alone. A Labor Zionist leader named Golda Meir recalled the tension: "Whenever I had to go from Tel Aviv to Jerusalem for a meeting—which was frequently—I kissed the children goodbye in the morning knowing that I might well never come home again, that my bus might be ambushed, that I might be shot by an Arab sniper at the entrance of Tel Aviv."[9] By autumn most of the countryside was in open rebellion against British rule and Jewish encroachment. The British brutally put down the insurrection, inflicting large casualties on the rebels. Like the Jews, the Arabs were willing to die for their country.

Yet even a nationwide rebellion could not stop the Jews from expanding their enterprise. They would continue to settle Palestine, even in the face of armed hostility. To overcome the problem, the Zionists devised a new method of creating settlements, known as tower-and-stockade villages. Since the land could not be settled slowly, as that would only invite attacks, the plan would have to be implemented in a single day. They would first build a watchtower and a wooden perimeter and then fill in the interior. An eyewitness described the process:

> Zero hour was fixed at 3:30 on a certain Tuesday morning, and the new group, accompanied by members of the neighbouring settlements, set out with portable structures in a procession of lorries, and nosed their way eastwards. . . .
>
> As they came closer, they made out the silhouette of a young boy seated on a tractor. The figure detached itself and came toward them.
>
> "Shalom, Shalom, Hacol Beseder! Hallo, hallo. Everything's ok!" he called, quite calmly. "Shalom," they replied.
>
> He was a youth of eighteen, a member of the new group. When the date of settlement had been decided, he had volunteered to go out some time before and crush out a path with the tractor. But he had a job in the town during the day, and besides it was felt advisable not to attract too much attention to the impending settlement of this area. The tractor had therefore been brought out four nights before and hidden amidst the weeds and he had decided to work it during the night.
>
> For three nights before the "great day," he had come out to this spot and carefully and quietly had worked, methodically burning

the weeds, then crushing them with the tractor. He was alone and completely unarmed. There was the ever-present danger that he would be surprised by Bedouin, in which case only his wits, his Arabic, and perhaps a cigarette would have saved him. . . . And they followed him to the newly-cleared site, and hastily prepared to build up their homestead.

By late afternoon, a new Jewish village had sprung up. Bungalows had been erected, barricades run up round the boundaries, and the wooden watchtower, complete with lamp and dynamo, put in position. When night fell the lamp was switched on mid dead silence. It threw a powerful beam across the surrounding waste. Its symbolism was apparent to all, and it was the only moment when they permitted themselves to be sentimental. It was the light of a new life and a new era. An area from which civilization had departed 2,000 years before was being reclaimed.

A new settlement had been established.[10]

In this manner, the Yishuv formed fifty-six tower-and-stockade settlements as the Arab Revolt raged for no fewer than three years, from 1936 to 1939.

The British resorted to heavy measures to crush the revolt, bringing in an additional twenty thousand soldiers to Palestine. One of them was named Orde Charles Wingate, one of the most colorful characters to ever walk the Holy Land. A short, blond, intense Scotsman, he was convinced that helping the Jews reclaim the land of the Bible was his sacred duty. "I count it my privilege to help you fight your battle," he told the Jews. "To that purpose I want to devote my life. I believe that the very existence of mankind is justified when it is based on the moral foundations of the Bible." Wingate wanted to train the Jews to fight the Arabs, but the British wavered—teaching the Jews military techniques could result in the Jews one day using their newfound skills against the British. But the Arab revolt grew worse. Finally, Wingate persuaded British commanders to allow him to put together a Jewish squad to attack Arab marauders, the so-called Special Night Squads. Under his leadership, the sns attacked the infiltrators, scoring major successes. Before going into battle, Wingate would read the soldiers biblical passages relating to their area of operations, testimony to their upcoming success. In doing so, Wingate trained many future leaders of the Israeli army. By 1939 the revolt was quashed, due ironically to British-Jewish cooperation.

During the height of the revolt, Britain sent a commission headed by Sir William Robert Peel to investigate the cause of the unrest. The commissioners toured Palestine, viewing Arab and Jewish cities, towns, and villages. At one Jewish agricultural settlement, they came across a man living in a rough ramshackle hut. Surprisingly, there was a piano and music sheets inside. One of the commissioners recognized the man. He was a well-known German musician who had once played at the British Embassy in Berlin. "This is a terrible change for you," the commissioner said. But to the commissioner's surprise the musician replied, "It is a change from Hell to Heaven."[11] He had fled Nazi Germany, where he had been hounded and cast out of society. Compared to that, Palestine was a blessing.

In July 1937 the Peel Commission released its findings, explaining how grave the situation was. "The disease is so deep-rooted that, in our firm conviction, the only hope of a cure lies in a surgical operation," the commission declared. "An irrepressible conflict has arisen between two national communities within the narrow bounds of one small country. About 1,000,000 Arabs are in strife—open or latent—with some 400,000 Jews. But while neither race can justly rule all Palestine, we see no reason why, if it were practicable, each race should not rule part of it." The report ended on a gloomy note: "Partition seems to offer at least a chance of ultimate peace. We can see none in any other plan."[12] Therefore, the Peel Commission recommended dividing Palestine into Jewish and Arab states. The Jews accepted the plan, while the Arabs rejected it. But the commission's recommendations were quickly overshadowed by events in Europe. With the winds of war stirring again, British policy became concerned with the threat of another conflict with Germany. Since the Arab states held much of the world's oil, British planners determined they could not afford to alienate these countries. Therefore, British policy in Palestine quickly veered toward the Arab's favor. In 1938 Britain formally rejected the partition plan. But even larger changes in British policy were to come.

"The Night of Broken Glass"

Meanwhile, the situation in Germany was growing worse for the Jews. The Nazis passed the Nuremberg Laws in 1935, depriving the Jews of German citizenship and forbidding intermarriage. More Jews fell under Nazi control with the unification of Austria and Germany in March 1938. The Nazis moved quickly to victimize their new prey. In Vienna ss troops rounded up elderly Jews and brought them to the Prater amusement park. An eyewitness described what happened. The victims "had to run in circles until they fainted and collapsed. Those pretending to have fainted in order to escape the ordeal were beaten until they got up and ran again. . . . Another favorite torture was the famous scenic railway in the Prater amusement park, where large numbers of Jews were forced into the carries, tied to their seats, and then driven at top speed until they lost consciousness. . . . Hundreds of Jewish people were taken to the hospital during the following days with severe heart attacks, and in no few cases these 'pleasure hours' brought about heart failure and death."[13] Like their brethren in Germany, Austrian Jews now lived under the cruelty and random violence of Nazi rule.

In October 1938 the Nazis expelled seventeen thousand Polish Jews who had been living inside Germany. These Jews were rounded up, put on trains, and then marched to the Polish border. A deportee recalled:

> When we reached the border, we were searched to see if anybody had any money, and anybody who had more than ten marks, the balance was taken from him. . . . We walked two kilometers on foot to the Polish border. They told us to go—the ss men were whipping us, those who lingered they hit, and blood was flowing on the road. They tore away their little baggage from them,

they treated us in a most barbaric fashion. . . . They shouted at us, "Run! Run!" I myself received a blow and fell in a ditch. My son helped me and he said, "Run, run dad—otherwise you'll die."[14]

Once across the border, only about half were admitted in their former country. The rest languished in Polish detention camps until the war began.

Then in November 1938 Hitler's Stormtroopers attacked Jews throughout Germany, in what became known as Kristallnacht (the Night of Broken Glass). For four days, Nazi henchman attacked forty-thousand Jews, dragging them out of bed, throwing them in jail, killing, maiming, and wounding innocent men, women, and children. Thousands of Jewish homes, synagogues, and stores were broken into and destroyed. An eyewitness recorded how the terror began in one German town: "Dead silence—not a sound to be heard in the town. The lamps in the street, the lights in the shops and in the houses are out. It is 3:30 a.m. All of a sudden, noises in the street break my sleep, a wild medley of shouts and shrieks. I listen, frightened and alarmed, until I distinguish words. Get out, Jews! Death to the Jews!"[15] The mobs ran down the streets breaking and looting Jewish homes.

A schoolgirl recorded the attack on her home: "Seconds later, there burst into this room a horde of violent monsters, their faces contorted into raving masks of hatred, some red, some pale, all screaming and shouting, eyes rolling, teeth bared, wild hands flailing, jackboots kicking. They were wielding axes, sledgehammers, stones and knives. They rushed about the room smashing, throwing, trampling. It seemed to me that there were hundreds of them bursting through the door, though I believe there were, in fact, only a dozen." The mob left, and the girl and her family waited in fear: "No one moved. The sounds continued awhile and then there was silence, though my mind still heard the noise. But there was silence, complete and sudden, with only broken furniture groaning and settling into place. We listened for a long time, not daring to breathe, expecting them to return any minute to kill us all. But they did not return." The girl and her family surveyed the damage to their house: "The piano on its side, its guts ripped out and scattered on the floor like the bones and sinews of some huge animal, every single oil painting hanging in strips out of its frames or lying impaled on the spikes of upturned furniture . . . books were torn, the pages scattered, furnishings were slashed with the stuffing welling out like flesh, old oak and walnut tables and chairs were legless, the carpets hacked, curtains torn down, floorboards splintered, and many windows smashed."[16]

The Nazis made a special point of attacking synagogues, the symbol of the Jewish faith. All across Germany, as Jewish houses of worship burned, the fire brigades looked on, only dousing flames if they spread to non-Jewish buildings. A non-Jewish German boy looked on as one such episode unfolded in front of him: "And there we saw the synagogue—or, more correctly, what was left of it. The red wall, the black slate roof, the well-kept lawn— the building—was gone. A burnt-out shell of smoke-blackened bricks, empty holes where the windows had been, a collapsed roof from whose splintered rafters plumes of black smoke drifted upward—that was all that remained. Across the street . . . a fire engine was parked. The hoses were rolled up; the firefighters sat on or leaned against their truck, dozing and staring wordlessly at the scarred ruin."[17]

The attacks on the houses of worship were not limited to grand synagogues in large cities. In a small village, a Jewish butcher named Michael watched as Stormtroopers attacked the town's synagogue near his home:

> After a while, the Stormtroops were joined by people who were not in uniform; and suddenly, with one loud cry of, "Down with the Jews," the gathering outside produced axes and heavy sledgehammers. They advanced toward the little synagogue, which stood in Michael's own meadow, opposite his house. They burst the door open, and the whole crowd, by now shouting and laughing, stormed into the little House of God.
>
> Michael, standing behind the tightly drawn curtains, saw how the crowd tore the Holy Ark wide open; and three men who had

smashed the ark, threw the Scrolls of the Law of Moses out. He threw them—these Scrolls, which had stood in their quiet dignity, draped in blue or wine-red velvet, with their little crowns of silver covering the tops of the shafts by which the Scroll was held during the service—to the screaming and shouting mass of people which had filled the little synagogue.

The people caught the Scrolls as if they were amusing themselves with a ball game—tossing them up into the air again, while other people flung them further back until they reached the street outside. Women tore away the red and blue velvet and everybody tried to snatch some of the silver adorning the Scrolls.

Naked and open, the Scrolls lay in the muddy autumn lane; children stepped on them and others tore pieces from the fine parchment on which the Law was written—the same Law which the people who tore it apart had, in vain, tried to absorb for over a thousand years.

When the first Scroll was thrown out of the synagogue, Michael made a dash for the door. His heart beat violently and his senses became blurred and hazy. Unknown fury built up within him, and his clenched fists pressed against his temples. Michael forgot that to take one step outside the house amongst the crowds would mean his death.

The Stormtroopers, who still stood outside the house watching with stern faces over the tumultuous crowd which obeyed their commands without really knowing it, would have shot the man, quietly, in an almost matter of fact way. Michael's wife, sensing the deadly danger, ran after her husband, and clung to him, imploring him and begging him not to go outside. Michael tried to fling her aside, but only her tenacious resistance brought him back to his senses.

He stood there, in the small hall behind the front door, looking around him for a second, as if he did not know where he was. Suddenly he leaned against the wall, tears streaming from his eyes, like those of a little child.

After a while, he heard the sound of many heavy hammers outside. With trembling legs, he got up from his chair and looked outside once more. Men had climbed on the roof of the synagogue, and were hurling tiles down—others were cutting the cross beams as soon as they were bare of cover. It did not take long before the first heavy grey stones came tumbling down, and the children of the village amused themselves as they flung stones into the many-colored windows.

When the first rays of a cold and pale November sun penetrated the heavy dark clouds, the little synagogue was a heap of stone, broken glass and smashed-up woodwork.

Where the two well cared for flowerbeds had flanked both sides of the gravel path leading to the door of the synagogue, the children had lit a bonfire and the parchment of the Scrolls gave enough food for the flames to eat up the smashed-up benches and doors, and the wood, which only the day before had been the Holy Ark for the Scrolls of the Law of Moses.[18]

In addition, about thirty thousand Jewish men were rounded up and sent to concentration camps. As they debarked the buses, a prisoner saw the brutal treatment that awaited them. "One man, who had apparently lost consciousness on the trip, was removed from the bus by an ss man pulling him by the ankles. This caused the man's head to hit each of the steps leading down from the bus. . . . After being dumped on the ground, he flailed his arms and legs through the air, thereby inadvertently kicking his tormentor. The latter, in a blind rage, jumped on his victim, stomping and kicking him into submission with his hobnailed boots."[19]

By the time it was over, 7,500 Jewish businesses and 275 synagogues had been destroyed or burned, along with an unknown number of homes. To make matters worse, the German government fined the Jews for the damage done during the attacks. The fine was equivalent to one-sixth of all property owned by Germany's Jews. Hitler's anti-Semitic policies had been harsh, but violence had not yet been a tool of state policy. Kristallnacht marked the beginning of the new policy, and it was precisely at this terrible moment that Britain unequivocally backed away from the Jewish state promised under the Balfour Declaration.

On February 7, 1939, with the threat of Nazi Germany growing greater by the day, David Ben-Gurion, Chaim Weizmann, and delegates from Egypt, Iraq, and Saudi Arabia arrived in London to meet with the British leadership. They had been summoned by British prime minister Neville Chamberlain, in order to explain the empire's new policy toward Palestine. Jewish immigration would end. The Jews would live under Arab rule in an independent state. Ben-Gurion erupted: "Jews cannot be prevented from immigrating into the country except by force of British bayonets, British police, and the British navy. And, of course, Palestine cannot be converted into an Arab state over Jewish opposition without the constant help of British bayonets!"

The British were aghast. The Jewish leader was threatening violence! But Ben-Gurion relished the moment: "For the first time in the history of Zionism and in the history of the Jewish people after the Roman conquest, we faced serious combat with a mighty power and did not rely only on pleading, requests for mercy, or appeals for justice. For the first time we used a new argument: our own strength in Palestine." The British "could hardly believe their ears."

Egyptian prime minister Ali Maher explained Arab opposition to Zionism:

> If Palestine were empty, we, the Arab states, would invite the Jews to come to Palestine and establish a Jewish state in it. For we understand the Jewish ideal. It is a beautiful and just ideal. It is necessary that the Jews also have a state, and it would be good for the Arabs too. But the country is not empty. Arabs have lived there for centuries. Go slowly. Halt immigration for a while, peace will be established, and you will win Arab friends. With their goodwill you can continue the activities later. Perhaps you will even become a majority. But do not hurry. Let there first be peace, and if for that purpose you have to slow down—is peace not worth it?

But the Jews could not wait under those circumstances. Moreover, the Yishuv had come too far. Ben-Gurion likened limiting immigration to asking a mother in labor to stop giving birth: "It is possible to kill the child or to kill the mother, but it is impossible to expect her to cease giving birth."[20]

Shortly after the meeting, the British made their policy official in the form of a White Paper that ended Jewish immigration, forbade Jewish land purchases, and declared an Arab majority state to be formed within ten years. The new policy meant an end to the Zionist hopes of a state of their own. It was a terrible blow to the Yishuv, even as their mortal Nazi enemy threatened to destroy world Jewry: "If the international Jewish financiers in and outside Europe should succeed in plunging the nations once more into a world war, then the result will not be the bolshevization of the earth, and thus the victory of Jewry, but the annihilation of the Jewish race in Europe," Hitler declared in January 1939.

With the rising Nazi threat and the end of legal Jewish immigration into Palestine, the Jews sought to bring in refugees clandestinely, but sneaking rickety old ships crammed with refugees past the Royal Navy was a difficult proposition at best. The British captured most of the ships before they could arrive in Palestine, placing the passengers in camps, first in the remote Indian Ocean island of Mauritius and later in Cyprus.

Against this bleak background, the dreariest World Zionist Congress ever assembled in Geneva in August 1939. Hundreds of desperate and frightened delegates from Europe listened as Ben-Gurion denounced the White Paper and declared it would not hold. "Too late!" the European delegates cried out. And yet, even as they despaired, another bombshell dropped on them: Hitler and Stalin agreed to a non-aggression pact, freeing Hitler to attack Poland whenever he saw fit.

The aged Chaim Weizmann took to the podium. "There is darkness all around us and we cannot see through the clouds," he said in a faltering voice. "The remnant shall work on, fight on, and live on until the dawn of better days. Toward that dawn I greet you. May we meet again in peace."[21] Then Weizmann and his bitter rival, David Ben-Gurion, embraced. Much as they argued with each other over the direction of the movement, they were bound by the threat of the Nazis. As they embraced, wild applause rang out. Many delegates sobbed. The vast majority did not survive the war.

One of the delegates from Palestine, Golda Meir, recalled her role in the Congress:

> I had spent most of my time closeted with the delegates of the labor movement's European youth organizations, planning ways in which we could stay in touch with each other when and if war broke out. Of course, neither I nor they knew then about Hitler's "Final Solution," but I remember looking into their eyes as we shook hands and said "shalom" to each other and wondering what awaited each of them when they returned to their homes.
>
> I have often replayed in my mind those relatively optimistic conversations we had in my room in Geneva toward the end of August 1939. All but a few of those dedicated young people perished later in Auschwitz, Maidenek, and Sobibor, but among them were the leaders of the Jewish resistance movements of Eastern Europe who fought the Nazis inside the ghettoes, outside them with partisans and finally behind the electrified barbed wire of the death camps. I can hardly bear to think of them now, but I believe with all my heart that one of the things that made it possible for them to go on fighting against such odds to the very end was the knowledge that we were with them all the time and so they were really never alone. I am not particularly given to mysticism, but I hope I will be pardoned for saying that in our darkest hours it was the memory of their spirit that gave us heart, inspired us to go on and, above all, lend validity to our refusal to be wiped out and to make life easier for the rest of the world. In the final analysis, it was the Jews of Europe, trapped, doomed and destroyed, who taught us once and for all that we must become masters of our own undertaking, and I think it can be said that we have kept faith with them.[22]

-5-

An Indifferent World, Cold and Cruel

Palestine and the Holocaust, 1939–1946

"A Most Profound Anguish": The Jews in World War II

The Jewish people's worst fears came true on September 1, 1939, as Hitler's legions invaded Poland, bringing most of Jewish civilization under Nazi control. Everywhere the German Army went, Jewish suffering followed. Jews were beaten, robbed, expelled, their homes attacked, their synagogues destroyed. The Nazis forced the Jews into ghettos, cut off from the outside world. The largest ghetto was in Warsaw, where up to half a million Jews were crammed into an area only a few blocks long and surrounded by a brick wall. Seven people lived in each room. The Germans allotted the Jews food amounting to roughly three hundred calories per day. Many soon succumbed to disease and starvation. Nazi crimes grew even worse when Germany invaded the Soviet Union in 1941. Mobile ss units followed the army, rounding up Jews wherever they lived and forcing them into the forests, where they were brutally murdered. In this manner, hundreds of thousands were killed. And yet the Nazi appetite for Jewish blood was not yet satiated.

As the Nazis overran Europe, Jews attempted to flee to Palestine, cramming onto whatever rickety old ship they could find, hoping to evade the Royal Navy. Some ships arrived safely, and their passengers were settled in villages and kibbutzim throughout Palestine. Most were intercepted, however. One such ship was the *Patria*. Eighteen hundred Jews had been crammed aboard the ship in Haifa Harbor, awaiting deportation to Mauritius. Outraged Haganah leaders decided on a drastic action. They smuggled a bomb onto the ship and placed it on the lower inner sidewall, hoping to disable the ship, rendering it unable to leave. Instead the old rusted outer hull collapsed, blowing an enormous hole in the ship's side. Water poured in, and the ship sank in fifteen minutes, with the loss of two hundred lives. Tragedy had begot tragedy. The British reluctantly allowed the survivors of the *Patria* to stay in Palestine, but it would not become British policy.

A short time later the British intercepted the *Atlantic*, packed with seventeen hundred European refugees. Before being interred at a prison camp, a passenger recorded his impressions as the ship was brought ashore in Haifa:

> How marvelous it is to stand on dry land once again, to breathe fresh air, and not to be sandwiched between bodies! The harbor was new and the customs hall, bustling with activity, was spotlessly clean. We were closely searched. All papers were impounded and receipts were issued.
>
> We were loaded into buses and Jewish drivers were taking us to disinfection stations. Our clothes were treated separately. Some people's heads were crawling with lice. All of us had our hair doused with a pungent liquid. We had a hot shower and our own doctors looked us over. It was only months later that I learned how worried they had been about my emaciated state and how delighted they were that I had pulled through. I had been in such poor condition that the doctors were not prepared to risk giving me typhoid and smallpox injections at the time. Dr. Kummerman thought that with my cough I would surely soon be released, anyway.
>
> Back on the buses, we were driven over well surfaced suburban roads. New buildings were rising everywhere. The street signs were in English, Hebrew, and Arabic. We passed modest-sized houses surrounded by colorful flowering shrubs. Heavily laden asses trudged along the pavements led by Arab boys. A wrecked

house here and there bore silent witness to the prevailing state of civil unrest. Buses full of children passed by.

A large Jewish school was being built. We saw the modern buildings of a rural kibbutz, set in obviously lovingly tended fields which contrasted with the barren land further away, where the monotony of the landscape was further enhanced by the scrub and the occasional corrugated iron roofed shack. We passed through ancient Akko, whose narrow streets were surrounded by a medieval wall. The town stands on the tongue of land, which is dominated by the green and golden roof of the mosque and by the minarets which gleamed in the sunshine. The bus skirted the town and we were relieved not to be taken to its infamous prison. Eventually the bus took a left turn and a barrack camp came into view, surrounded by a barbed wire fence.

We were taken to the "Office for Refugees" which seemed reassuring inasmuch as there was another office which dealt with political prisoners. We were told that we would have to do our own cleaning, cooking and baking. Police supervised the issue of rations and the preparation of the food. The wooden barracks had corrugated iron roofs and accommodated thirty men each.[1]

The refugees had fled the Nazis, endured a torturous sea voyage, and then been put into prison camps. They hoped to be released in Palestine, but it was not to be. Instead British troops surrounded the camp one morning. When the refugees realized they were being deported, they began physically resisting. Those who fought the troops were beaten to the point of unconsciousness and had to be carried out on stretchers. The young and elderly were brutally shoved onto awaiting trucks and then loaded onto ships. Their destination was the distant Indian Ocean island of Mauritius. The men and women were kept in separate camps, and it was not until two years later that the women were allowed to briefly visit their husbands, fathers, and sons.

But the worst was yet to come. In December 1941 a cattle boat called the *Struma* left Europe with 769 refugees packed into an area intended for no more than 100 people. The conditions aboard were appalling. There were no showers, no sleeping quarters, no lifeboats, and only one toilet. Even breathing fresh air required waiting in line to stand on the crowded upper deck. The sea-unworthy vessel chugged into Istanbul. At the port, its leaking hull and defective engines stalled its journey to Palestine. The British informed the Turks they would not let the vessel into Haifa. Zionists leaders frantically lobbied the British to allow the ship in, but to no avail. Finally the Turks ordered the *Struma* out of their port and back onto the high seas. But sailing the Black Sea during wartime was dangerous. The *Struma* exploded, torpedoed by a Soviet submarine. With no lifeboats, all except one passenger perished.

The Zionists were aghast. Moshe Shertok wrote the British colonial secretary of state an angry letter. "A group of Jews manages to escape from death and torture at the hands of their Nazi oppressors," he reminded the secretary. "All the resources of the democratic world which is fighting Nazi oppression, including the Mandatory Government of Palestine, fail to provide them a haven of refuge; all avenues of rescue being closed to them, they are forcibly sent back into the inferno from which they have fled: in the end . . . fate administers them the coup de grace and they all drown." Then Shertok explained why the Zionist cause was so important: "Jews cannot possibly conceive that anything of that sort could have happened if those fugitives had belonged to a nation which has a government—be it even one in exile—to stand up for them."[2]

As bad as the refugee crisis was, the Nazi menace soon reached Palestine itself. Throughout 1941 and 1942 Erwin Rommel's Afrika Corps repeatedly sent the British reeling back through the North African deserts. If Rommel reached Palestine, the plan was to make a last-ditch Masada stand at Mount Carmel, south of Haifa. Fortunately, in November 1942, British forces attacked Rommel at El Alamein, lifting the threat to Palestine. But even as the Nazi threat to Palestine receded, newspapers in Palestine began reporting on large-scale massacres and killings of Jews in Europe, amounting to systematic murder. Were the stories true? They seemed so outrageous. Could anyone do such a thing—even a deranged madman like Hitler? Nobody knew for sure. But it was true. In early 1942 Adolf Hitler approved "the final solution to the Jewish question": the systematic murder of all Jews under Nazi control. The Nazi official in charge of the operation, Heinrich Himmler, explained the twisted logic behind the decision to slaughter men, women, and children in a secret speech to party members:

> This destructive pestilence is still in the body of our people. The sentence, "The Jews must be exterminated," is a short one, gentlemen, and is easily said. For the person who has to execute what this sentence implies, however, it is the most difficult and hardest thing in the world. . . . We had to answer the question: What about the women and children? Here too, I had made up my mind, to find a clear-cut solution. I did not feel that I had the right to exterminate the men—that is, to murder them, or have them murdered—and then allow their children to grow into avengers, threatening our sons and grandchildren. A fateful decision had to be made: This people had to vanish from the earth.[3]

It was a policy Himmler intended to carry out to the last. Nearly six million would perish across Nazi-occupied Europe. A Jewish resident of Palestine named Abba Eban described the sentiment as the truth came to light:

> What plunged Palestinian Jewry into its most profound anguish was the horrifying news that began to reach it in 1943 of the Jewish holocaust in Europe. At first the ears refused to hear and the mind to believe the stupendous nature of the catastrophe. But there were too many witnesses coming out of Europe to allow any comforting illusion to persist. The facts were hideous, but inescapable: millions of Jews—men, women, and children in the Jewish communities of Nazi-occupied Europe, all the way from Norway to Greece, and especially in the densely populated Jewish centers in Poland, Romania, and the Soviet Union were being herded like cattle into railway trucks, shipped off to special camps and there simply destroyed like useless rubbish. In those coun-

tries, to be a Jew in Europe meant that a man would be dragged out of his home, put into a cattle truck with thousands of others, deported to a distant camp, separated from his family, beaten and humiliated for a few days, weeks, or months of forced labor, after which his emaciated, wrecked and shambling body would be dispatched into a gas chamber, where he would be scientifically asphyxiated, his hair shaven off to make mattresses, his bones crushed and melted down to make soap. The gold fillings from his teeth would be assembled to sustain the declining German war effort. In the meantime, his wife and children would be submitted to similar agonies, tortures and murders in specially constructed camps. Particularly unbelievable, yet patently true, was the fact that a million Jewish children were being flung into furnaces and burned to death. Years after, mountains of their little shoes would be preserved in museums to testify that the inhumanity of man had no finite limit.[4]

The Allied war effort, once so close to collapse, took on a new life with the entry of the United States into the fight against Germany. And American Jews, fighting patriotically for their country against Germany, could now be expected to support a Jewish state in Palestine. Ben-Gurion decided it was time for a dramatic move. On May 9, 1942, over six hundred Jewish American delegates gathered at the Biltmore Hotel in New York City. They were all supporters of the Zionist program, but they did not know that Ben-Gurion planned for them to play a historic role in the history of Zionism that very day. For as they took their seats in the grand banquet hall, Ben-Gurion was preparing an explicit statement calling for a Jewish home in Palestine. Herzl's first World Zionist Congress had called for a Jewish home, but the "Biltmore Program" called for a Jewish commonwealth. By making the declaration in the United States, Ben-Gurion hoped American Jews would press their government for a Jewish state in Palestine and—through their government—press the British as well. Britain desperately needed America in the war. The British Empire could ill afford to antagonize large segments of American society. Ben-Gurion was well aware of these facts. His move was a masterstroke. Until that point American Jewry had been somewhat indifferent to Zionism. But with the rise of Hitler and the threat to the majority of the world's Jews in Europe, their American brethren quickly began to realize the need for a Jewish safe haven. America might have been the "Golden Land," but it could not house all the world's endangered Jews—only a Jewish state could. America's Jews quickly became the leading non-Palestinian Zionists. Their support would prove crucial in the years to come.

Palestine's Jews had eagerly joined the British Army, hoping for a chance to fight against their Nazi antagonists. But British Mandate authorities feared they would only be training the Jews to fight against them when the war ended. As a result, the thirty thousand Jewish volunteers from Palestine were kept out of the action, relegated to guard duty in remote locations. After the successful Allied landing in Normandy in June 1944, it seemed like the Jewish Brigade would not get a chance to fight before the war ended. Prime Minister Winston Churchill changed the situation, however. Churchill's support had been crucial in establishing the Mandate in the 1920s. His backing now made a Jewish fighting force possible. Earlier in the war he had written:

> None has suffered more cruelly than the Jew, the unspeakable evils wrought on the bodies and spirits of men by Hitler and his vile regime. The Jew bore the brunt of the Nazis' first onslaught upon the citadels of freedom and human dignity. He has borne and continues to bear a burden that might have seemed to be beyond endurance. He has not allowed it break his spirit: he has never lost the will to resist. Assuredly in the day of victory the Jews' sufferings and his part in the struggle will not be forgotten. Once again, at the appointed time, he will see vindicated the very principles of righteousness which it was the glory of his fathers to proclaim to the world.[5]

In late 1944 the British trained the Jewish Brigade with live ammunition for the first time. The brigade went into battle in Italy in the closing months of the war, sweet retribution against the Nazis.

More importantly, the men gained combat experience, experience that would prove invaluable in the coming wars with the Arabs.

The Plight of the Displaced Persons

When the Second World War ended, the issue of Palestine and the Jews, relegated to the background during the war years, was immediately thrust into the foreground. The fate of the shattered remnant of European Jewry, now known as "displaced persons" and living in camps throughout Europe, would be the first postwar battle. An American official reported, "Three months after v-e Day . . . many Jewish displaced persons and other possibly non-repatriables are living under guard behind barbed-wire fences, in camps of several descriptions (built by the Germans for slave-laborers and Jews), including some of the most notorious concentration camps amidst crowded, frequently unsanitary and generally grim conditions, in complete idleness, with no opportunity, except surreptitiously, to communicate with the outside world, waiting, hoping for some word of encouragement and action in their behalf."[6] Their families had been killed, and they had no homes to return to—Palestine was their only hope. The Zionists intended to use all means available to bring them to Eretz Yisrael.

In October 1945 Ben-Gurion went to assess the situation in Germany. An American Jewish chaplain named Judah Nadich drove Ben-Gurion to a displaced persons camp near Dachau. The inmates erupted when they saw him, even though they did not know he was coming. Nadich wrote, "Suddenly, one of the Jews . . . happened to peer into my automobile and, recognizing the strong face and the white shock of hair, suddenly screamed in an unearthly voice, 'Ben-Gurion! Ben-Gurion!' Like one man, the entire group turned toward the car and began shrieking, shouting the name of the man who was accepted by all of them as their own political leader." Nadich assembled the inmates in the camp auditorium:

In a few minutes, I led Ben-Gurion into the large jammed hall, all the seats occupied, all the aisles filled, every inch of space packed, those unable to enter, standing near the doors and leaning across the window-sills. As I led Ben-Gurion into the hall, the people spontaneously burst into song—'Hatikvah,' the hope that had never died, the hope that was unquenchable in their breasts, the hope that had kept them alive. As Ben-Gurion stood on the platform before them, the people broke forth into cheers, into song, and finally, into weeping. For the incredible was true; the impossible had happened. Ben-Gurion was in their midst and they had lived despite Hitler, the Nazis, and all their collaborators, with all the diabolical instruments of destruction at their command— they had lived despite them all to this day when they could welcome Ben-Gurion![7]

Another writer explained, "He was the embodiment of all their hopes and aspirations. The black night was over, and the first rays of a new dawn were bursting over the skies of their miserable camp."[8] The displaced persons (DPS) sang, cheered, and wept as Ben-Gurion told them they would soon come home to Zion.

While he was in Germany, the Jewish leader also saw the very sites where the "Final Solution" had been carried out.

Ben-Gurion stood in silence at the edge of the mass grave at Bergen-Belsen concentration camp, tears rolling down his cheeks. A British major stood at his side and described the scene of horror he had witnessed when he entered the camp as it was liberated six months before, on April 15, 1945. There were piles of corpses between the long lines of barracks. One of the heaps of bodies was higher than the roof of the barracks. On the pathways lay hundreds of living skeletons. Thousands were dying of starvation and disease inside the huts. In the five days that followed, 14,000 inmates died of typhus and dysentery. The British army lacked the means to cope with a disaster of such dimensions. To wipe out the typhus epidemic, they had to burn the barracks. They rounded up German civilians from the vicinity and ordered them to bury the corpses. The Germans picked up the bodies and threw them into the pit. "This is where they were buried," said the major, pointing at the roped-off mound of loose earth in front of them.[9]

Ben-Gurion never recovered from the trauma of his trip to postwar Germany. His distress was clear when he returned to Jerusalem and gave a report on his trip. In a quavering, restrained voice, he told the Representative Assembly of the Jews of Palestine:

> I was in Dachau and Belsen. I saw the gas chambers, where every day they poisoned thousands of Jews, men and women, the aged and the elderly, infants and children, led them naked as if they were going to take showers. The gas chambers are really built as if they are shower rooms, and the Nazis would peep in from the outside to see the Jews writhe and struggle in their death throes. I saw the furnaces in which they burned the bodies of hundreds and thousands and millions of Jews from all of the countries in Europe . . . I saw the gallows at Belsen, on which they would hang a number of Jews at once for sins such as coming two minutes late for forced labor, and all the other prisoners had to gather and watch the display. I saw the kennels where they bred the savage dogs that were trained to be set on the Jews on their way to work or to be killed. I saw the platforms, on which naked Jewish men and women were laid and the camp commanders would stand and shoot them in their backs, and I saw the few remnants, the survivors of the six million who were slaughtered in the sight of the world, an indifferent world, foreign, cold, cruel.[10]

Many in the audience cried and moaned during the speech.

Meanwhile, roughly 250,000 homeless Jews languished in Europe's displaced person camps, mostly in Germany. The first major postwar attempt at a solution to the refugee crisis was an Anglo-American Committee of Inquiry in 1946. The members inspected the situation in Europe and Palestine. Before touring one of the displaced person camps, questions arose whether the refugees really wanted to go to Palestine or were under Zionist influence. One of the committee members decided for himself upon arriving at the camp:

> Even if there had not been a single foreign Zionist or a trace of Zionist propaganda in the camps, these people would have opted

for Palestine. Nine months had passed since [v-e Day] and their British and American liberators had made no move to accept them in their own countries. They had gathered them in centers in Germany, fed them and clothed them, and then apparently believed that their Christian duty had been accomplished.

For nine months, huddled together, these Jews had had nothing to do but to discuss the future. They knew that they were not wanted by the western democracies. They were not Poles anymore; but as Hitler had taught them, members of the Jewish nation, despised and rejected by "civilized Europe." They knew that far away in Palestine there was a National Home willing and eager to receive them and to give them a chance of rebuilding their lives, not as aliens in a foreign state but as Hebrews in their own country. How absurd to attribute their longing for Palestine to organized propaganda! Judged by sober realities, their only hope of an early release was Palestine.[11]

In Palestine, the committee members met with both Jewish and Arab representatives. It was a distinct change from the Arabs' tactics with the Peel Commission, which they had mostly boycotted. Now the Arab Office presented an eloquent argument for their opposition to a Jewish state and partition: "The whole Arab people is unalterably opposed to the attempt to impose Jewish immigration and settlement upon it, and ultimately to establish a Jewish State in Palestine. Its opposition is based primarily upon right. The Arabs of Palestine are descendants of the indigenous inhabitants of the country, who have been in occupation of it since the beginning of history; they cannot agree that it is right to subject an indigenous population against its will to alien immigrants, whose claim is based upon a historical connection which ceased effectively many centuries ago."[12]

The British, sensitive to Arab opposition, continued to refuse the refugees' entry to Palestine, even after the Anglo-American Committee recommended allowing immediately one hundred thousand displaced persons into Palestine. Golda Meir captured the Yishuv's sentiment: "It may have been extremely naive of us to have believed that now everything would change, but it was certainly not unreasonable—especially in the light of the horrifying spectacle of hundreds of thousands of emaciated survivors tottering out of the death camps into the arms of the liberating British forces."[13] For the Jews of the Yishuv, it was the last straw—six million of their people had been murdered, and their remnants languished in camps in the land of their killers. They needed to be brought into Palestine. Force was now the only option.

-6-

Nothing Can Keep Us from Our Jewish Homeland

End of the British Mandate, 1946–1947

"Black Saturday"

For the first time, the Haganah and its right-wing counterparts, the Irgun and Stern Gang, joined together. They blew open a British detention camp, letting out two hundred illegal immigrants. They sabotaged the railroad in Palestine and blew up a British coast guard vessel. The largest operation came on the night of June 17, 1946, when the Haganah's strike force—the Palmach—simultaneously blew up eleven bridges connecting Palestine and the surrounding territories. The Jews hoped that these measures would convince the British to allow more refugees in.

Britain's response was quite different. On June 29, 1946, on what became known as "Black Saturday," the British struck back, deploying tanks, armored cars, and troops throughout the cities and kibbutzim of the Yishuv. They cut the phone lines and closed the borders. British troops attempted to root out the Haganah and Irgun by breaking into homes and searching for hidden weapons in floors, walls, and cellars. Suspected Haganah members and supporters were arrested, thrown into detention camps, and beaten or tortured.

The Haganah's efforts had failed, and the refugee crisis worsened. British policy remained strict: the quota on Jewish immigration was enforced. Still, the ships came. One immigrant ship, upon being halted by British vessels outside Haifa, unfurled a long banner declaring, "We survived Hitler. Death is no stranger to us. Nothing can keep us from our Jewish Homeland."[1] That ship, along with thirty-five others, was halted, and their cargos of fifty thousand displaced Jews were forced into prison camps on the island of Cyprus. The conditions in the camps were crowded, hot, and miserable. An American journalist reported:

> You had to smell Cyprus to believe it. You had to smell the latrines for twenty thousand people to believe it—and you didn't believe it. You had to smell the sweat of men and women as they cooked the food over open stoves and the sweat poured into their pots and pans; you had to smell the garbage which piled up waiting for the trucks which didn't come to believe it—and you didn't believe it. Each evening I left the prison camp for the Savoy Hotel and showered for an hour, but I felt I could never wash the smell away. . . . There was no water in Cyprus. All day, some twenty thousand adults and two thousand orphaned children stood at the barbed wire and looked out at the Mediterranean which creamed their shore, but they no water. Each day a few small boys stood in the midday heat, clutching the gate with their hands, they eyes fixed on the road outside the barbed-wire boundary of the camp. Behind them, down the long rows of silent nameless streets, the population retreated in the thin shadows of tents and huts, trying to escape the burning assault of the sun.[2]

And yet the refugees continued to live their lives, even bringing babies into the wretchedness of the camps. By doing so, they were defying Hitler and keeping Israel alive. When doctors warned about the possibility of mass deaths among children there, Jewish Agency representative Golda Meir went to see the camps for herself. She was appalled by what she saw:

> The camps themselves were even more depressing than I had expected, in a way worse than the camps for DPS that were being run in Germany by the US authorities. They looked like prison camps, ugly clusters of huts and tents—with a watchtower at each

end—set down on the sand, with nothing green or growing any-where in sight. There wasn't nearly enough water for drinking and even less for bathing, despite the heat. Although the camps were right on the shore, none of the refugees was allowed to go swimming, and they spent their time for the most part, sitting in those filthy, stifling tents, which, if nothing else, protected them from the glaring sun. As I walked through the camps, the DPS pressed up against the barbed-wire fences that surrounded them to welcome me, and at one camp two tiny little children came up with a bouquet of paper flowers for me. I have been given a great many bouquets of flowers since then, but I have never been as moved by any of them as I was by those flowers presented to me in Cyprus by children who had probably forgotten—if they ever knew—what real flowers looked like.[3]

The Saga of the Exodus

On July 18, 1947, another refugee ship, this one a rickety old river steamer from the United States, chugged toward the port of Haifa. Although it was designed to hold 400 people, no fewer than 4,500 concentration camp survivors were crammed together in the most unsightly and unsanitary manner imaginable. Renaming their ship the *Exodus 1947*, they had departed France a few days before. As it neared Haifa, a British armada of six destroyers and one cruiser bore down on the *Exodus*. The British captain hailed the refugee ship: "I must warn you that illegal entry of your pas-sengers into Palestine will not be allowed; and your ship will be arrested if you try to do so. We do not want to hurt anyone, but if you resist force will be used . . . I repeat force will be used if our sailors are attacked. Your leaders and all sensible passengers must stop the hot heads from futile resistance."

The refugees defiantly retorted:

On the deck of this boat, the *Exodus*, are more than 4,000 people, men, women, and children, whose only crime is that they were born Jews. We have nothing against your sailors and officers, but unfortunately they have been chosen to implement a policy to which we shall never acquiesce, for we shall never recognize a law forbidding Jews to enter their country. We are not interested in the shedding of blood, but you must understand that we shall not go to any concentration camp of our own free will, even if it happens to be a British one.

The battle lines were drawn. The Jews would not surrender; the British would not allow them entry into Palestine. The British captain gave the orders. The armada machine-gunned the *Exodus*. Still the ship would not surrender. Two destroyers rammed the fragile ship from opposite sides, smashing into its upper deck. When this too failed to deter the refugee steamer, British sailors stormed the ship. The British captain recalled the ensuing melee:

> The boarding parties soon learned what they were up against. Those that got over were assaulted from all angles, stream jets were turned on them, the side decks coated in oil to make them slippery, smoke bombs, fireworks and a variety of missiles hurled at them and tear canisters thrown. An Ordinary Seaman reported back: "I tried to get on board three times but there was too much opposition in the shape of big Yids. I was forced to draw my revolver and fired eleven warning shots. One of the last shots, however, I used to stop a lad of 17 or 18 from collecting my scalp with a meat axe. He got it in the stomach."[4]

The boarding party fanned out on the old tub and clubbed the captain to death, killed two others, and wounded many more. Still, the ship refused to surrender. Only when the continued ramming of the ship threatened to sink it did the *Exodus* give finally give in after three hours of fighting. Riddled with holes and listing badly, the ship was towed into Haifa harbor. At the dock, a crowd of several thousand Jews looked on and cheered their brethren while the passengers sang "Hatikvah." As reporters and photographers looked on, American journalist Ruth Gruber described the horrific state of the *Exodus*:

> The ship looked like a matchbox that had been splintered by a nutcracker. In the torn, square hole, as big as an open blitzed barn,

we could see a muddle of beddings, possessions, plumbing, broken pipes, overflowing toilets, half-naked men, women looking for children; railings were ripped off; the lifesaving rafts were dangling at crazy angles. . . .

A child came off, with large frightened eyes. He carried a potato sack with his belongings; a blanket was strapped across his back. A man and a child came down, hand in hand. The child broke away and ran back up the gangway, looking for his mother. He was sobbing with fright. The soldiers gently pulled him down the gangway again. No one was allowed to return to the ship. . . .

The people trickled down the gangways in little groups and milled about on the dock like frightened animals. They looked weary and shattered, mourning their dead and hundreds wounded. Surrounded by troops to prevent their escaping into Haifa, they made their first step on the dreamed-of soil. They breathed the air deeply and tiredly. . . .

On the pier, the British took off every bandage and examined every wound to make sure that only the serious cases stayed. Some of the wounded screamed with pain as their head dressings were untied and then tied up again. A military ambulance waited on the dock. When the army doctor nodded his head, a patient was placed on one of the ambulance gurneys. To be sent to Haifa's hospitals, they had to be more to the dead than to the living. . . .

The refugees looked up at Mount Carmel and seemed to say to themselves, *This land is mine. Soon it will be mine forever. They're only taking us to Cyprus. We'll be there only a year or two. Then we'll come back with visas. We'll come back forever.* . . .

By this time the heat had become suffocating. The babies, who had been incredibly quiet, began to cry. Men looked dazed and ready to collapse as red-bereted soldiers shoved them along the last mile. Members of families, separated for the search pens, were taken to different transports. They were reassured that they would be reunited the next day in Cyprus.[5]

But the British government had no intention of sending the refugees to Cyprus. His Majesty's Government wanted to make an example to discourage further immigration attempts. They placed the refugees on prison ships and sent them back to their port of origin in France. The British insisted the French forcibly disembark the passengers. The French government, sensitive to the plight of the survivors of Hitler's Final Solution, adamantly refused. The refugees refused to disembark, stating, "We will go ashore in Europe only as dead men." In the suffocating mid-summer heat, a contagion of rashes and boils broke out among the passengers. The French government offered them medical care, but that meant leaving the ship. The refugees refused, insisting they would disembark only in Eretz Yisrael. After the heat wave, heavy rains rocked the ships for four days. Below deck in the prison cages, there was not enough room for the refugees to lie down. They were forced to stand upright against each other as the rain streamed against their bodies. When the storms ended, the heat returned.

The British had been convinced that the heat and storms would force the refugees to disembark the ships. Yet the Jews continued to defy them. The British then announced that those who did not leave the ships would be taken to Germany. The British were certain that the Holocaust survivors would not willingly go back to the land of their murderers. Once again, they were wrong. The refugees voted to stay on board. "The stand taken by the immigrants in their struggle has written a brilliant page in the history of the Jews' fight for their freedom," the Haganah extoled.

As the ships were awaiting the trip to Germany, journalist Gruber was allowed on board. She described the refugees' plight as she was led down to the ship's prison hold, which was essentially a large iron cage:

> Squeezed between a green toilet shed and some steel plates were hundreds and hundreds of half-naked people who looked as though they had been thrown together in a dog pound. Trapped and lost, they were shouting at us in all languages, shattering each other's words. Some pressed their faces against the slanted fencing and their bodies looked broken and distorted. We watched

the cage grow tighter and wilder as more people forced their way from somewhere in the bowels of the ship and pushed against the people already inside the narrow cage. The hot sun filtered through the grillwork, throwing sharp lines of light and darkness across the refugees' faces and their hot, sweaty, half-naked bodies. Women were nursing their babies. Old women and men sat weeping unashamed. There were no beds in the hold. Each man, woman, and child slept on a brown army blanket folded neatly on the slimy floor. The blanket was each person's living space, his dining room, his bedroom and his study. Sometimes three or four people lay on a single blanket. Each man's space was bounded only by the dimensions of his body.[6]

Nonetheless, when a French journalist asked if the refugees wanted to get off the ship, the reply came back: "We will come down willingly only in Palestine. Here we will come down as corpses."

The ships set sail for Germany. The refugees described the trip there as the most interminable part of their entire ordeal:

We got two meals a day. We would send a couple of men out of the prison cage for the food. For breakfast it was salty tea and we each got a package of British C-ration biscuits from New Zealand, an inch and a half by an inch and a half, ten in a package. When you broke them open to eat them, there were maggots in them. The evening meal was potato soup with the C-ration biscuits soaking in the soup, and for protein, the maggots were swimming around in it. When you're hungry, you eat it, maggots and all.[7]

When the ships arrived in Hamburg, Germany, British soldiers awaited them on the docks, as did members of the media. The British demanded the passengers disembark. Once again, they refused. Gruber recorded the ensuing chaos: "Inside the holds, the people joined hands and danced the hora, singing passionately. Hundreds of troops were rushed aboard. The soldiers ran down the steps to the holds and with clubs and hoses forced the refugees against the walls. Bucket-brigade fashion, they passed the people up the slippery stairs, across the deck, and down gangway to the wharf. Some were beaten with batons, others were kicked, pulled by the hair, and rolled down like felled trees. One of the refugees, dragged down the gangplank, shrieked, 'They shall not keep us from our homeland.'"[8] The Holocaust survivors were then placed into displaced person camps in the very land of their people's murderers. The saga of the *Exodus* was finally over. It had lasted two months and shocked the world.

"Freedom or Death!": Jewish Dissidents Strike

By now the Jewish dissident groups had had enough of the British. A recent Polish immigrant named Menachem Begin, the new leader of the right-wing dissident Irgun militia, decided to take decisive action. Slight of stature and bespectacled, Begin was hardly an imposing figure. British intelligence described him as a "hump-backed, hawk-nosed former law student with thick horn-rimmed glasses and bad teeth." But Begin saw himself as a great military leader, the heir to Vladimir Jabotinsky's Revisionist legacy. Begin called for a revolt against the British, declaring, "War to the end!" and "There will be no retreat. Freedom—or death!"[9] The Haganah had attacked British installations but had tried to avoid causing casualties. Begin felt obligated to no such restrictions. He ordered attacks against British personnel, with devastating consequences.

On a hot July morning in 1946, seven Irgun members disguised as Arab porters smuggled milk crates filled with 250 kilos of explosives into the King David Hotel in Jerusalem. The hotel housed the Mandate's headquarters. It was the very symbol of British rule in Palestine, the target Begin wished most to attack. At 12:37 p.m. a tremendous explosion shook West Jerusalem. The southwest wing of the King David Hotel bulged outward, and then all six floors collapsed. An Englishman relaxing in the bar's hotel recalled: "There was the most appalling roar . . . Everything went completely black and there was the noise of smashing glass and wrenching furniture and through the blackness one could feel the atmosphere was full of smoke and dust . . . from above came the most terrifying sound I have ever heard: the sound of falling masonry, and we could only assume we were about to be crushed."[10] The massive blast killed ninety-one people, including British, Arabs, and Jews. The British government was outraged by the attack, but it had the effect that the Irgun had hoped it would: the British began to reevaluate their position in Palestine.

Not all Irgun operations achieved their objectives, however. Four Irgunists attempted to attack the British airport at Lydda, only to run into a roadblock, where they were apprehended. While they were imprisoned, one of the men managed to smuggle out an account of what they had endured:

> The driver lost control of the car and it ran into a barbed-wire barrier set up on the road by the Army. . . . At that moment a Bren-gun opened fire on us from behind, and then the car was surrounded by "anemones" (British paratroopers) with their revolvers aimed at us. We had no choice but to leave our car with our hands up. Eliezer got a bullet in his back, and Mordechai (the driver) in his shoulder. . . . As we came out I got a blow in the back and rolled into the ditch. As I lay I heard a revolver-shot and I saw a soldier pointing his revolver at Mordechai. He fired, missed Mordechai and killed his brother Britisher. He at once hit Mordechai over the head with his revolver and threw him on to me in the ditch. We both got to our feet while, with their revolvers trained on us, they kicked us. . . .
>
> Then began the chapter of beatings which ended only the next day at seventeen hours—about twenty hours consecutively.
>
> Amid blows, we were taken into a small armored car, each of us guarded by a soldier. The guards at once emptied our pockets, ordering us to keep our hands up. . . . When they had done with this, they all began to hit us. They aimed particularly at our faces and stomachs. When we doubled up from the blows to the stomach they would hit us in the face to straighten us up again. . . .
>
> This journey ended in a camp I do not know. They shoved us out and took us to an open field. They stood us in a row, about ten soldiers formed a line in front of us and loaded their rifles. I must mention that we all stood the test, and nobody lowered his head.

At that moment an officer came running up and reprimanded the soldiers, who had apparently really meant to finish us off. . . .

They began an organized attack for which they had apparently got an officer's permission or orders. They hit each of us in turn and then all together. Four or five soldiers took part in this. When they got tired, they were relieved by others. They hit us with their fists in the head and the feet, and they kicked us in all parts of the body, not even omitting the testicles. Among the beaters were two policemen, who had apparently been sent to guard us. One of them moved around with a big baton which he brought down on our backs, or legs, or stomachs. . . . This went on until late at night. An officer came in and ordered them to stop hitting us, to wash us and give us blankets for sleeping. They poured water over our heads and each of us had to wash the other. . . . The four of us, wet and naked and shivering with cold, lay down on one blanket and covered ourselves with two other blankets. . . . But no sooner had we dozed off than the guard came, kicked us awake, and pulled off the blankets. We had such visits about every fifteen minutes.

Toward morning, they ordered us to get up and "wash" again. The blanket we had lain on was soaked with blood and had changed its color . . . covered in our rags, we were made to run all the way to the "hospital-room." On the way every soldier we met hit at us with his fists or his rifle-butt, and our guards did not spare us either. We ran with our hands above our heads. In the dispensary they kept us for about three-quarters of an hour with our hands up until the doctor came. . . . They made us run back the same way to the place we had come from. They again undressed us and took us outside, and there poured slop-water over us. Then soldiers standing around were invited to volunteer to hit us, and there was no lack of volunteers. . . . All day the police came and went and meantime the soldiers did not stop "playing" with us . . . a giant corporal came in and ordered us to do all kinds of humiliating things. When we refused, he beat us mercilessly.[11]

The four men were not beaten to death, but they were executed. But instead of deterring the dissidents, the result was still more violence. The Irgun attacked the British officers club and the Haifa oil refinery, and they made an audacious attack on Acre Prison, where Irgun members were being held. Menachem Begin called it the "greatest jailbreak in history," and the episode made headlines worldwide. Three of the Irgunists were captured in the prison break and hanged. In retaliation the Irgun kidnapped and hanged two British sergeants. A British intelligence officer recorded the grisly discovery of his two comrades in a eucalyptus grove:

> Their faces were heavily bandaged so that it was impossible to distinguish their features . . . their feet were about 6 inches to one foot off the ground. . . . They were wearing just their trousers and one wore a vest. One of them had a pair of shoes on, the other was wearing some thick socks.
>
> Their bodies were a dull color, and blood had run down their chests which made us at first think they had been shot.
>
> The sappers had swept a path up to the bodies, and the press were allowed to take photographs of the spectacle. When this had been completed it was decided to cut the bodies down. . . . As the body fell to the ground, there was a large explosion . . . the two trees had been completely blown up and there was a large crater where the roots had been. One body was found horribly mangled about twenty yards away . . . the other body disintegrated, and small pieces were picked up as much as 200 yards away. . . . The one remaining body was put on a stretcher and carried away. Any remains of the other corpse were also collected and put on a stretcher.[12]

Menachem Begin bluntly explained his actions: "We repaid our enemy in kind. We had warned him again and again. He had callously disregarded our warnings. He forced us to answer gallows with gallows."[13]

"A Long, Weary, and Blood-Drenched Jewish Journey": The United Nations Vote

By early 1947 the British had had enough of Palestine and its warring factions. They turned the issue over to the United Nations.

Palestine's fate would be decided by the newly formed world body. In the summer of 1947 the United Nations Special Committee on Palestine (UNSCOP) arrived in Palestine to listen to testimony and gather evidence amid continued Jewish attacks against the British. The secretary general of the Arab League explained his position: "The Zionist pretends that he has got a particular civilizing mission with which he returns to a backward, degenerate race in order to put the elements of progress into an area which has no progress. The Arabs simply stand and say 'no.' We have a heritage of civilization and of spiritual life. We are not going to allow ourselves to be controlled either by great nations or small nations or dispersed nations."[14]

David Ben-Gurion presented the Jewish case. A state of their own was necessary for their survival. "The homelessness and minority position make the Jews always dependent on the mercy of others. The 'others' may be good and may be bad, and the Jews may sometimes be treated more or less decently, but they are never masters of their own destiny; they are entirely defenseless when the majority of people turn against them." He then turned to the Holocaust: "What happened to our people in this war is merely a climax to the uninterrupted persecution to which we have been subjected for centuries by almost all the Christian and Moslem peoples in the old world."[15]

The Arab Office explained its opposition to the partition of Palestine into Jewish and Arab states:

> The idea of partition and the establishment of a Jewish state in part of Palestine is inadmissible for the same reasons of principle as the idea of establishing a Jewish state in the whole country. If it is unjust to the Arabs to impose a Jewish state on whole of Palestine, it is equally unjust to impose it in any part of the country. Moreover . . . there are grave practical difficulties in the way of partition: commerce would be strangled, communications dislocated, and the public finances upset. It would also be impossible to devise frontiers which did not leave a large Arab minority in the Jewish state. This minority would not willingly accept

its subjugation to the Zionists, and it would not allow itself to be transferred to the Arab state. Moreover, partition would not satisfy the Zionists. It cannot be too often repeated that Zionism is a political movement aiming at the domination at least of the whole of Palestine, to give it a foothold in part of Palestine would be to encourage it to press for more and to provide it with a base for its activities. Because of this, because of the pressure of population and in order to escape from its isolation it [a Jewish state] would inevitably be thrown into enmity with the surrounding Arab states and this enmity would disturb the stability of the whole Middle East.[16]

The Arab Office responded to the issue of the Holocaust by stating, "The Arab people are second to none in regretting the woes which have been inflicted on the Jews of Europe by Europeans. But the question of these Jews should not be confused with Zionism, for there can be no greater injustice than solving the problems of the Jews of Europe by committing another injustice on us, the Palestinian Arabs. The Europeans should not solve their own problems by creating problems for other people."

During the hearings, four UNSCOP members went to Haifa just as the *Exodus* was being towed into port by British ships. They watched as British soldiers used rifle butts, hose pipes, and tear gas on the death camp survivors. These people were then locked up in cages and shipped out of Palestine. The four UNSCOP members returned to Jerusalem pale with shock. Ultimately, UNCSOP recommended the partition of Palestine into Arab and Jewish states.

On November 29, 1947, all of Palestine—Arab and Jew— gathered around their radios to listen to the General Assembly of the United Nations vote on the UNSCOP proposal for the partition of Palestine into Arab and Jewish states. If it passed, the Jews would finally have their state. If it failed, the Jews would be forced to live in a single state of Palestine as a minority dominated by the Arabs. The outcome of the vote was very much in doubt. The entire Muslim world opposed partition. Moreover, a two-thirds majority was required for the motion to pass. Behind the scenes, however, American diplomats worked hard to push it through. In the end, the tally was thirty-three in favor, thirteen opposed, and ten abstentions. The motion carried.

All across Jewish Palestine, spontaneous celebrations erupted. In the cities, towns, and villages, everyone poured into the street laughing, singing, and cheering. The crowds lifted children in the air. Men and women wept openly. Abba Eban was overwhelmed by the moment:

> What a long, weary and blood-drenched Jewish journey it had been across the infinities of space and time since the nation had first been born under that very sky! There had been generations in which kings and prophets flourished and then the seemingly final end, when Jerusalem crumbled before the legions of Titus Vespasian. And across all the intervening centuries the beat of Jewish hearts had everywhere been quickened by the prospect of the return! Now the hour of choice had come, imminent and implacable. And, no matter how it fell, something of a great moment would be enacted of which future Jewish generations would never cease to speak of and dream.[17]

And yet, the "great moment" would unfold under the shadow of violence. This eventuality was not lost on most Jews. Ben-Gurion could not bring himself to join the celebrants. A young soldier named Moshe Dayan recorded his conflicting emotions:

> I felt in my bones the victory of Judaism, which for two thousand years of exile from the Land of Israel had withstood persecutions, the Spanish Inquisition, pogroms, anti-Jewish decrees, restrictions, and the mass slaughter by the Nazis in our own generation, and had reached the fulfillment of its age-old yearning—the return to a free and independent Zion. We were happy that night, and we danced, and our hearts went out to every nation whose UN representative had voted in favor of the resolution. We had heard them utter the magic word "yes" as we followed their voices over the airwaves from thousands of miles away. We danced—but we knew that ahead of us lay the battlefield.[18]

Dayan was correct. Violence erupted between the Arabs and Jews of Palestine almost immediately. The British, committed to a withdrawal by the following summer, only reluctantly and occasionally intervened as the violence spread. The two sides were on their own.

-7-

The Darkest Moment of Our Struggle

War between the Jews and Arabs of Palestine, 1947–1948

Arabs Take the Offensive

Less than a month after the fateful vote, a large crowd gathered in an Arab village near Jerusalem, eager with anticipation. They had come from all over the country, rifles at their sides, ready to take action. Even though the Arabs represented two-thirds of the population, the UN had voted to vivisect their country, handing half of it over to the Jews. Now the time was at hand for the Arabs to take back what they felt was rightfully theirs. At noon, a car pulled into the village.

As the passenger emerged, the crowd erupted, piercing the air with shrill Arab war cries, pushing each other just to touch the man at the center of their attention: a modest-looking figure wearing a black-and-white Bedouin headdress. They had good reason to be excited, for Abdul Khader Husseini was not only Hajj Amin al-Husseini's cousin, but he was also the best military leader the Arabs of Palestine had. He had proved himself many times during the revolt against Britain a decade earlier. He was brave, often leading charges himself. He was educated, unlike most other Arab leaders. Most of all, he was charismatic, an indispensable quality for a tradition-based society such as Arab Palestine.

Abdul Khader was led into a house where a banquet had been prepared in his honor. Surrounded by other local leaders, they feasted on a whole roast lamb spread out on a bed of rice. Once the meal was over, it was time to get down to business. Abdul Khader was not prone to wild boasting or exaggeration. Serious and soft-spoken, he addressed his followers matter-of-factly: "Diplomacy and politics have failed to achieve our goals." They had only one choice: "We shall keep our honor and our country with our swords."[1]

He brought out a map of Palestine and outlined his strategy. The most vulnerable targets were isolated Jewish settlements. They would first ambush supplies to these settlements, closing the roads completely when they had built sufficient strength. In this manner, he hoped to take a group of four small Jewish settlements south of Jerusalem, the Etzion Bloc. But his ultimate goal was a much larger prize. The largest Jewish settlement was West Jerusalem, home to one hundred thousand Jews, one-sixth of the entire Yishuv. It was also the most vulnerable Jewish city, isolated from the rest of the Yishuv and ringed by Arab settlements. It was supplied by road from Tel Aviv. Abdul Khader meant to cut off this road. "We will strangle Jerusalem," he told his followers.

It was not mere rhetoric; Abdul Khader had the means at his disposal to make good on his words. The coastal road from Tel Aviv began a sharp ascent at Bab el Wad (Gate of the Valley), where the twisted gorges and narrow canyons provided excellent ambush positions for the Arab fighters from the surrounding villages. Abdul Khader would get word when a convoy was coming, and then his men would swing into action. They would place a roadblock behind the convoy to prevent its escape. Then they would put another barricade in front of the convoy and begin shooting. Hearing the gunfire, hundreds of Arab villagers would descend on the site, hoping to gain some loot for themselves. It proved an effective system.

For the Jews making the run to Jerusalem, the trip was a nightmare. It was only sixteen miles from Bab el Wad to Jerusalem, but it usually took three hours, marred by shooting and explosions. To protect themselves, the Jews constructed homemade armored cars—known as "sandwiches" because of the iron plating on their sides. Some armored cars were enclosed, but others were exposed from the top. The convoys were protected by the elite force of the Haganah, the Palmach. A passenger on a convoy described one harrowing journey:

As the convoy was being organized in the plain below, trucks heavily laden with essential supplies took their positions. Up front were some sandwich armored trucks, their Palmach guards joking with each other; among them, standing beside their cars were several girls armed with Sten guns. The boys wore woolen caps knitted for the armed forces by willing "aunties," members of the soldier welfare organization; the girls draped Arab head cloths around their shoulders. This gave them a decidedly unmilitary appearance; however, beneath the surface, their hearts were as ready as ever for action.

At last the order was given. The convoy lurched out, its overloaded trucks trailing smoke from their straining exhausts, their engines at full power to overcome the drag. Armored cars rolled out, their hatches still open; boys and girls hung out of the openings on top. The wind played with their long hair and cooled their sweat covered faces. The Palmach fighters subdued the tension gnawing at their insides by laughing and presenting a reckless attitude, and exchanging greetings with the onlookers in the villages they passed.

The convoy soon left the Jewish area behind and approached Arab territory. The road passed through orange groves and olive orchards, reaching out to the hilly ground before Bab el Wad, the entrance to the mountain pass through which ran the only approach road to Jerusalem. Arab ambushes were frequently concealed in the hills, overlooking the road from both sides. As the convoy entered the narrow pass, action stations were taken automatically and hatches closed one after another until the fighters inside the armored trucks were completely enclosed in their steel hulks. A feeling of acute isolation prevailed, as if they were sitting in a dark cellar. Tense eyes peered through the narrow slits, trying to detect any danger which loomed ahead. . . . The crew of a

British armored car, parked by the water pumping station beside the road waved to the convoy as it rolled by.

As the trucks climbed the mountain road, engines straining as they negotiated the steep and winding slope, some of the larger trucks could barely keep station. The convoy reached a bend and suddenly, the firing started. The shooting, almost welcome after the long and tense wait, grew heavier from minute to minute. The front car hit a mine and overturned; the survivors crawled for cover to the ditches beside the road. The Palmach fighters, their small Sten guns poking through the slits, did their best to return fire but they had little hope of hitting anyone. The ranges were far too long to be effective, but at least they kept the enemy at bay. Truck after truck was hit, some of them bursting into flames, the wounded cried for help, but to no avail, the area was completely covered by dense fire.

The situation worsened by the minute, with no help in sight. Some of the support crews took up firing positions in the ditches, dodging Arab bullets pinging around them. Some were hit as they rushed across the road. The whole convoy was now stalled, at the mercy of the Arabs above on the hill tops. By now the enemy started to descend downhill; Arab women and children carrying sacks followed by their armed husbands and fathers, waiting to pillage the stricken vehicles on the road below. The handful of defenders braced themselves for the last stand, crouching in the ditches, rapidly running out of ammunition.

As all hope seemed to disappear, a different kind of sound was suddenly heard from above. High on the hill, a company of Palmach troops had come to the rescue, picking off the pillagers on their way down. Now it was the Arabs turn to be desperate. Deserting their half-filled sacks hurriedly, they scurried off to the west and disappeared. As the rescuers descended the steep slope, order was already being resumed. Wounded were carried to those trucks still running, damaged cars were pushed aside, and the remainder of the convoy was soon ready to roll. As the first trucks reached Jerusalem, throngs of people—who had already been informed of their plight—crowded the entrance to the city, shouting and waving to the haggard fighters who had run the gauntlet once more to bring the vital supplies. Seeing their faces, the fighters knew that it had been worth it.[2]

Such encounters were commonplace. Jerusalem required thirty trucks a day to feed it. As the weeks went by, fewer and fewer finished the trip. The road to Bab el Wad was soon littered with wrecked hulks, burned by homemade bombs and stripped of every part. One soldier wrote, "The iron skeleton is as quiet as my friend. Bab el Wad! Remember our names forever. Bab el Wad on the road to the city." Abdul Khader's plan seemed to be succeeding. But the worst was yet to come.

Meanwhile, a campaign of bombings spread across the land. Arab and Jew attacked civilian and military targets. The worst violence occurred in the Holy City, Jerusalem. On a stormy winter night, the Haganah bombed the Semiramis Hotel, the Arabs' headquarters, in the neighborhood of Katamon. The Haganah had received word that Abdul Khader himself was there that night. A young Arab woman named Hala al-Sakakini, daughter of Khalil al-Sakakini—one of the Palestinians' leading intellectuals—recorded:

> We had terrible weather last night—rain, lightning, thunder and a violent howling wind. About a quarter past one we were awakened by an awful explosion that lighted the sky and shook the house. This explosion was followed by shots so near we had to leave our beds and creep to the corridor. . . . The eastern wing of the Hotel Semiramis was completely destroyed. It was nothing but a heap of rubble. In spite of the pouring rain and bitter cold a large crowd had gathered at the scene. All faces were drawn and pale with sadness and fury. Women wept and men muttered curses. . . . All day long you could see people carrying their belongings and moving to safer ones in Katamon or to another quarter altogether. They reminded us of pictures we used to see of European refugees during the war. People were simply panic-stricken. The rumor spread that leaflets had been dropped by the Jews saying that they would make out of Katamon one heap of rubble. Whenever we saw people moving away we tried to encourage them to stay: "You ought

to be ashamed to leave. This is just what the Jews want you to do; you leave and they occupy your houses and then one day you will find that Katamon has become another Jewish quarter!"[3]

Abdul Khader was not at the hotel, but twenty-six people died in the explosion. The inevitable retaliation came on the morning of February 22, 1948, at Ben Yehuda Street in the heart of Jewish Jerusalem. Three trucks loaded with TNT exploded, sending a flash of white light across the morning sky and shattering the dawn silence. The devastation was enormous. Entire buildings collapsed from the power of the blast. Apartments had their facades torn off, revealing bleeding, crying people, many who had been asleep when the explosion hit. Windowpanes shattered for a mile around the blast area, followed by sheets of flame. The entire city shook.

Shortly after the carnage at Ben Yehuda Street, the Haganah High Command gathered in Tel Aviv. The meeting was led by Yigael Sukenik, a former archaeology student turned soldier, who had changed his name to Yigael Yadin. Although he was only twenty-nine years old, he had impressed Ben-Gurion with his keen intellect. Ben-Gurion named him the Haganah's chief of operations. Yadin was not pleased with the current state of affairs: "The enemy is freely choosing the place and intensity of action. Our loss of strategic initiative at this stage of development will cause an extremely dangerous situation in the stages to come."[4] By "stages to come," Yadin meant when the British evacuated, for that was when full-scale fighting was expected, both from Arabs inside and outside of the country. Therefore, Yadin and his staff drafted a new operational plan. Whereas previous plans dealt solely with defense of Jewish settlements, Plan D also addressed how to deal with Arab towns and villages. "The objective of this plan is to gain control of the territory of the Hebrew state and defend its borders." Simply defending against Arab attacks would not be sufficient: if Arab towns or villages occupied strategic points, routes of communications, or were used as enemy bases, Plan D called for the "destruction of the armed forces and the expulsion of the population outside the borders of the state." In all of Israel's turbulent history, no single document has ever been as controversial.

Before the Jews could implement Plan D, however, they needed more arms. And that meant money. There was only one source for the money: American Jewry. Golda Meir, having grown up in Milwaukee, was dispatched to the United States on a desperate mission to raise the money. She arrived with no luggage and no prepared speech for a meeting of Jewish fund-raising organizations in Chicago. The audience did not know who she was. The stout, determined woman from Palestine told her listeners:

> The Jewish community in Palestine is going to fight to the very end. If we have arms to fight with, we will fight with them. If not, we will fight with stones in our hands.
>
> I want you to believe me when I say that I came on this special mission to the United States today not to save seven hundred thousand Jews. During the last few years, the Jewish people lost six million Jews, and it would be audacity on our part to worry Jews throughout the world because a few hundred thousand more Jews are in danger.
>
> That is not the issue. The issue is that if these seven hundred thousand Jews in Palestine can remain alive, then the Jewish people as such is alive and Jewish independence assured. If these seven hundred thousand people are killed off, then for centuries we are through with the dream of a Jewish people and a Jewish homeland.
>
> My friends, we are at war. There is no Jew in Palestine who does not believe that finally we will be victorious. That is the spirit of the country . . . but this valiant spirit alone cannot face rifles and machine guns. Rifles and machine guns without spirit are not worth very much, but spirit without arms can, in time, be broken together with the body. Our problem is time . . . the question is what can we get immediately. And when I say immediately, I do not mean next month. I do not mean two months from now. I mean you cannot decide whether we should fight or not. We will. The Jewish community in Palestine will raise no white

flag for the mufti. That decision is taken. Nobody can change it. You can decide one thing: whether or not we shall be victorious in this fight, or whether the mufti will be victorious. That decision American Jews can make. It has to be made quickly, within hours, within days.

And I beg of you—don't be too late. Don't be bitterly sorry three months from now for what you failed to do today. The time is now.[5]

The audience wept and pledged money. By the time her trip was over, Meir had raised $50 million—twice as much as she had hoped for. The funds were then used to purchase arms in Europe. But the arms purchases would take time. Meanwhile, the situation in Palestine deteriorated.

At dawn on March 24, forty trucks loaded with supplies began the slow, dangerous ascent up Bab el Wad. Arab sniping and ambushes had taken their toll. Leaders in Jerusalem were warning of panic and food riots if more supplies did not come in. The meat, sardines, margarine, bread, and oranges crammed into the trucks would prevent that. But this convoy would be different. No fewer than three hundred Arab fighters were waiting on the ravines above Bab el Wad. As the convoy inched forward, a barricade of stones and logs barred their way. A special armored car with blades—a "blockbuster"—moved ahead to break the blockade. Once it did, the convoy could move along.

But the blockbuster ran over a hidden mine. The powerful blast knocked the blockbuster off the road and into a gulley. A second blockbuster hit a mine and collapsed on its side, effectively blocking the convoy. Several passengers were killed as they tried to escape the vehicle; others remained trapped inside. Meanwhile, gunfire and grenades pounded the trucks and armored cars along the highway. The soldiers in the armored cars, firing blindly into dark pine trees and huge rocks through the narrow slits in the sides, could not offer an effective defense. Several Arabs reached the overturned truck and set it on fire. It went up in a blaze of orange flames, killing the trapped passengers. The other trucks in the convoy bunched up on each other, making for easy targets.

Radiator fluid from their engines oozed out on the road, and white puffs of steam filled the air. The sound of tires exploding from gunfire was all around. Several drivers panicked and tried to turn around. As they did, their cars fell into the gulch below the road, adding to the number of vehicles already filling the sides of Bab el Wad. Still, command refused to allow the trapped convoy to retreat. They knew how important the supplies were to Jerusalem. Inside the armored cars the men stripped to their undershorts in the unbearable heat. They began to run low on ammunition. Swarms of villagers descended on the convoy, taunting the men trapped inside with broken Hebrew chants of "Yitzchak, Yitzchak, today death will find you."

After six hours of shooting, the convoy was finally ordered to withdraw. The trucks rolled back in reverse with their tires shot out, riding on their rims. As the convoy slowly retreated, the victorious Arabs ran down from their hiding positions in the hills, shrieking cries of joy, and then descended upon the supply trucks. Jubilant with their victory, they looted sacks of flour, sardines, meat, and oranges. It was an unexpected bonanza. They had intended to defeat the Jews, but in doing so they had gained more food and goods then they were accustomed to in their poverty-stricken villages. They would feast that night in homes, celebrating their success, while the Jews of Jerusalem would go hungry. Back at the safety of Kibbutz Hulda, the Jews wiped the blood off the armored cars, wrapped the dead in white cloth, and attempted to repair the damaged vehicles.

Three days later, Arab irregulars ambushed another convoy returning to Jerusalem from the isolated Etzion Bloc. Yadin called it "the darkest moment of our struggle." Ben-Gurion too realized the gravity of the situation. Calling the high command of the Haganah together in Tel Aviv, he explained that the fall of Jewish Jerusalem would be fatal to the Yishuv. Therefore the Jerusalem road had to be opened no matter how great the risks involved were.

Ben-Gurion proposed that for the first time the Haganah act as a regular army instead of a militia. They would move into the open and capture the villages around Jerusalem, freeing the road below to convoys. It was an audacious plan that almost didn't get off the ground. The operation was saved only by the arrival of rifles and machine guns from a plane landing on a recently vacated British airfield and a shipload of arms hidden under onions and potatoes. The number of weapons only totaled a few hundred, but they were enough. The operation was set to begin on April 6. It would have been hard to believe that from this tiny, stuttering step, the Jews would shatter Palestinian society within the next few weeks.

The Jews Take the Offensive

On a dark, rainy April night, 180 Haganah men raced toward the Arab village of Kastel, overlooking the Jerusalem road. Kastel was in many ways typical of the Arab villages in the region. The homes were small stone huts surrounded by stone fences and terraces. The villagers grew figs, olives, and vegetables; a few kept sheep in their pastures. None of the villages in the area had water or telephones, and only a few had electricity. Therefore Abdul Khader's bands relied on horses and foot messengers to coordinate their attacks. These villages also provided the bands with food, supplies, and auxiliary manpower that could be quickly summoned into battle. In line with Plan D guidelines to deprive the enemy of bases, the Haganah would take the villages, expel their residents, and raze the buildings to the ground. Kastel would be the first village to be attacked.

The Haganah men quickly overwhelmed the local irregulars and took up strong defensive positions. For the first time, an Arab town was under Jewish control. With Kastel's fall, a convoy rushed up to Jerusalem. The first trucks rumbled through the city outskirts, and news spread quickly that a convoy had finally arrived. It had been two long weeks since the last convoy, and people had been subsisting on a few ounces of dried meat and potatoes, with only a drop of margarine. Men, women, and children stopped whatever they were doing. Some hung cheering out of their windows, others climbed up roofs and balconies to get a view of the most welcome sight they had ever seen: a massive column of loaded trucks, as far as the eye could see, carrying the very means that would save all their lives. Hundreds of hungry, joyous, singing people mobbed the convoy; women still in bathrobes, religious Jews with their prayer shawls on their shoulders after morning services, excited schoolchildren all rushed the trucks. Men wept openly, children handed out flowers, and young ladies kissed the drivers.The city was saved, but only temporarily. Abdul Khader Husseini was in Damascus, unsuccessfully trying to acquire more arms from his Arab brothers, when he received word that Kastel fell. He ordered his men to retake the village and rushed back to Jerusalem. His men launched a spirited attack but ran out of ammunition. Back from Damascus, Abdul Khader himself led the next attack. With three hundred fighters supported by four mortars, his men began to push back the seventy defenders, taking the buildings slowly but surely. After the first row of houses had been retaken, Khader ordered his men to dynamite the mayor's house—the largest building in the village—but the mining party fled upon hearing the defenders voices. Khader entered the house, thinking his men had taken it. Instead, he was an easy target for the remaining Jews.

The next morning, the Arabs frantically looked for Abdul Khader. He was nowhere to be found. As word spread of his disappearance, Arab men from Jerusalem, Hebron, Ramallah, and every village in between dropped their work, grabbed their rifles, and headed straight to Kastel. Before long, two thousand men had assembled at Kastel. They quickly defeated the Jewish fighters, who clamored down the hill and fled. But as the Arabs reached the crest of the hill, a cry of *"Allahu Akbar"* went out as they came upon Abdul Khader's lifeless body. The Arab victory suddenly turned into a tragedy; men gathered around the body, some kissed his dead face, others banged their heads with rifle butts in remorse. The men placed him on a stretcher and carried him down the hillside back to East Jerusalem. As they did, the Jews took back Kastel.

Silence fell over Arab Jerusalem as news of Abdul Khader's death became public. Thousands poured in from the countryside to mourn their leader. "Palestine has never seen such a huge funeral," Khalil al-Sakakini recorded.[6] A massive throng gathered outside the Old City, where they passed Abdul Khader's coffin from hand to hand, as is Muslim tradition. The lamenting procession entered the Old City and slowly made its way through the heart of the Old City to the Haram al-Sharif, the Temple Mount. Their destination was the Dome of the Rock. There, Abdul Khader was given the rare privilege of being inhumed in the shrine where the Prophet himself is said to have ascended to heaven. The death of Abdul Khader was more than simply the loss of the Arabs' most capable leader: in a society that revered the individual, he was irreplaceable. A contemporary recorded: "There is something in our blood that ascribes such importance to the man—such hero worship to the leader—that when he dies, everything collapses."[7] These words would prove prophetic in the next few days.

Around the same time Abdul Khader's men were mourning their leader, another assault was being planned on a nearby Arab village. About 150 men of the rightist dissident militia groups, the Irgun and Stern Gang, joined together on the morning of April 9 to attack the last Arab village not yet under Jewish control. The men began the assault with high hopes; it was the first time they had ever participated in a formal military operation. Their target was an important one, for if the village of Deir Yassin were taken, the heights above the Tel Aviv–Jerusalem Highway would firmly be in Jewish hands, securing the Holy City.

The attack immediately bogged down, however. Almost every male citizen of Deir Yassin had a firearm and knew how to use it. In contrast, the men of the Irgun and Stern Gang were not trained for coordinated military operations—their only experience had been throwing bombs into unarmed groups of civilians. They were taking more losses then they expected. With the attack stalled, they decided to change tactics. They began dynamiting any building offering armed resistance. This would eliminate the threat coming from within. But the same houses also held civilians, who were killed in the blasts. The Irgun dynamited fifteen houses in this manner. The militiamen threw grenades into the houses when they ran out of dynamite, effectively stifling any armed opposition. When the operation was over, the survivors were taken to West Jerusalem, paraded in the streets, and then dumped in Arab East Jerusalem.

The first witness to arrive at the scene was a Swiss Red Cross worker. The militiamen told him they were still in the process of cleaning up the village. But his impression was quite different: "Everything had been ripped apart and torn upside down. There were bodies strewn about. They had done their 'cleaning up' with guns and grenades and finished with knives—anyone could see that." A short time later, Haganah officers came to take the village from the Irgun. One officer remarked, "All of the killed, with very few exceptions, were old men, women, or children." He noted, "The dead we found were all unjust victims and none of them had died with a weapon in their hands." Another Haganah commander sneered, "You are swine," and ordered his men to surround the militiamen. A tense standoff ensued as the Haganah commanders debated about forcibly disarming the dissidents and shooting them if they refused. At last, the Haganah commander ordered the Irgun to clean the village and bury the dead. They carried the bodies to a rock quarry and set them ablaze. "It was a lovely spring day," the Haganah commander recorded. "The almond trees were in bloom, the flowers were out, and everywhere there was the stench of the dead, the thick smell of blood, and the terrible odor of the corpses burning in the quarry."[8]

The next day, the Haganah commander issued a communiqué: "For a full day Etzel [Irgun] and Lechi [Stern] soldiers stood and slaughtered men, women, and children—not in the course of the operation, but in a premeditated act which had as its intention slaughter and murder only. They also took spoils, and when they finished their work, they fled."

Irgun and Stern leaders denied that any deliberate killings of civilians occurred at Deir Yassin. Menachem Begin noted that they had set up a loudspeaker at the entrance of the village, warning civilians to leave: "By giving this humane warning, our fighters threw away the element of complete surprise, and thus increased their own risk in the ensuing battle. A substantial number of the inhabitants obeyed the warning and they were unhurt. A few did not leave their stone houses—perhaps because of the confusion. The fire of the enemy was murderous—to which the number of our casualties bears elegant testimony. Our men were compelled to fight for every house; to overcome the enemy they used large numbers of hand grenades. And the civilians who had disregarded our warnings suffered inevitable casualties."[9] The Jewish Agency did not accept Begin's explanation and immediately condemned the killings. Regardless of which view was correct, the events at Deir Yassin would have a more far-reaching impact than anyone could have imagined.

Arab retribution was swift and terrible. Six days after Deir Yassin, a bus convoy carrying eighty nurses and doctors headed toward Hadassah Hospital on Mount Scopus, set off slightly from the rest of Jewish Jerusalem. To get there, the convoy had to cross through Arab neighborhoods. Therefore, several armored cars escorted the buses. But the lead armored car hit a huge mine and tumbled into a crater, blocking the rest of the vehicles. Soon, Arab gunmen swarmed over the site, screaming, "Deir Yassin!" They began shooting at the trapped convoy, killing the passengers one by one. An attempt by the Haganah to rescue the trapped convoy failed. Some Arabs reached the vehicles and set them on fire, burning the passengers inside alive. The convoy's agony was clearly visible to the civilians watching from rooftops and balconies around the city. The shooting went on for six hours, until the British finally authorized a force large enough to extricate the convoy. By the time they arrived at the scene of the devastation, there were only six survivors.

It might have seemed that the episode that began at Deir Yassin the week before was over, but it was only beginning. The situation in Arab Jerusalem had been deteriorating for several months. Its citizens may not have been on the brink of starvation like their Jewish counterparts in West Jerusalem, but their situation was terrible nonetheless. In late March, Khalil al-Sakakini wrote:

The whistle of the bullets and the thunder of the shells do not stop day or night. We heard nothing like that during the two World Wars. Every time we enter our homes, we expect them to be shelled and fall on our heads; every time we walk the streets, we keep close to the walls and the sandbags for fear of a stray bullet. In this situation, it is hardly surprising that the residents are considering moving to another neighborhood or another city in order to free themselves of this permanent anxiety and danger. This is why many of our neighbors had moved either to the Old City, or to Beit Jalia, or to Amman, Cairo or other places. Only a handful of affluent people remained. . . .

The artillery shelling and machine-gun fire do not stop day or night, as if we were on an ever heating battlefield. . . . Night falls and we cannot close our eyes. We say that if we live to see the day, we will leave this neighborhood, Katamon, to another, or leave this country altogether.[10]

By April roughly eighty thousand Arabs, the elite of Palestine had fled. By doing so, they undermined all of Palestinian society. Among those who left was the family of Khalil al-Sakakini, whose daughter Hala had so vehemently decried those who had fled only a few months earlier. Without their leaders, landholders, educators, and professionals, those who remained were mostly undereducated peasants and workers. By the time of Deir Yassin, Palestinian society had become extremely brittle, although it was not yet outwardly obvious. But overnight, the cracks in Palestinian society became clear for all to see.

The Jews Triumphant

It began in Jerusalem with the broadcast by the Arab Higher Committee of the news of Deir Yassin in gruesome detail. The Arab Higher Committee had hoped to shock the surrounding Arab nations to join the fight, but the tactic backfired. Instead the broadcasts terrified the remaining Palestinians. Fear spread quickly, fueled by word of mouth, exaggerated rumors, and above all, the uncertainty of war. Families began to pack their belongings and flee. They did not feel they were leaving permanently; they planned to be back soon, behind the victorious Arab armies who would take back their land from the Zionists. Soon, masses of people clutching a few suitcases or just sacks filled with a few belongings began departing their homes on crammed buses, taxis, bicycles, donkeys, or even on foot. They thought that their Arab neighbors would take them in for the short period before the Jews were defeated. Few if any could have guessed they would never return to the homes and villages they and their ancestors had lived in for generations.

The Jews had gone on the offensive in the center of the country; they would now do so in the north. The two sides had been fighting inconclusively in the Galilee for several months by the time of the fateful events of April. The largest city in the north was Haifa, gateway to Palestine, home to some sixty-two thousand Arabs and a roughly equal number of Jews. But by the start of the war, the flight of the Arab elite and rumors of a massacre had reduced Haifa's Arab population in half by the time the British announced their evacuation from the city on April 21. The two sides moved to take the city. The Haganah held the higher ground and began shelling Arab positions. As the Haganah infantry advanced, Arab civilians began fleeing to the British-held areas. A rumor among the Arabs that the British would transport anyone to safety led to a massive run to the port area. Men, women, and children were trampled in the mad rush; several boats capsized due to overcrowding. At a British-brokered truce meeting, the Arab heads of Haifa declared "that they were not in a position to sign a truce, as they had no control over the Arab military elements in the town and that, in all sincerity, they could not fulfill the terms of the truce, even if they were to sign. They then said that as an alternative that the Arab population wished to evacuate Haifa . . . man, woman and child."[11] They also requested British assistance for an evacuation. Explaining their decision not to sign a truce, one witness claimed the Arabs told him they believed that signing it would mean certain death at the hands of their people or other Arab leaders. Within days, only a few thousand Arabs remained in what was shortly before the second largest Arab city in Palestine.

There would be no such requests to evacuate Jaffa, the largest Arab city in Palestine. Realizing the town's importance, the Arabs reinforced Jaffa's defenses, and artillery and snipers struck at Tel Aviv. With the largest Jewish city under threat, the militias planned to strike at Jaffa. This time, however, the offensive was led by the Irgun. Menachem Begin relished the moment. With over six hundred men at their disposal, the Irgun was no longer acting as an underground, but as an army. On the morning of the battle, Begin addressed his soldiers:

> Men of the Irgun! We are going out to conquer Jaffa. We are going into one of the decisive battles for the independence of Israel. Know who is before you, and remember whom you are leaving behind. Before you is a cruel enemy, who has risen to destroy us. Behind you are parents, brothers, children. Smite the enemy hard. Aim true. Save your ammunition. In battle, show no more mercy to the enemy than he shows mercy to our people. But spare women and children. Whoever raises his hands in surrender has saved his life. You will not harm him. . . . You have only one direction—forward![12]

Despite Begin's oratory, the Irgun attack quickly bogged down. While mortars pounded Jaffa's rear, the Irgun frontally attacked strong positions that were defended by several rows of machine guns hidden in ruined buildings. Several Irgun assaults were beaten back. "Our frontal attack had yielded no results commensurate with the effort," Begin wrote. But as the casualties mounted, Begin did not despair: "You do not know the spirit of Irgun soldiers," he declared and then ordered more frontal assaults. Meanwhile, the mortars increased the pace of the shelling. Begin recorded what happened next:

> Then, a strange phenomenon was revealed before our eyes: the mass flight from Jaffa. Arab civilians and a variety of Arab "fighters" suddenly began to leave the town in panic.
>   There appeared to have been two causes for this epidemic flight.

One was the name of their attackers and the repute which pro-paganda had bestowed on them. The Beirut correspondent of the United Press cabled that when the first boat-load of refugees arrived there from Jaffa they reported that the information that this attack was being made by the Irgun had thrown the popula-tion into a state of abject fear. The second factor was the weight of our bombardment. . . . Our shelling made the free movement of enemy forces impossible and forced them to seek doubtful shel-ter in buildings. It disrupted telephone communications, cut the electricity supply, and broke water mains. Confusion and terror, deepened by the noise of the battle raging at no great distance from the central streets, reigned in the town. Thus the morale of the enemy was broken, and the great flight began, by sea and land, on wheels and on foot. It started with thousands, but very quickly tens of thousands were sucked into the panic flood. British sources reported numerous casualties in all parts of the town. A concentration of Iraqi "volunteers" suffered a direct hit and more than a hundred of them were killed or injured. The enemy was given no rest and could find no shelter.

The British military authorities tried to calm the panic stricken Arabs. Jaffa was in utter confusion. The streets were flooded, the houses gaping and tottering, looting and murder were rife. There was no authority that could now prevent the complete evacuation of the town.[13]

A Swiss Red Cross observer described the panic that gripped Jaffa: "Immediately everyone was consumed with terror, and soon the evacuations started. In the hospitals, the drivers of cars and ambulances took their vehicles, assembled their families, and fled in complete disregards of their responsibilities. Many of the ill, nurses, even physicians, departed the hospital wearing the clothes they had on, and fled to the countryside. For all of them the one obsession was to escape at any cost."[14] Jaffa fell on May 13, with only a few thousand Arabs left of the eighty thousand who had lived there a few weeks before.

After the fall of Haifa and Jaffa, the Haganah launched more offensives in the north. The focus of the attack was Safed, home to twelve thousand Arabs. The operation was successful, and by May 12 the town was taken. Nearly all the Arab civilians had fled during the fighting. With only a few days left before the end of the Mandate, Jewish commanders resorted to psychological methods. Haganah commander Yigal Allon explained, "The protracted battles reduced our forces, and we faced major tasks in blocking the invasion routes. We, therefore, looked for a means that would not oblige us to use force to drive out the tens and thousands of hostile Arabs left in Galilee and who, in the event of an invasion, could strike us from behind."[15] Allon's means was fear. He spread rumors among the Arabs that if they did not leave, they would be slaughtered and their daughters would be raped. As Allon hoped, it was highly effective, and nearly all the Arab villagers in the eastern Galilee fled to Lebanon and Syria.

The pace of the flight surprised even Zionist officials. One of them wrote, "Our army is steadily conquering Arab villages and their inhabitants flee like mice. You have no idea what is happening in the Arab villages. It is enough that during the night, several shells will whistle over them and they flee for their lives. Villages are steadily emptying, and if we continue on this course—and we shall certainly do so as our strength increases—then villages will empty of their inhabitants."[16] After visiting the Arab villages, he found them "in ruins. No one has remained. The houses and huts are completely destroyed. . . . Among the ruins echoed the cries of an abandoned chicken, and a miserable and orphaned ass strayed along the village paths."[17]

Many of the villagers fled from the shock of warfare as the enemy armies attacked. According to one Arab villager: "We were awakened by the loudest noise we had ever heard, shells exploding . . . the whole village was in panic . . . women were screaming, children were crying. . . . Many of the villagers began to flee with their pajamas on. The wife of Qassim Ahmad Sa'id fled carrying a pillow in her arms instead of her children."[18] Khalil al-Sakakini recorded their plight: "People left their country dazed and directionless, without homes or money, falling ill and dying while wandering from place to place, living in niches and caves, their clothing falling apart, leaving them naked, their food running out, leaving them hungry. The mountains grew colder, and they had no one to defend them."[19] Another Haganah offensive cleared out the western Galilee, simultaneously driving out Arab opposition and expanding the borders of the future Jewish state. A Jewish army commander observed the panicked flight of Arab civilians:

> They abandon the villages of their birth and that of their ancestors and go into exile. . . . Women, children, babies, donkeys—everything moves, in silence and grief, northwards, without looking to right or left. Wife does not find her husband and child does not find his father . . . no one knows the goal of his trek. Any possessions are scattered by the paths; the more the refugees walk, the more tired they grow—and they throw away what they had tried to save on their way into exile. Suddenly, every object seems to them petty, superfluous, unimportant as against chasing fear and the urge to save life and limb.
>
> I saw a boy aged eight walking northwards pushing along two asses in front of him. His father and brother had died in the battle and his mother was lost. I saw a woman holding a two-week-old baby in her right arm and a baby two years old in her left arm and a four-year-old girl following in her walk, clutching at her dress. . . .
>
> I saw suddenly by the roadside a tall man, bent over, scraping with his fingernails in the hard, rocky soil. I stopped. I saw a small hollow in the ground, dug out by hand, with fingernails, under an olive-tree. The man laid down the body of a baby who had died in the arms of his mother, and covered it with soil and small stones.[20]

The Jews had won a stunning victory in the six weeks leading up to the British withdrawal. By mid-May not only had armed Palestinian resistance been crushed, but Palestinian society lay in tatters. But neither the Jewish victory nor the Palestinian defeat was complete at this point. The Arab states promised to liberate Palestine once the British were gone on May 15. Had the Arabs states and the Palestinian Arabs been able to combine their attacks, the Jewish state might have been stillborn. Yet the British, simply by their presence, prevented the Arab states from invading until the Mandate was over. This allowed the Jews to fight their enemies in two separate rounds. Round one was over. But round two had just begun.

-8-

We Shall Triumph!

Israel's War of Independence, 1948–1949

Statehood or Truce?

On May 12, 1948, David Ben-Gurion gathered the Provisional Council in Tel Aviv for what was the most important meeting in Israel's history, if not the entire three-thousand-year span of Jewish history. The outcome of their meeting would decide the fate of the Jewish state. A few days earlier, the U.S. State Department had warned the Jews that they were outnumbered and could not prevail in a war with the Arab states. They recommended the Jews accept a truce. But while a truce would prevent an Arab invasion, it would postpone the establishment of a Jewish state. To Ben-Gurion, the proposal was anathema. After two thousand years in exile, he would not consider postponing the creation of a Jewish home. But others in the Provisional Council wavered. They feared an Arab invasion would mean the death of all their hopes. The diminutive leader had guided the Jewish Agency through many crises in the past. With his iron will, magnetism, and boundless energy, Ben-Gurion was the undisputed leader of the Yishuv. Yet his style was often dictatorial. He chafed at any hint of opposition. Determined to win the vote, Ben-Gurion went so far as to fly a cabinet member in from besieged Jerusalem to Tel Aviv, as he knew he could count on his vote. Even with this extraordinary measure, the outcome of the vote remained uncertain.

The ten members of the council gathered. Ben-Gurion sat at the head, with his usual open-collared shirt and unruly hair. Moshe Sharett spoke first, relaying the American suggestion to not proclaim a state. Ben-Gurion then played the first of his two cards designed to sway the vote in favor of statehood. Golda Meir reported on her secret mission to dissuade Jordan's King Abdullah from war. The negotiations had failed—Jordan would invade. The mood in the room darkened. Ben-Gurion's first gambit had failed. Next, the Haganah command gave a military assessment. Yigael Yadin explained:

> The conventional forces of the neighboring states, with their equipment and weapons, have an advantage. But one must not make a purely military determination of weapon against weapon and unit against unit. The question is, to what extent our people will be able to prevail against that force, considering the morale and ability of the enemy and our own tactics plan. It's been proven many times that the numbers and the formations are not always decisive. If I wanted to sum it all up and be cautious, I'd say at this moment, our chances are about even. If I wanted to be more honest, I'd say that the other side has a significant edge.[1]

There was a stunned gasp in the room. It seemed to the council members that delaying statehood was the only way to prevent their destruction. Privately, Ben-Gurion fumed at Yadin's report. But then the Jewish leader played his trump card. He knew something that the Americans did not know when they issued the warning. He opened two files containing reports from agents he had sent to Europe to purchase arms. Slowly and dramatically, he read the contents of the reports, reading out the figures for maximum effect. His agents had purchased 30,000 rifles, 5,000 machine guns, over 200 artillery pieces, 12 mortars, 10 tanks, and 30 airplanes. Calling a truce would mean depending on the mercy of others at the very time when the youth were being conscripted and heavy arms were coming in. "If we can increase our forces, widen training, and increase our weapons, we can resist and even win," Ben-Gurion declared.[2] The Jews might not ever get another chance at statehood. Now was the time. "I dare to believe in victory. We shall triumph!"[3]

Silence permeated the room as the members digested the news, transfixed by their leader's radiance and confidence. If they voted to accept the truce, they would not have a state but might live to fight another day. If they rejected the truce, they would have their state, with a bloody battle to secure it. The moment of truth arrived. Ben-Gurion called for a vote. By six to four, the council rejected the American proposal. They would announce the establishment of a Jewish state two days hence. The great leader had prevailed again.

All that was left was to decide on a name for the state. The final choices were Zion and Israel. Ben-Gurion urged the latter name—it was a fortunate choice. One official explained, "The moment the name was proclaimed, everyone realized instinctively that it could in fact have no other. The children of Israel, the people of Israel, the land of Israel, the heritage of Israel—all these had existed, in reality and metaphysically, for so many thousands of years, they had exercised such influence on the evolution of mankind that the State of Israel was their logical consequence and culmination."[4]

The high price of rejecting the truce became apparent the very next day. The isolated Etzion Bloc south of Jerusalem had been under attack by Arab irregulars. They had taken many losses but had held out. With the arrival of a regular army, the Jordanian Arab Legion with their armor and artillery, the defenders stood no chance. All the Haganah command in Jerusalem could do was listen in anguish as radio reports came in: "We are heavily shelled. Our situation is very bad. Their armored cars are 300 yards from the fence. Every minute counts. Hurry the dispatch of planes." An hour later: "Heavy fire of artillery, mortars, and machine guns. The birds [airplanes] have not yet appeared. We have about 100 killed and many wounded. Establish contact with the Red Cross or help in any other way."[5]

But there would be no help. The only airplane sent turned back due to mechanical failures. As the battle raged, more reports came in: "The Arabs are everywhere, there are thousands of them. They are blackening the hills." And: "The Arabs are in the kibbutz. Farewell." The last message received in Jerusalem read, "A desperate Masada battle was waged in the village."[6] The Etzion Bloc had fallen. The triumphant Arabs ordered the remaining defenders to lay down their arms and line up for a photograph. As they did, an Arab gunman shot all fifteen captives. Approximately 150 had died defending the Etzion Bloc. The Jewish state was being born under the very threat of annihilation.

On May 14, 1948, leaders of the Jewish Agency gathered at a museum in Tel Aviv. For one of the few times in his life, David Ben-Gurion wore a suit and tie instead of an open-collared shirt, underscoring the importance of the occasion. At 4:00 p.m., the Jewish leader rose and stood underneath a picture of Theodor Herzl. He rapped the table in front of him three times with a walnut gavel. Solemnly, he read the Declaration of Independence of the State of Israel, explaining the historical, legal, and moral justification for the Jewish state:

> In the land of Israel, the Jewish people came into being. In this land was shaped their spiritual, religious, and nationalist character. Here they lived in sovereign independence. Here they created a culture of national and universal import and gave to the world the eternal Book of Books.
>
> Exiled from the land of Israel, the Jewish people remained faithful to it in all the countries of their dispersion, never ceasing to pray and hope for their return and the restoration of their national freedom. Impelled by this historic association, Jews strove throughout the centuries to go back to the land of their fathers and regain their statehood. In recent decades, they returned in their masses. They reclaimed the wilderness, revived their language, built cities and villages, and established a vigorous and ever-growing community, with its own economic and cultural life. They sought peace, yet were prepared to defend themselves. They brought the blessings of progress to all inhabitants of the country and looked forward to sovereign independence.

In the year 1897 the First Zionist Congress, inspired by Theodor Herzl's vision of the Jewish State, proclaimed the right of the Jewish people to national revival in their own country. This right was acknowledged by the Balfour Declaration of November 2, 1917, and re-affirmed by the Mandate of the League of Nations, which gave explicit international recognition to the historic connections of the Jewish people with Palestine and their right to reconstitute their National Home. . . .

It is the self-evident right of the Jewish people to be a nation, as all other nations, in their own sovereign state. By virtue of the natural and historic right of the Jewish people and of the Resolution of the General Assembly of the United Nations, we hereby proclaim the establishment of the Jewish State in Palestine to be called Israel.

The formalities were over. The State of Israel had come into being. Ben-Gurion and the rest of the leadership quickly moved to the matters at hand. There was no time to celebrate. A war of life and death was coming. There "was no joy in my heart," Ben-Gurion said later. "I was thinking of only one thing: the war we were going to have to fight."[7]

Blood and Fire: The Arab Invasion

The somber mood in Israel contrasted sharply with the mood in the surrounding Arab states. One Jordanian Arab Legion officer recalled, "How beautiful was this day, May 14, when the whole world held its breath, anticipating the entry of seven Arab armies into Palestine to redeem it from the Zionists and the West. On this day, Arab forces broke forth from all sides and stood as one man to demand justice and to please God, conscience, and the sense of duty."[8] Similarly, the British commander of the Arab Legion, John Baggot Glubb, captured the excitement that permeated the army and civilians:

It was a sultry May day, with a haze of dust hanging over the roads. In the city of Amman and in every village along the road the people were gathered, cheering and clapping wildly, as each

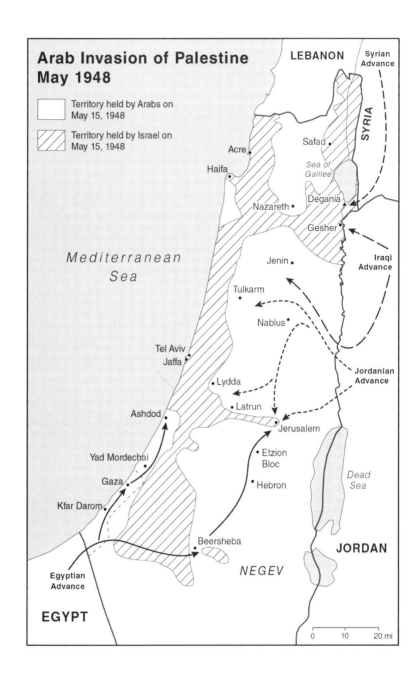

2. Arab Invasion of Palestine, May 1948. Map adapted from Benny Morris, *Righteous Victims* (New York: Random House, 2001). Erin Greb Cartography.

unit drove past. The flat roofs and the windows were crowded with women and children, whose shrill cries and wavering trebles could be heard above the roar and rattle of the vehicles, and the cheering of the crowds of men beside the road. The troops themselves were in jubilation. In some trucks, the soldiers were clapping and cheering. In others, they were laughing and waving to the crowds as they passed. Many of the vehicles had been decorated with green branches or bunches of pink oleander flowers, which grew beside the road. The procession seemed more like a carnival than an army going to war.[9]

The newly born state faced invasions on several fronts. In the south, the Egyptians—the largest army—aimed to take Tel Aviv via the coastal highway. In the east, the formidable Jordanian Arab Legion sought to take the greatest prize of all: Jerusalem, with the holy Muslim sites. Smaller units of Iraqis, Syrians, and Lebanese invaded the north. Although the population of the Arab states greatly outnumbered the Jewish state, the amount of soldiers they committed to the fight was only slightly larger than the Jews could muster. The Haganah was not aware of this at the time, however. The military and civilian leadership bitterly debated how best to distribute the resources to repel the attack. Ben-Gurion saw Jerusalem, the spiritual heart of the Judaism as the key. Operations chief Yadin saw Egypt as the greatest threat. They had the largest invading army, attacking along a coastal road with no natural obstacles. They were driving toward Tel Aviv, the largest Jewish city. If Tel Aviv fell, so would Israel.

Therefore, in the immediate aftermath of the British withdrawal from Palestine on May 14, Yadin ordered most troops south. In doing so, the Haganah left the British police fort at Latrun, overlooking the Tel Aviv–Jerusalem highway, unguarded. Jordan's Arab Legion came in and took the fort unopposed. The road to Jerusalem was closed again, and it was held by a regular army, not untrained guerillas. Jerusalem's supplies began to dwindle. Meanwhile, the city fell under siege, shelled relentlessly by Jordanian artillery and mortars.

The first major crisis of the war, however, came from neither the Jordanians nor the Egyptians, but from the Syrians in the north. Their force of thirty armored vehicles was far more than anything the Haganah could muster and seemed unstoppable. The juggernaut began by overrunning two Jewish settlements before attacking forty-two defenders holed up at a British police fort at Zemach. The defenders put up a fierce fight, but all forty-two were killed. Nonetheless, they held up the Syrians for two crucial days.

As the Syrian column advanced toward Kibbutz Degania on the Sea of Galilee, two representatives from the besieged kibbutz reached high command in Tel Tel Aviv. Once there, they begged Ben-Gurion for planes, artillery, and armored cars. But the prime minister replied, "We don't have enough artillery, enough airplanes. Every front needs reinforcements. The situation is extremely grave in the Negev, in the Jerusalem area, and in the Upper Galilee." The two men broke down upon the prospect of their homes and family being wiped out. Ben-Gurion sent them to Yadin. "We are aware of the situation," he told them. "There's no other way than to let the Arabs approach within twenty or thirty meters of the gates of Degania and then throw Molotov cocktails on them." The two men exploded at Yadin. They told him he was condemning Degania's defenders to certain death.

Yadin was shaken by the encounter. "I was suddenly shocked at that moment, when I realized what the fall of Degania would mean, that the whole north of the country might be lost. In the south, the Egyptian army was advancing on Tel Aviv, Jerusalem was cut off, and the Iraqis were putting pressure on the middle of the country. This was a moment that I suddenly felt that the dream of generations was about to disintegrate."[10] Yadin stormed into Ben-Gurion's office and demanded that four recently arrived artillery guns be sent north. The guns were intended for Jerusalem, which Ben-Gurion viewed as the key to the war. The two strong-willed men argued for three hours until Yadin pounded Ben-Gurion's glass table with his fist, shattering it into pieces. The old man finally relented. He allowed two of the guns to go north.

In the early-morning hours of May 20 the Syrian column attacked Degania. The armored cars and infantry advanced, backed by flamethrowers. The defenders could fire back with only small arms and homemade bombs. The fighting was ferocious. Despite their tenacious defense, the kibbutz was on the verge of being overrun. At this crucial hour, the two artillery pieces arrived. The defenders set them up as fast as they could and pointed them at the Syrian forces. But the ancient guns didn't even have aiming sights: they were firing blind. Nonetheless, the noise and shock of the guns was more than the Arabs had ever encountered. Although they missed their targets, the guns set the dry fields on fire, causing panic among the attackers. They fled in terror, leaving behind a tank that remains in Degania to this day, a reminder of how close the kibbutz, and perhaps the entire Galilee, came to falling. The two artillery pieces were then shipped south to relieve an Iraqi attack on another settlement. As before, the din of the guns sent the Arabs fleeing.

The north of Israel might have been secure, but the situation in the south and center grew worse. The same day that Degania was saved, Haganah officials cut rations in Jewish Jerusalem to nine hundred calories a day, hardly enough to live on. The water pipeline had been destroyed, leading to strict rationing. The water trucks could move only at night, for fear of shelling. There was not enough for bathing or sanitation. Meanwhile, the shelling continued incessantly. All this was duly reported to headquarters in Tel Aviv.

Ben-Gurion reached his breaking point: "At last we had a state, but we were about to lose our capital. If ever the people of the country saw Jerusalem fall, they would lose their faith. They would lose their faith in us and in our hopes of winning." On the night of May 22 he summoned Yadin. "I want you to occupy Latrun and open the road to Jerusalem," he told the operations chief bluntly.

Yadin was shocked. Latrun was a well-fortified position, standing on high ground and manned by heavily armed Arab Legionaries. Yadin felt an attack would be suicide. "You simply cannot take Latrun by a frontal attack. We have to take a longer period and hit them by the flanks."

"Jerusalem can't hold out," Ben-Gurion retorted. "By the time we capture Latrun under your plan, there won't be any Jerusalem left to save!"

"Listen," Yadin bristled back, "I was born in Jerusalem. My wife is in Jerusalem. My father and mother are in Jerusalem. Everyone I love is there. Everything that binds you to Jerusalem binds me even more. I should agree with you to send everything we have to Jerusalem. But tonight I don't, because I'm convinced they can hold on with what we've given them and we need our forces for situations far more dangerous than the one in Jerusalem." Yadin was referring to the larger Egyptian army making its way up the coast, attacking and shelling Jewish settlements along the way. None of the settlements had fallen, but they hadn't been able to stop the Egyptians, either. At that very moment, the Haganah was sending reinforcements south to fortify the Egyptians' next target, Yad Mordechai. But the old man's mind was made up. "Take Latrun!" he ordered.[11]

Yadin tried to delay the attack again two days later, citing lack of men and organization, but Ben-Gurion would not hear of it. Reports from Jerusalem warned of a worsening situation. Moreover, the British had opened the refugee camps on Cyprus, and some of the new immigrants would be sent into the battle.

As the Haganah prepared its men, a young platoon commander named Ariel "Arik" Scheinerman described the new arrivals from Cyprus:

> Suddenly a convoy of trucks stopped next to us and unloaded new, foreign-looking recruits. They looked slightly pale, and were wearing sleeveless sweaters, gray pants, and striped shirts. A stream of languages filled the air, names like Herschel and Yazek, Jan and Maitek were thrown around. They stuck out against the backdrop of olives, rocks, and yellowing grains. They'd come to us through blocked borders, from Europe's death camps. I watched them. Watched them strip, watched their white bodies. They tried to

find fitting uniforms, and fought the straps on their battle jackets as their new commanders helped them get suited up. They did this in silence as though they had made their peace with fate. Not one of them cried out: "Let us breathe the free air after the years of terrible suffering." It is as if they'd come to the conclusion that this is one final battle for the future of the Jewish people.[12]

The plan was to attack under the cover of night, backed up with artillery. But nothing went as planned. First, the buses to take the soldiers to the front were late. Then the artillery never showed. Despite the lack of fire support, the operation was ordered forward. But the first bus in the convoy bungled its navigation route, losing more hours of darkness. By the time the attack finally began, it was nearly dawn. As the soldiers approached the fort, the last veil of darkness lifted, leaving them exposed. A seventeen-year-old soldier in Scheinerman's platoon named Ya'akov Bugin recorded the horrific ordeal that unfolded:

All of a sudden, a lethal burst of fire was leveled at us. It was massive, planned, and orchestrated, and coming from different angles. The fire caught our platoon—which was first—on a vulnerable stretch. I remember bullets and shells flying through us like raindrops. The whole slope was like a firing range. Suddenly, I was thrown to the ground. I felt dizziness, heat, chills, and a deafening ringing. I'd caught a bullet in the chin and I closed my eyes and waited for the end. To my good fortune a man named Rami, from Magdiel, Arik's deputy, crawled to me under fire along with a medic. The two of them bandaged me, and then Rami dragged me down the hill, under a barrage of fire. I noticed that the rest of the company had retreated and taken cover behind the hill; only we, Arik's platoon, were caught on the exposed slope. We galloped down the hill. Arik found a little fold in the contours of the valley where we could hide from the ceaseless fire. Only later did we realize that it was a death trap.[13]

Scheinerman's platoon was trapped and its only radio was destroyed by a Jordanian bullet, leaving the men unable to communicate with the rest of their army. And it was still just dawn. As the sun rose, their positions became more visible to the Jordanians firing down from high ground. Artillery and mortar shells exploded around them, sending earth and shrapnel flying. Machine gun fire punctured the air. They were stuck in a muddy gully, but it did provide some cover. Nonetheless, every now and then an Arab bullet would find its mark, hitting an exposed limb or other body part. The merciless sun beat down on the men, most of whom were by now injured. They soon ran out of water. From above, clouds of black mosquitoes and gnats bit their blood-soaked wounds. From below, ants crawled all over them. After two hours, the men heard Arab soldiers moving toward them from a vineyard, screaming, "Kill the Jews!" The men waited until the enemy was in range, thirty to forty yards away, and opened fire with all they had. Several Arabs fell, and the rest retreated. Scheinerman's men beat back several other attacks that morning.

Despite the pounding they were taking, Scheinerman kept his men prepared for another offensive. His spirits soared when he heard the IDF's antiquated artillery pieces open fire on the Jordanians early in the afternoon. After hours of agony, it was a welcome sound. Scheinerman thought it was a signal that the offensive was starting again, so he ordered his men to get ready and waited for reinforcements to arrive. But instead of a counterattack, an eerie silence descended on the battlefield. Scheinerman looked to his right, where another Israeli company was supposed to have been. In their place, he saw Arabs wearing headdresses, holding their rifles in the air in celebration. Scheinerman realized that the Israelis he was counting on had retreated, and the Arabs were swooping over the bodies of the dead, looting them. The artillery shots had been covering fire for the men to retreat under, not a prelude to another assault. His men were now alone and surrounded.

Arab Legion soldiers and Palestinian irregulars advanced on the isolated unit from all sides, their gunfire completely overwhelming what the small platoon could return. Scheinerman shouted for a retreat. The nearest cover was a wheat field three hundred yards behind them across open ground, and the men ran for it in a disorderly rabble. They were covered by a boy who could not move and stayed behind, firing with his last bit of strength. Many of the men fell and did not get up. Scheinerman could only crawl; his knees were badly torn up by the rocks in the field. He was shot in the stomach and thigh but carried on. Ya'akov Bugin ran as fast as he could and made it to the wheat field, where he began crawling between the rows of stalks, hidden from the Arabs. As he crawled, he heard someone moaning nearby. It was Scheiner-man; he was lying on his back, soaked in blood. Bugin's jaw was shot so badly he could not speak. Wordlessly, he helped Scheiner-man onto his feet. Scheinerman could not move on his own; he had to lean on Bugin. And that meant they both had to stand up and expose themselves in the wheat field. As they stood up, they saw Arabs shooting their wounded comrades only a few feet away. The Arabs saw the two wounded men but did not bother finishing them off. They were too busy plundering the bodies of the dead.

The two wounded men limped on. When they reached stone terraces, Bugin pushed his commander over, then slowly and painfully crawled over the walls himself. They had no water and were terribly thirsty. Scheinerman found a pool of foul water; it may have been contaminated, but he drank anyway. Bugin's jaw was too badly injured to allow him to open his mouth and quench his thirst. On they limped for hours in the searing sun. The fields around them were on fire from artillery shells, making them even hotter. Several artillery rounds exploded nearby. Occasionally, other retreating Israeli soldiers stumbled by on their way back to the starting point, but they did not offer to help the two men. Scheinerman told Bugin several times to leave and save himself, but the wounded teen did not seriously contemplate leaving his commander. "In my heart I'd reached a conclusion. I would not let this man die," he later explained.[14] Bugin was good to his word; he brought Scheinerman back to base, where the commander collapsed and was taken to a hospital in Tel Aviv.

The name Ya'akov Bugin was not widely known, but by saving his commander, he saved one of the most important figures in modern Israeli history. A few years later, Ariel Scheinerman changed his name to Ariel Sharon, the future general and prime minister.

The assault on Latrun was a dismal failure. The Haganah lost eighty men and 250 rifles. The road to Jerusalem remained closed. Three days later, the disaster Ben-Gurion feared befell the Jews. For two weeks the outnumbered Haganah soldiers had tried in vain to fend off the Arab Legion inside the walls of the Old City. Out of the two hundred soldiers, only thirty-five remained uninjured. They had almost no bullets left, no electricity, no medical supplies, and no method of waste disposal. There were almost out of water. The putrid smell of garbage and rotting flesh hung over the quarter, since there was no way to bury the dead. Cut off from the New City, they were on their own. And they were losing the battle, slowly being pushed back street by street by the superior firepower and greater numbers of the Arab Legion. Seventeen hundred Jewish civilians remained, huddled mostly in the basement of the three largest synagogues in the Jewish Quarter.

The climax came on May 28. The Arab target was the Hurva, the largest and oldest synagogue in the Old City. The offensive began as the Arab Legion blew an enormous hole in the synagogue wall. A few Haganah fighters held off the legionaries with their last hand grenades as they entered the breach, but they ran out of ammunition. The Hurva was taken. The Arab Legion planted their flag on the roof, in full view of the Jews in the New City. But it was only the beginning. A massive explosion shook the Old City, and billows of white smoke filled the sky. When it was over, it became clear what had happened. The Arab Legion had demolished the Hurva, altering Jerusalem's skyline.

There was no other option. The Jews of the Old City surrendered. Under the agreement, they were allowed to leave unharmed. As the civilians departed two by two through the Zion Gate into the New City, two thousand years of Jewish settlement in the Old City came to an end. No one knew when they would return. But as the refugees huddled together, they still held out hope. "Out of blood and fire Judea will fall, and out of blood and fire it will be reborn," they sang prophetically.

The loss of the Jewish Quarter was devastating to the new state. Its fall reinforced Ben-Gurion's determination to open the Jerusalem road before the New City also fell. He ordered a second attack on Latrun, on May 30. This time, Ben-Gurion appointed a commander with experience in the Second World War to oversee the operation. General David "Mickey" Marcus had served under Dwight Eisenhower. By appointing him head of the IDF, Ben-Gurion believed he had found a leader that all the disparate factions would accept. Marcus meticulously planned the second assault on Latrun. This time the assault was better planned and executed. Under cover of night, an armored column approached the fort unseen. They reached the gates, and an assault team ran out of the trucks and began to storm the fort's gates. To deal with the Arab gunners located on the fort's roof, a flamethrower shot out great sheets of orange flame. The attack seemed to be succeeding. But the flames also set fire to the roof, illuminating the night and making the armored vehicles an easy target for the Arabs. Firing their anti-tank guns from a short distance, the Arab Legion set armored vehicle after armored vehicle ablaze. Meanwhile, the assault team fought a vicious hand-to-hand battle with grenades, knives, and guns. They were overwhelmed by the defenders, and the ground floor of the fort was littered with the bodies of dead Jews. None of the assault team's members survived. The few who had survived in the armored vehicles scrambled out and retreated into the darkness as Jordanian bullets whizzed around them. The second attack on Latrun had failed. The police fort again proved too formidable a position. Another method would have to be found to save Jerusalem. But time was running out.

Meanwhile, the fight for Tel Aviv intensified. The spearhead of the Egyptian thrust reached kibbutz Yad Mordechai, where about one hundred lightly armed defenders faced off against a much larger Egyptian army that was backed with artillery, mortars, and armored cars. In the ferocious battle that followed, the Egyptians leveled all the buildings in the kibbutz, leaving the defenders fighting in caves and tunnels. Yet they put up a tenacious defense, repelling wave after wave of attack. They managed to hold off the Egyptians for five days before retreating. While the Egyptians celebrated after capturing their first Jewish settlement, they had paid a high price in blood. Moreover, the staunch defense gained the Jews time, during which more arms came in, including aircraft that would prove invaluable.

The Egyptian army approached the town of Ashdod, a mere twenty miles from Tel Aviv. In order to slow down their advance, the Israelis sent four newly arrived planes south. The planes hadn't even had time to practice taking off before their first operation. Chaim Weizmann's nephew, Ezer, was one of the four pilots:

> We set off at dusk; four planes, four pilots. It was a very short distance from Tel Nof to the battlefield near the Ashdod Bridge. No sooner had we taken off than we were swooping down on the Egyptian column. Anti-aircraft fire pursued me as I dived toward my target. Hurtling downward, I was astounded and even somewhat frightened as I caught a glimpse of the Egyptian force, whose size exceeded all my expectations; thousands of soldiers and hundreds of military vehicles lined the highway to Tel Aviv.
>
> I dropped two bombs and began the steep climb. With the anti-aircraft fire still at my back, I dived once more, heading toward the row of armored vehicles. As I dropped more bombs, I saw Egyptian soldiers fleeing in all directions.
>
> When I pulled out of my dive, I caught a glimpse of my number two, Eddie Cohen, a volunteer from South Africa. As I watched, Eddie's plane plunged downward, dipping lower and lower until it crashed. Eddie's first mission for the Israeli air force was also his last.
>
> Our attack had been successful; it did delay the Egyptian column.[15]

An intercepted Egyptian radio message stated, "We have been heavily attacked by enemy aircraft, we are dispersing."[16] The Israelis followed up the successful air attack with a ground assault on at the column at Ashdod. Although the attack did not defeat the

Egyptians, it stopped their forward movement. A failed Egyptian attack on the kibbutz of Negba ended all further plans of taking another offensive. The Egyptians dug in. Tel Aviv was saved, but the situation in Jerusalem was worsening.

With no trucks coming in, Jerusalem's rations had to be cut again. Each citizen received 150 grams a day: four thin slices of bread and a few beans and peas. When these were gone, there would be nothing left. But fortune presented a new solution. Two soldiers making their way down from Jerusalem stumbled on a goat path. If the path could be widened, convoys could make their way to Jerusalem bypassing Latrun. But it would not be easy. The Jews had only two bulldozers; most of the work would have to be done with picks and shovels. The Jordanians might be able to shell the lower part of the path. But with Jerusalem facing starvation, the military leaders felt they had no choice.

Ben-Gurion, however, pressed for a third attack on Latrun. Only the combined entreaties of Yadin, Marcus, and Palmach commander Yitzchak Rabin convinced him to approve the bypass road instead. With Ben-Gurion's reluctant approval, they set out to work in round-the-clock shifts. Using the few bulldozers and tractors at their disposal and aided by sheer muscle, the engineers labored to carve out a viable road. At night, as Jordanians shelled them, hundreds of porters noiselessly carried food and supplies to waiting trucks, jeeps, and mules. Live cattle were herded along the route, because Jerusalem desperately needed meat.

As the engineers labored on constructing the "Burma Road" to Jerusalem, the UN proposed a four-week ceasefire. For Ben-Gurion, it was an easy decision. The Haganah was low on supplies. They had suffered two defeats at Latrun and lost the Old City. A truce would allow the Jews time to bring in arms, regroup, and recruit soldiers. Moreover, Jewish Jerusalem would be saved from starvation. UN supervisors would allow trucks to Jerusalem so long as they did not carry arms. And when the fighting started again, they could use the new Burma Road to supply food to the city. The Jews also planned to rebuild the water pipeline up to Jerusalem.

The Arabs also had reason to accept the truce. The Egyptians had gained a fair amount of territory but were low on ammunition. They were not sure if they could maintain their gains without a chance to rearm. The Jordanians had already accomplished most of their war aims. They had taken most of the territory on the west bank of the Jordan River, and most of all, East Jerusalem, home of the Muslim holy sites, was under their control. The Arabs, therefore, agreed to the proposal.

The cease-fire was to go into effect at 10:00 a.m. on June 10. In Jerusalem, gunfire intensified in the hours leading up to the cease-fire, as both sides emptied their armories. But around the designated hour the shooting began to slack off and finally ended. It was the first quiet the city had experienced in at least a month. The dazed citizens began to leave their homes. The city needed to be cleaned. As the pall of war lifted, so did the menace of famine. Trucks rolled in unmolested, carrying in the food Jerusalemites had been craving for weeks. The city would never be threatened with starvation again. But the man most responsible for its rescue would not live to see it: General Marcus was shot by one of his own men. His lack of Hebrew had prevented him from responding to a sentry's entreaty in the darkness of the night, as the general stepped outside wrapped in a white bedsheet to relieve himself.

Meanwhile, an uneasy silence settled over the land. Jerusalem had been the eye of the storm, but the entire state had come under attack. In addition to the large battles against Jordan, Egypt, and Syria, the Jews had engaged in smaller battles with the Lebanese and Iraqis in the north. These engagements were not decisive, but they did keep the Arabs out. And although it was not clear when the truce began, Israel had survived what would be its closest call. There would be other times when Israel's existence hung on a knife's edge, but never more so than in the spring of 1948 when Jerusalem was besieged and the entire country nearly overrun. But Masada had not fallen. And soon, the tide of war would change.

But before it did, Jew and Jew would come to blows, threatening to destroy the state from inside.

"There Can be No Compromise!": The Altalena *Incident and the Arab Refugee Crisis*

On the morning of June 21, David Ben-Gurion called an emergency meeting of the Provisional Council, the interim government of the State of Israel. At issue was the fate of the *Altalena,* a ship loaded with weapons that had arrived in Haifa the day before. Although the *Altalena* carried 5,000 rifles and 270 light machine guns that Israel desperately needed, the ship was under the Irgun's command. Irgun leader Menachem Begin refused to hand the weapons over to the Israel Defense Forces. Ben-Gurion had formed the IDF not only to replace the Haganah, but to replace all the militias, including the Irgun. There would be only one army from now on.

But Begin's insistence that the weapons aboard the *Altalena* go to the Irgun challenged Ben-Gurion's plan. As the ship sailed from Haifa to Tel Aviv, picking up Begin along the way, Ben-Gurion told the Provisional Council that it was "an attempt to destroy the Army and kill the State. If the Army and the State surrender to an independent force the Government might just as well pack up and go home." Others in the council sought to avoid bloodshed and counseled compromise. Ben-Gurion replied:

> I am as much a compromiser as the rest of you. But there are things on which there can be no compromise, for the very soul of the state is at stake. They must agree to turn over the ship, to accept the authority of the Government. Once they agree, we will be generous; we will not harm anyone. At most, there will be a few arrests. All of us want to avoid bloodshed, but there is no room for negotiations. They must turn over the ship to the Government and accept the authority of the Army. It is our Army. If they do so, there will be no battle. If the affair is really over, there will be an amnesty. But there is no room for compromise or negotiations: the future of the war effort is at stake.[17]

The philosopher Max Weber defined that the government of a state as the only body with a legitimate monopoly on the use of force. The Irgun was challenging the monopoly of the state's authority to use force. Ben-Gurion may or may not have read Weber, but he instinctively understood the dictum. Either the established government controlled all weapons, or there would be armed militias challenging the authority of the state. Despite the desperate shortage of weapons to fight the Arabs, Ben-Gurion was prepared to send all the guns on the *Altalena* to the bottom of the sea before he surrendered the authority of the government to anyone.

That afternoon, the *Altalena* came to rest in Tel Aviv on top of the ruins of a sunken ship. Ben-Gurion brought in reinforcements and gave them orders to fire if the Irgun did not surrender the ship. Menachem Begin addressed the local population from a loudspeaker on the ship: "People of Tel Aviv, we of the Irgun have brought you arms to fight the enemy, but the government is denying them to you." Then he addressed the army gathered on the beach: "Use your heads. Help us unload these arms, which are for the common defense. If there are differences among us, let us reason later."[18]

But the army had their orders. They cleared civilians from the area. Violence seemed imminent. The motor launch from the *Altalena* reached shore and unloaded its weapons unmolested. It looked like the IDF would not fire on other Jews. But as the launch returned with more weapons, an IDF machine gun opened fire. The Irgunists responded in kind, and a gun battle broke out all along the waterfront as Jew fought Jew. At his headquarters, Ben-Gurion received news of the gun battle. "There's no other way. We must shell her," he said.

IDF artillery opened up on the *Altalena*. As appalled citizens of Tel Aviv looked on, the *Altalena* went up in smoke. The Irgunists began fleeing the sinking ship. One of them wrote:

> There were soon internal explosions and a lot of smoke. . . . Mr. Begin got hysterical, stating that he wished to go down with the

ship. It was explained to him that the ship could not go down, only up, and the Captain, who kept his cool, literally had Mr. Begin dumped overboard. Afterwards we all abandoned ship, the deck—which was of metal—was burning the soles of our feet. We all jumped overboard and swam to the shore. The small arms fire from the hotel balcony continued and a few people were hit in the water. The ship's propeller was threshing furiously as the captain was trying to free the keel and get out to sea. A young volunteer from Morocco, with whom I had been friendly on board, was hit in the water and was sucked into the path of the propeller. He did not survive.[19]

In all, thirteen died in the shootout on the beach at Tel Aviv. Most of the arms blew up in the explosion. It was a high price to pay for a country in the midst of a life-and-death struggle for its survival. But by monopolizing the legitimate use of force, Ben-Gurion effectively ended all internal threats to the state. "Irgun soldiers will not be party to a fratricidal war," Begin said that night. The dissident militia disbanded, never to return. Moreover, arms began flowing into Israel in large quantities: machine guns, rifles, artillery, ammunition, and even tanks and planes. The IDF doubled its manpower, due in part to the new arrivals from the detention camps in Cyprus, as well the continued influx of overseas Jewish volunteers. Unlike the detainees from Cyprus, the overseas volunteers had, for the most part, served in the Second World War. Many had particular expertise they were able to put to use in serving the Jewish state's army, despite their lack of knowledge of Hebrew. In all, about five thousand Jewish volunteers came from overseas. By the time the truce ended on July 9, the IDF was a much more potent force than it had been at the end of the Mandate.

Although the next round of fighting lasted only ten days, the newly enlarged IDF made gains on all fronts, pushing back the Syrians in the north, the Egyptians in the south, and most importantly, the Jordanians in the center. The target of the central offensive was the key Arab towns of Lydda and Ramle. They sat beside the east-west highway as well as the north-south railway, threatening Israel's lines of communications in both directions. Lydda housed the only international airport in the country. Moreover, the large enemy populations were close to Tel Aviv, Israel's largest city, endangering its civilian population. These were the military considerations as the offensive began. The human dimension would prove more complex.

On July 11 an armored column led by Moshe Dayan prepared to break the Arab defenses. At the head of the column was a heavy armored vehicle captured from the Arab Legion the day before. Mounted with a machine gun, it was nicknamed "the Terrible Tiger." The unit moved into Lydda and encountered heavy resistance from fortified Arab positions. The column opened fire with their machine guns, and the IDF's firepower overwhelmed the defenders. In his memoirs, Dayan recalled how position after position collapsed, sandbags crumbled, smoke rose, and Arabs ran from the scene. What Dayan did not record, or did not know, was that during the course of the attack, roughly one hundred civilians were killed by the rapid machine gun fire. In less than an hour of heavy fighting, Lydda was in Israeli hands. Under an Israeli-imposed curfew, Lydda's terrified civilians sought shelter in the town's mosques and cathedral.

The next day a small force of Arab Legion vehicles accidently entered the city. The town's inhabitants erroneously took their presence as a sign that the Legion was coming to save them. At midday they opened fire on the Israeli soldiers in the city. The soldiers responded with overwhelming force, shooting in all directions, throwing hand grenades into buildings and homes. One soldier fired an anti-tank weapon into a mosque, killing seventy civilians. In all, roughly two hundred Arabs inhabitants were killed in the melee. News of the fighting soon reached high command. David Ben-Gurion, Yitzchak Rabin, and Yigal Allon were all unanimous in wanting to expel the population. In a report, Allon explained that by doing so they would relieve a long-term threat to Tel Aviv, clog the routes of any advance from the Arab Legion, and add the burden on the Arab economy of caring for forty-five thousand people.[20] Allon refrained from issuing a direct order to expel the residents of the town to the brigade commander, however. Instead, an Arab delegation composed of residents, terrified after two days of fighting, occupation, and killing, requested that the town's residents be allowed to leave. The military commander agreed, providing the people moved quickly.

In a flurry, Lydda's residents grabbed their suitcases, stuffed them with their most important possessions, and loaded them onto horse-drawn wagons, donkeys, and mules. Most of them were not particular in what they took with them, believing they would be back in a couple of days, on the heels of the victorious Arab Legion. Behind them they left the very essence of their lives: stone homes furnished with couches, tables, rugs, family pictures, and clothing; their kitchens overflowing with spices, dates, pastries, and tea leaves; their olive groves, lemon trees, and fig fields. They did not know it, but they would never return. All the while, Israeli soldiers banged on their doors, shouting for them to leave for King Abdullah in Jordan. Some of the forty-five thousand refugees were driven by bus to Latrun and herded off toward Jordan. Others had to walk the entire distance, urged on by Israeli soldiers firing over their heads. The heat was unbearable, with temperatures up to one hundred degrees in the cloudless midday sun. The roads were narrow and jammed with people. The way to Jordan was uphill, adding to their misery. Few had enough water. The old, sick, and young fainted. An estimated 335 died on the way.

Many Israelis expressed reservations about the removal of the civilians from Lydda and Ramle. One party leader did not accept Allon's position that strategic needs justified the removal of thousands of women, children, and old men from their homes. A hardened military leader of the operation recalled his conflicting emotions: "For years you've trained for this day," he explained. "You've been told there is an inevitable war coming. You've been told that the Arabs will have to go. And yet you are in shock. In Lydda, the war is as cruel as it can be. The killing, the looting, the feelings of rage and revenge. Then the column marching. And although you are strong and well-trained and resilient, you experience some sort of mental collapse. You feel the humanist education you received collapsing."[21] Like Deir Yassin, Lydda remains one of the most controversial episodes in Israel's history, causing much debate and internal anguish to this day, and continued condemnation from the Palestinians, more proof in their eyes of Zionist aggression.

Lydda added to the Palestinian refugee crisis that was already under way. The war created some seven hundred thousand Arab refugees. International pressure began to demand that Israel accept some of the homeless. There were those inside Israel who agreed. But at a cabinet meeting Ben-Gurion explained his position: "As for the return of the Arabs, not only can I not accept the opinion of encouraging their return, but I think that one should prevent their return. War is war," he told the cabinet, "and those who have declared war upon us will have to bear the consequences after they have been defeated."[22] To Ben-Gurion and the majority of the cabinet, the thought of several hundred thousand hostile Arabs seeking the Jews' destruction being allowed to enter the State of Israel was unacceptable. Shortly afterwards, he made his policy clear in response to a UN repatriation proposal: The refugee question could only be settled as part of an overall peace treaty between Israel and the Arab states, he declared. During the course of those negotiations, the long-term interests of the Arab and Jewish populations would be considered, and the Jewish state would take into account the destruction of Jewish life and property by the Arabs in their war of aggression, as a counterclaim against Arab charges of lost property. Ben-Gurion also made clear that not all Arab refugees would be allowed to return to the area now under Israeli control.

As with the *Altalena*, there would be no compromise. The security of the state was at risk. Most Israeli officials agreed with Ben-Gurion. But while the integrity of the state might have been secured, the flight of the refugees opened a chapter that remains unresolved to this day, leaving a trail of blood and tears in its wake.

A reporter described the conditions in a refugee settlement in Jordanian-held territory:

> The tent camp in the Jordan Valley on the approach to Jericho had perhaps 20,000 inhabitants. . . . I looked at their filthy habitations—brush for mattresses, a torn blanket or two, a larder empty except for a pinch of meal, a pat or two of lard. The camp was talking about an Arab businessman from Haifa. The day before, he had taken his two sons from the tent, shot them through the head, and turned the gun on himself. . . . The Jews had taken his home and business, and refused to allow his return, even to liquidate. He was penniless and couldn't stand watching his children's bellies bloat. The tent camp in Ramallah was even worse. Icy winds off the Judean hills whipped through the torn flaps. The widow from Ramle wore an old flour sack, and her legs were blue with cold. Her five children emitted a monotonous wail; she was on the move perpetually, swabbing their runny noses. Her husband, a Ramle carpenter, had been killed in the war. . . . Agonized, she asked me what happened to her home. I could have told her it was probably occupied by a [Jewish] family from Bulgaria or Poland, but stalled with a don't know answer.[23]

The Palestinian refugees languished in makeshifts camps, dependent on the United Nations Relief and Works Agency (UNRWA) for food, water, health services, and jobs. Meanwhile, their homes in Israel were settled by Holocaust survivors from Europe, were demolished, or fell into disrepair.

The war continued for the rest of 1948. The focus of the battles shifted south, where Israel pushed back Egyptian forces, taking most of the Negev desert. By the time the war finally ended in early 1949, Israel had expanded its borders on nearly every side. But the quest for long-term security was just beginning. The Arab states remained hostile, refusing to negotiate face- to-face with Israelis at the armistice meetings. The borders may have been tentatively agreed upon, but they were tense and awkward, nowhere more so than in Jerusalem. After the IDF's Moshe

Dayan and Arab Legion's Abdullah Tall demarcated the lines in the Holy City, the IDF's Jerusalem commander wrote:

> In the heart of the city, this separation was emphasized by a stone wall designed to prevent sniping. In the no man's lands, it was a series of barbed-wire entanglements, minefields, and make-shift obstacles.
>
> These no man's lands were created because Dayan and Tall had used a thick china marker to delineate the City Line on a map. The line was two or three millimeters wide on the map—which translated to forty to sixty meters on the ground. Their line covered houses and even whole streets indiscriminately.
>
> In the heat of the summer, the marker tends to melt and had covered certain area, thus widening the City Line even further. Neither side could agree on what belonged to whom, and people were killed because of the thickness of a pencil.
>
> Guests at the reconstructed King David Hotel stay on the terrace or on their room's balcony overlooking Jordanian sentries perched on the city wall within small-arms distance. The intervening no man's land turned into a mass of concertina wire, garbage, and putrefying animals that been blown up by the mines. Nothing could be rebuilt along the front line—it was simply too dangerous.[24]

Similar tensions plagued Israel's other borders. The Arab states refused to accept Israel's existence, seeing it as an imperialist entity foisted upon them by outsiders. Palestinian society lay in ruins, its people scattered across the region, biding their time in squalid refugee camps for the chance to reclaim their honor and homes from the Jews, who they blamed for stealing their homes. The war became known to them as *Al Nahkba* (the Catastrophe). They had lost everything but refused to acquiesce to those they viewed as invaders who had stolen their homeland. The Jews had their state, but it had cost them six thousand dead, 1 percent of the entire Jewish population. Moreover, it was not clear if they could endure in the sea of hostility that surrounded them.

-9-

A Heavy Burden

The Jewish State Fights to Survive, 1949–1957

The Ingathering of the Exiles

The new state faced innumerable challenges. They had to hold elections, form a government, build the economy, establish foreign diplomatic contacts, and build schools. All this had to be done under the threat of hostile neighbors. But one priority overshadowed all others: the "ingathering of the exiles." In the Bible, Jewish exiles returned from the Babylonian exodus, and so, too, would modern Jews. After all, that was the very purpose of the establishment of the State of Israel. For the state to survive, it was also vital that it increase its population. Israel's Arab neighbors greatly outnumbered it. More people would provide for a larger army and economy, and the country's population doubled in its first four years. At first, most of the new arrivals were from European displaced persons camps, Holocaust survivors. The next wave came from Arab lands. Some had been driven out after the Israeli War of Independence. Others immigrated for economic or ideological reasons. No matter their motive, it was difficult for many of them to reach the Promised Land. Still, their situation was so dire that they risked life and limb to make the journey.

Israeli reports from this time bear out the horrendous living conditions of the Jews in North Africa:

The situation of the Jews in the Moroccan Atlas Mountains is beyond description. Mere reading or hearing about it cannot convey the reality that such conditions exist in our time. Whoever has not seen a family of eighteen huddled in one room, five meters long, which serves for living quarters, kitchen and workshop, whoever has not visited rooms in which hundreds of children, all half-naked and with eye diseases which will never be treated, are taught together; whoever has not met the "teacher," whose only method of teaching is the whip; whoever has not smelled the peculiar smell of the entire quarter—would never believe that such wretchedness can exist, and that fellow human beings be allowed to live like this.[1]

A Jewish Agency report from 1949 described the situation of the Jews in Casablanca: "There are 80,000 Jews in this city, 50,000 of which live in the ghetto. The crowding in these quarters is atrocious, and the hygienic conditions frightful. Congenital syphilis is widespread, and so are trachoma and a scalp disease. In one town at the foot of the Atlas Mountains, we found an entire community that was blind. Whoever was still able to see would soon go blind, because of the ubiquitous trachoma. There is no helping them, because there are no doctors and no one treats the disease." Another report read:

The situation of the Jews further inland is particularly bad especially in Cyrenaica [Libya], where the Arabs are openly threatening to massacre them when Sheikh el-Senoussi comes to power. In small towns and villages, Jewish girls are often forced to convert to Islam. A typical case happened just two weeks ago: a local Jewish girl whom an Arab wanted to marry got on one of our ships. When the Arabs in her town discovered this, they demanded that the Jewish community supply them with fifty Jewish virgins within a week. That night more than fifty Jewish families fled that town and came with their daughters to Tripoli.[2]

After fleeing their homes in North Africa, the migrants arrived in transit camps set up by the Jewish Agency. Conditions there were appalling. One such camp in Algiers was typical: "In the *Alliance Israelite* building and the little alley behind it live masses of people, crowded like animals. From top to bottom, and even on the stairs, you see people sitting with their belongings. They live, cook, fall ill, give birth and die, men and women, young and old, all of them together. More than fifty people live in one room of four or five square meters."[3]

From the transit camps, the migrants were taken to Marseilles on ships, where conditions were severe. The immigrants had virtually no possessions to begin with, nor were they issued any food. There were not enough beds, forcing the migrants to sleep on the floors with no blankets and no warm clothing.

As difficult as the journey of the North Africans was, Yemenite Jews had at least as hard a time. They walked miles on foot across the deserts and mountains of Yemen's interior to reach the port of Aden. Along the way they were attacked and robbed by bandits, while starvation and thirst made the journey even more dangerous. At Aden they gathered into primitive camps, where Arab nationalists threatened them with knives raised. Finally, they boarded planes to take them to the Holy Land. They had never seen planes before. Some preferred to sit in the aisles, as the seats were too soft for them. Others lit portable stoves in midair to cook their meager rations, much to the horror of the flight crews. But they finally arrived in Israel as part of "Operation Magic Carpet," fulfilling the biblical prophecy of their return on "eagles' wings." They were a colorful people. The men were dressed in white robes with caps and side curls, the women in colorful flowing dresses and hand-carved necklaces and earrings. After centuries of suffering in the remote wastes of Yemen, they were returning home. Although they had never seen planes before, they were arriving in them en masse.

Their hardships were far from over, however. Bringing in vast numbers of immigrants strained the small state well beyond its limited capabilities. Israel was forced to cram hundreds of thousands of immigrants into transit camps, known as *ma'abarot*. They had no privacy whatsoever, and living conditions were squalid. At first the immigrants lived in tents, later in canvas huts, and then in wooden huts. There were only a few water taps in the camps, and the whole population had to share them. The poor-quality water had to be boiled before it was fit for human use. The schools lacked basic features such as desks, chairs, blackboards, chalk, and textbooks. The health clinics were perpetually understaffed and lacked medicine. The camp residents suffered from intense heat and dust in the summer, and they wallowed in the mud and cold during the winter. At one point, there was no grain left and no money to pay for another shipment.

Perhaps the worst feature of the camps was the sanitation. One resident wrote:

> Nobody washes. In some camps there are hot showers, but in others there is no installation for hot water at all, so that all through the winter it is impossible to bathe, even if they want to. There are entire camps with thousands of men, women, and children, where there is not a single shower room, not even for cold water. And when there is a wretched little bathroom, it is occupied by inmates who have nowhere else to stay. . . . In many camps, therefore, the toilets are nothing more than holes in the ground, lined with sheets of tin, without any sewage or running water. These holes soon fill up and stink up the atmosphere, but in the absence of any other facility, people keep using them, though they overflow with excrement.[4]

Israel's economists—Levi Eshkol, in particular—advised against the massive migrations. He called large-scale immigration suicide and warned that the people in the camps would starve due to a lack of money. But Ben-Gurion would not consider scaling back the ingathering. Israel had to bring in all the Jews they could in as short a time as possible. The Jews in many Arab nations faced imminent crises. Moreover, Israel itself faced another possible war and needed to build up its own strength before the next round. Faced with another crisis, Ben-Gurion turned to one of his most trusted advisers: Labor Minister Golda Meir. He sent Meir to the United States on a fund-raising trip. The American-reared minister had collected $50 million from American Jewish donors prior to the War of Independence, money that proved decisive in allowing Israel to acquire much-needed arms. She had saved the country once; now she was being asked to do so again. Meir told her American audience:

> I went to our Parliament two weeks ago last Tuesday, and presented a project for 30,000 housing units by the end of this year. Parliament approved it, and there was great joy in the country. But actually I did a strange thing: I presented a project for which I didn't have the money.
>
> What we want to do is give each family a luxurious apartment of one room; one room which we will build out of concrete blocks. We won't even plaster the walls. We will make roofs, but no ceilings. What we hope is that since these people will be learning a trade as they build their houses, they will finish them, and eventually, one day, add on another room. In the meantime, we will be happy, and they will be happy, even though it means putting a family of two, three, four, or five into one room. But this is better than putting two or three families in a single tent. . . .
>
> It is an awful thing to do—to forge a signature to a check, but I have done it. I have promised the people at home and the people in the camps that the government is going to put up these 30,000 units, and we have already started to do so with the little money we have. But there isn't enough for these 30,000 units. It is up to you either to keep these people in camps and send them food packages, or to put them to work and restore their dignity and self-respect.[5]

America's Jews contributed generously, but it was still not enough. Immediate action needed to be taken. There was only one institution capable of organizing a massive building effort: Ben-Gurion turned to IDF chief of staff Yigael Yadin. Yadin vigorously threw himself into organizing a rescue mission headed by the army. The results were impressive. In a mere four months, the army built more permanent housing and schools. They installed water and sanitation and provided medical care to the one hundred or so camps in the country. Using the army for social services carried a cost, however. The IDF's battle readiness declined, and Arab infiltrators entered the country at will. Moreover, even the army's efforts could not settle all the new refugees. The burden on Israel's small economy was too large. Another solution presented itself, but its very nature nearly split the Jewish state apart.

January 7, 1952, was the most explosive Knesset (parliament) session in Israel's history. Even before David Ben-Gurion took the podium, the country was in an uproar. Word had leaked out that Israel and West Germany had negotiated reparations for Holocaust victims, a sum total of $865 million (roughly $8 billion in 2015 dollars). Opponents derided it as "blood money." Opposition leader Menachem Begin refused to take his seat at the Knesset, gathering a large crowd at a nearby square. Ben-Gurion opened the session by explaining it was not blood money—they were asking for compensation for lost Jewish property during the Nazi era. "Let not the murderers of our people also be their inheritors," he said, referencing a biblical passage. Many in the Knesset remained viciously opposed. Even as the debate raged in the Knesset, Begin whipped his supporters into a frenzy: "This will be a war of life and death. Today I give the order: Blood!"

With these words ringing in their ears, Begin's supporters marched toward the Knesset. The government had anticipated potential unrest; police were deployed en masse around the Knesset, armed with tear gas. Roadblocks had been set up around the building. A newspaper recounted the ensuing melee: "As road blocks were removed forcibly by the marchers, the police—who had been ordered to observe extreme self-restraint in dealing with the demonstrators—fell back to positions around the Knesset. The crowd showered the police with stones; and even Magen David Adom ambulances rushing first aid to the injured were stoned and halted. . . . A car parked outside the Knesset was overturned by the demonstrators. As the gasoline poured out of the tank, a tear-gas bomb apparently ignited it."

The violence in the street reached the Knesset a few moments later: "The shouting of a mob not far off, the intermittent wail of

1. The Fortress of Masada,
site of the Zealot's last stand.
(Moshe Milner, Goverment
Press Office, State of Israel)

2. Theodor Herzl,
the father of Zionism. (Israel
Government Press Office)

3. (*Opposite top*) Jewish survivors of the Nazi
concentration camps in Europe in Palestine,
April 1944, still wearing the signs of their
ordeal on their tattered clothing. (Zoltan Kluger,
Israel Government Press Office)

4. (*Opposite bottom*) The crowded illegal immigration ship *Exodus*, carrying Jewish refugees
from war-torn Europe, enters Haifa port on July
18, 1947, after three hours of combat with the
British navy. (Hans Pinn, Israel Government
Press Office)

5. (*Above*) David Ben-Gurion reads Israel's Declaration of Independence on May 14, 1948.
(Zoltan Kluger, Israel Government Press Office)

6. The *Altalena* on fire as it sits off the coast of Tel Aviv, June 22, 1948. (Hans Pinn, Government Press Office/State of Israel)

7. Arab villagers flee the fighting in the Galilee, 1948. Roughly seven hundred thousand Arabs became refugees during the war. (David Eldan, Israel Government Press Office)

8. General Moshe Dayan with jubilant soldiers in Sharm el-Sheikh, 1956. (Israel Government Press Office)

9. Nazi war criminal Adolf Eichmann standing trial in Jerusalem, 1960. "As I stand before you, judges of Israel," the prosecutor declared, "I do not stand alone. With me in this place and at this hour stand six million accusers." (Israel Government Press Office)

10. Israeli paratroopers stand in awe at the Western Wall, in Jewish hands for the first time in two thousand years, on June 7, 1967. (Photographer: David Rubiner. Israel Government Press Office)

11. Israeli armor crosses the pontoon bridge that allowed the IDF to cross the Suez Canal and turn the tide of the Yom Kippur War, October 1973. (Israel Government Press Office)

12. A typical intifada scene: youthful demonstrators burn tires, throw stones at IDF troops, wave Palestinian flags, and chant slogans. (Government Press Office, State of Israel)

13. Yitzchak Rabin and King Hussein shake hands as Bill Clinton looks on at the Israel-Jordan Peace Treaty ceremony, October 1994. (Avi Ohayon, Israel Government Press Office)

police cars and ambulance sirens, sporadic explosions of gas grenades and the glow of flames from a burning car came through the windows of the Knesset building, and later the window panes were splintered by rocks, and fumes of tear-gas bombs from the battle-scarred street outside permeated the chamber. One member was hit in the head by a stone."[6]

Menachem Begin then strode into the chamber, decrying the reparations deal as shameful. He then shouted at Ben-Gurion, "You are a hooligan!" With the Knesset in chaos, the session was disbanded.

Over the next few days, the rhetoric cooled, but the debate was not over. A government minister explained what the reparations would mean for Israel: "They would permit us to exploit the Negev mines, broaden agriculture, develop transportation, shipping and fishing, increase electrical output, develop basic industries, and build homes for *ma'aborot* residents. The people who wanted to exterminate us are forced to bear some of the burden involved in creating a new Jewish center of strength and a place of rebirth."[7] The preamble to the agreement bore this out, noting "the heavy burden" the State of Israel was assuming by taking in the refugees of Nazi terror.

The Knesset reconvened and approved the agreement by a vote of sixty-one to fifty. The reparations proved key to Israel's development. Within a few years, the transit camps disappeared, Israel's industries grew, and the economy improved. In many ways, it was the 1933 Transfer Agreement debate redux. Both times, pragmatists led by David Ben-Gurion argued that Israel's development and security were more important than emotion and honor. Both times they had been opposed by right-wing parties unwilling to compromise. And both times, the pragmatists narrowly prevailed, allowing the Jewish state's establishment and subsequent survival.

Infiltrators and Commandos

Yet Israel's survival in the 1950s remained very much in doubt. The most immediate threat was infiltration. From 1951 to 1956

Israel recorded more than six thousand illegal border crossings into its territory, with more than four hundred citizens killed. The infiltrators had different goals. Some were Arabs farmers trying to reclaim their old possessions and crops. But many were fedayeen (guerillas) seeking to harm Israelis in the hope of driving them out. The army, weakened by the demands of the massive influx of immigrants, seemed incapable of stopping the infiltrators. When a retaliation was mounted, they ended up as failures. The army units were generally unable to find their targets at night and wandered aimlessly. On occasion, they did find the targets and fired a few shots before withdrawing.

But that would soon change. The army set up a special squad led by Ariel Sharon to deal with the infiltrators, known as Unit 101. Sharon carefully picked his men and rigorously trained them for action behind enemy lines. In short order, he felt they were ready. When infiltrators from the Jordanian town of Kibbiya killed a Jewish mother and her two infants, the government ordered Unit 101 to strike back. It was time for action: "The orders were clear," Sharon recorded. "Kibbiya was to be a lesson. I was to inflict as many casualties as I could on the Arab home guard and on whatever Jordanian army reinforcements showed up. I was also to blow up every major building in the town. A political decision had been made at the highest level. The Jordanians were to understand that Jewish blood could no longer be shed with impunity. From this point on, there would be a heavy price to pay."[8]

Sharon and his men set off on the night of October 14, 1953, carrying packs loaded with explosives. They hiked over rough terrain for five miles before arriving at the Arab home guard positions at Kibbiya. Sharon ordered his men to attack:

> In the firefight in front of the Arab trenches, ten of the home guards were killed. Then we moved on toward Kibbiya itself. Just as we arrived, a jeep with two Jordanian soldiers in it wheeled down the main road in our direction, but a burst of fire from the paratroopers killed both of them, sending the jeep to a skidding halt.
>
> In a few more minutes, we were in the village proper. As we

walked through the streets, an eerie silence hung over the place, broken only by the strains of Arab music coming from a radio that had been left playing in an empty café. A report came in from one of the roadblocks that hundreds of villagers were streaming along the road. Kibbiya seemed completely deserted.[9]

Around midnight, the soldiers began to demolish the village's big stone buildings. At each building, a soldier checked if anyone was inside. When a building was found empty, charges were set in place and the building was dynamited. Sharon's soldiers found two children hiding in the corners and moved them out. The process of demolishing the buildings took several hours. The soldiers returned back, where they were met by an Israeli officer. Sharon told the officer than they had demolished forty-two buildings and inflicted ten or twelve casualties among the Arab home guard and the two soldiers in the jeep.

But Sharon was wrong. A total of sixty-nine Jordanians died at Kibbiya, including women and children. Sharon denied any deliberate killing, stating that the Arab families must have hid in the attics and cellars of the stone buildings and were killed in the demolitions. With the world in an uproar over the action, the Israeli government distanced itself from the raid. According to Sharon, Kibbiya was a tragedy, but also a turning point. The army and public now knew they had the ability to strike back. They would be helpless victims no more. Ben-Gurion agreed. "This is going to give us the possibility of living here," he told Sharon.[10]

After Kibbiya, Unit 101 merged with the paratroopers and—under Sharon's command—struck back at target after target inside Arab territory. They quickly became Israel's heroes, the front line of defense against the implacable foes that wantonly attacked and killed innocent civilians. But the attacks did not end. Instead, there was a spiraling cycle of cross-border violence. Fedayeen entered Israel and attacked civilians; the paratroopers would attack Arab military installations and fedayeen camps. The Gaza Strip, in particular, became a center of fedayeen activity. From Gaza, the infiltrators could attack targets in the center of the country, including

Tel Aviv. Israel's government felt the fedayeen were protected by Egypt's army, if not outright encouraged. When infiltrators killed a civilian near Tel Aviv in February 1955 and left behind papers linking them to Egyptian intelligence, the government decided on its largest-scale reprisal raid yet, targeting Egyptian military positions in Gaza.

As usual, Sharon led the assault. His units marched across the border under the cloak of darkness, through orange groves heavy with the scent of citrus. They reached their destination without detection. Then Sharon gave the order and the night exploded in an inferno of missiles, flares, and bullets. The Israelis had gained the advantage of surprise and quickly drove off the defenders. They dynamited a water pumping station, which crumbled in on itself. An Egyptian truck filled with soldiers attempted a rescue but tripped a wire booby trap and was turned into a flaming hulk. Other Egyptian units opened fire, however, and several paratroopers were struck dead as they made their way back across the border. By the time the operation was over, thirty-eight Egyptians and eight Israelis had been killed. Militarily the operation had been a success. The IDF had achieved its objectives, inflicting heavy damage on Egyptian infrastructure and personnel.

Israel's leadership hoped that the harsh reprisal would convince Egyptian president Gamal Abdul Nasser to rein in the fedayeen. Instead, Nasser was humiliated. Viewing the raid as a disaster, Nasser decided to take drastic measures. In September 1955 Egypt and Czechoslovakia announced a massive arms deal, including three hundred tanks, two hundred fighter planes, fifty bombers, artillery, naval equipment, and other weapons. It was far more than the Jewish state's meager inventory. Israeli leaders worried that when Nasser received all the weapons, Egypt would overrun the defenseless Jewish state. In addition to the massive arms deal, fedayeen from Gaza continued to infiltrate Israel's borders, Egypt blocked the Straits of Tiran leading to Israel's southern port of Eilat, and the Suez Canal was closed to Israeli shipping. The sum total of these provocations made Israeli leaders feel their state was in mortal danger from Egypt. But Israel's tiny industries could not supply it with adequate weapons. Israeli statesmen desperately searched for a patron who could supply it with arms. But the United States and the USSR remained aloof, wary of alienating the Arab world. Had it not been for Nasser himself, Israel might have not been able to find an ally.

War in the Desert

On July 26, 1956, President Nasser addressed a massive crowd in Alexandria on the anniversary of the coup that brought him to power. He seemed to be at a low point: his negotiations with the United States and Britain for a loan to build a dam at Aswan had failed. The Eisenhower administration refused to loan money to a government tied to the Soviets. "Go choke on your fury," he scolded the Americans. Egypt was involved in a "battle against imperialism and the methods and tactics of imperialism, and a battle against Israel, the vanguard of imperialism," he told the crowd. Moreover, Nasser found a different way of getting the money for his cherished dam. At the climax of his delivery he declared, "At this moment as I talk to you, some of your Egyptian brethren . . . have started to take over the canal company and its property to control shipping in the canal—the canal company and its property and to control shipping in the canal—the canal which is situated in Egyptian territory, which . . . is part of Egypt and which is owned in Egypt."[11] Egyptian troops had nationalized the Suez Canal from British control. Egypt would take the revenues from the canal and use it finance the dam. That night, wild celebrations erupted throughout Egypt. Finally someone was standing up to the European imperialists, who had humiliated and used them as pawns for so long. Nasser instantly became the hero of the Arab world.

But Nasser's moves entailed risk. The Suez Canal was a vital British interest. Moreover, Nasser was supporting Algerian rebels in their fight against France. The two European powers decided that military action was the only solution. They needed a regional ally—one that was also threatened by Egypt. Israel fit the bill. France began supplying Israel with the arms, tanks, armored vehicles, and planes it needed to counter the growing Egyptian menace. Meanwhile, the situation along the Egyptian border worsened, as waves of fedayeen continued to kill civilians while Egyptian artillery struck into Israel.

Time was running short. In the third week of October, Nasser moved army units into Gaza. The Egyptian leader publicly announced that he would regain the right of the Palestinians by force. Israel's leaders uniformly agreed that Nasser would attack shortly. Against this backdrop, Israel's highest military and political leaders met with their French and British counterparts secretly in a villa outside Paris, where they hastily drew up a war plan. Israel would attack Egypt and push toward the canal. The British and French would land their troops in the Canal Zone a few days later. Egyptian military power would be crushed, the canal would return to British control, and Nasser might even topple from power.

The war began on October 29, as paratrooper elements landed at the Mitla Pass in the western Sinai. A larger force led by Ariel Sharon drove across the desert to join them. Other Israeli offensives began in central Sinai toward Abu Agheila. In the north an offensive would go into the Gaza Strip, home of the fedayeen. Sharon linked up with the rest of the paratroopers outside the Mitla Pass. His orders were to wait outside the pass and avoid any battles. But Sharon felt the flat terrain outside the pass was a poor defensive position. When a report came in of an Egyptian armor unit nearby, he ordered most of his armor to go into the pass to find better defensive ground. "I didn't expect opposition inside Mitla Pass," Sharon explained, and he sent in a unit led by Motta Gur. Sharon was gravely mistaken, as he himself recalled:

> But within a mile of the entrance the first half-track was slammed by a volley of fire from hidden positions high on the defile walls. The driver was killed instantly and the half-track swerved sideways and stopped. The second half-track moved up and was also hit and stopped.
>
> Had some unit other than the paratroopers been involved, that

might have been the end of it. They might have withdrawn to assess the situation without getting themselves further involved. But the paratroopers were trained differently. For long years I had drummed it into them that they could never leave wounded or dead on the field. Never. It was one of the axiomatic lessons that I had preached constantly. The result was that when the half-tracks were hit, their natural reaction was to move forward to get the casualties out. This Motta Gur did, regardless of his orders not to get involved in a battle. And as the paratroopers moved to rescue their friends, they found themselves in the middle of a vicious firefight.

It was an act I never blamed Motta for, despite the eventual consequences.[12]

The consequences were heavy losses: "With Motta Gur still pinned down, the reconnaissance unit skirted the cliffs above the right side hoping to come down on the Egyptians from above. But when they got to the ridge, they were hit by a hail of bullets from caves and hidden ledges on the far side. Unable to identify the source of the fire, they assumed it was coming from below them and stormed down the wall. Here, some of them fell to their deaths, while others were caught by fire from the positions below as well as those opposite them."[13] With the armor unit pinned down by enemy fire, Sharon sent in his infantry. They scrambled up the sides of the pass and had to take each emplacement in hand-to-hand fighting, under heavy fire from the emplacements on the opposite ridges. After seven hours of heavy fighting, the Egyptians retreated back to the canal. It was the single bloodiest engagement of the war: forty Israelis and over two hundred Egyptians fell at the Mitla Pass. Once the darling of the IDF, Sharon fell into disfavor. It would take another war with Egypt for him to regain his previous stature.

In the central front, Israeli armor and infantry attacked the strong fortress at Abu Agheila, a vast and complex system of camps and bunkers surrounded by barbed wire, minefields, and artillery extending for seven miles on each side. The strongest single position at Abu Agheila, the Um Cataf stronghold, held off several Israeli attacks. Dayan expressed disappointment at what he saw as halfhearted efforts. He ordered another assault on Um Cataf, and to the attackers' surprise, the garrison was empty. The Egyptian commander had ordered a retreat. Israeli efforts at the rear of Abu Agheila were more successful. Bren Adan commanded an armored force against the Ruefa Dam, another well-fortified position.

Adan led an audacious attack. In order to reach the dam, his unit had to drive through a narrow defile impassable to wheeled vehicles. Adan left his supplies, ammunition, and fuel behind as the tracked armor raced up the defile. The tanks and armored vehicles rolled right over the Egyptian position's barbed wire perimeter and opened fire on the surprised defenders, inflicting heavy losses. The Egyptians quickly recovered from their initial surprise and returned fire, knocking out several tanks and vehicles. The crews of the immobile tanks continued to fire their guns, while the few remaining operable vehicles stormed the compound. Fuel and ammunition dumps went up in massive balls of flame, creating huge explosions that reverberated around the battlefield. The battle raged on for an hour, with heavy casualties on both sides. Under continuous heavy fire, Egyptian resistance finally broke. As the defenders emerged from the bunkers and trenches with their hands up, their faces were lit by the fires that continued to glow from the huge explosions. The route was now open to the Suez Canal in the central front. Israeli armor pressed forward.

The most successful Israeli operations occurred in the north, where IDF forces led by Israel Tal attacked the well-fortified Egyptian positions near the coast. Several armored vehicles struck mines in front of the forts, and the attack halted while sappers—under heavy artillery and tank fire—disarmed the mines, clearing a path for the armor. The armor moved slowly, hampered by a narrow path, Egyptian fire, and enemy mines, taking five hours of careful maneuvering before reaching the rendezvous point, the coastal road that ran from Gaza to the canal. A second Israeli unit found their way blocked by rolls of concertina wire. Under heavy

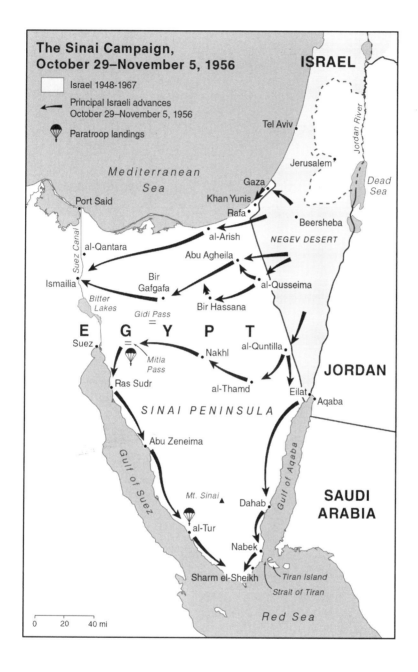

The Sinai Campaign, October 29–November 5, 1956

Israel 1948-1967

Principal Israeli advances
October 29–November 5, 1956

Paratroop landings

ISRAEL

Tel Aviv

Mediterranean Sea

Jerusalem

Jordan River

Dead Sea

Gaza

Port Said

Khan Yunis

Rafa

Beersheba

al-Arish

NEGEV DESERT

al-Qantara

Abu Agheila

Suez Canal

Ismailia

Bir Gafgafa

al-Qusseima

Bitter Lakes

Bir Hassana

Gidi Pass

E G Y P T

Suez

Nakhl

al-Quntilla

Mitla Pass

JORDAN

Ras Sudr

al-Thamd

Eilat

Aqaba

SINAI PENINSULA

Abu Zeneima

Gulf of Suez

Mt. Sinai

Dahab

Gulf of Aqaba

SAUDI ARABIA

al-Tur

Nabek

Sharm el-Sheikh

Tiran Island

Strait of Tiran

Red Sea

0   20   40 mi

3. The Sinai Campaign, October 29–November 5, 1956. Map adapted from
Howard Sachar, *A History of Israel* (New York: Alfred E. Knopf, 1996).
Erin Greb Cartography.

machine gun fire, the soldiers cut the wires, clearing the way for the tanks. The tanks moved forward and took the Egyptian fortifications, as well as a large British storage depot left behind from World War II.

With the Egyptian strongholds taken, the Israeli units jubilantly met each other at the coastal road, celebrating their triumph. There they joined forces and turned down the coastal road to the Suez Canal. Along the way, they captured nearly four hundred vehicles, including forty tanks and sixty armored cars, a huge windfall for the IDF's small inventory. Israeli forces also destroyed the bases in Gaza that the fedayeen had used for their attacks into Israel. Intelligence provided the names of suspected terrorists, and many were summarily executed. Gaza's two hundred thousand inhabitants, many of whom were refugees from the 1948 war, were now under Israeli control.

The final offensive of the war aimed at a single objective: capturing the Egyptian guns at Sharm el-Sheikh, responsible for closing the Straits of Tiran to Israeli shipping. But it would not be easy. The mission would have to proceed along an old camel trail that was not suited to the heavy wheeled and armored vehicles the IDF needed to take Sharm el-Sheikh. The trail was littered with boulders, descended into large ravines, and in many places followed deep sand. The route was 150 miles long and could only be resupplied by sea at Dahab. The battalion would therefore have to carry its own supplies, water, and gas over the rough terrain. Despite these difficulties, Israel's leaders remained determined to carry out the operation. By closing the Straits of Tiran to their ships, Egypt was successfully challenging Israel's legitimacy. Indeed, for Ben-Gurion it was the most important operation of the war.

Two hundred vehicles and eighteen hundred men set out from Eilat on October 29. Led by Avraham Yoffe, it became known as the "Long Trek." They advanced the first sixty miles without incident. But then the terrain abruptly changed uphill, and the hard ground gave way to sand. The vehicles sank into the soft ground. Yoffe ordered the tires deflated to give them better traction, and then they were pushed and pulled free. The vehicles that could not be salvaged had to be abandoned. As the expedition neared the oasis of Dahab, several men raced out front without vehicle support and were felled by Egyptian camel forces. At Dahab, the men rested as supplies came in from the sea. Refreshed, they set out again. Their next obstacle was a narrow goat track flanked by steep walls, where the Egyptians shot at the unit with machine guns and bazookas. After the Egyptians were driven off, the pass had to be widened for the armored vehicles. Demolition teams went to work, and the expedition moved on. When they finally reached Sharm el-Sheikh, they defeated the Egyptians stationed there and disabled the guns that had closed the straits to Israeli ships. For the first time, the Straits of Tiran were open to Israeli shipping.

By the time the fighting ended on November 5, Israel had captured one hundred tanks, two hundred artillery pieces, one thousand other vehicles, along with large amounts of ammunition and fuel. Egypt's army had been defeated before it could be unleashed on the Jewish state. In addition, the fedayeen had been mostly eliminated, and the Straits of Tiran were open. Golda Meir recalled her impressions as she visited the area:

> I shall never forget my first sight of the elaborate Egyptian military installations—built in defiance of the United Nations itself—at Sharm al Shaykh, for the sole purpose of maintaining an illegal blockade against our shipping. The area of Sharm al Shaykh is incredibly lovely; the waters of the Red Sea must be the bluest and clearest in the world, and they are framed by mountains that range in color from deep red to violet and purple. There, in that beautiful tranquil setting, on an empty shore, stood the grotesque battery of huge naval guns that had paralyzed Eilat for so long. For me, it was a picture that symbolized everything.
>
> Then I toured the Gaza Strip, from which the Fedayeen had gone out on their murderous assignments for so many months and in which the Egyptians had kept a quarter of a million men,

women, and children (of whom nearly 60% were Arab refugees) in the most shameful poverty and destitution.

I was appalled by what I saw there, and by the fact that those miserable people had been maintained in such degrading condition for over eight years only so that the Arab leaders could show the refugee camps to visitors and make political capital out of them.

Those refugees could and should have been resettled at once in any of the Arab countries of the Middle East—countries, incidentally, whose language, traditions, and religion they share. The Arabs would still have been able to continue their quarrel with us, but at least the refugees would not have been kept in a state of semi-starvation, or lived in such abject terror of their Egyptian masters.[14]

The Jewish state had accomplished all its military objectives. The diplomatic battle would be a very different story. The allies assumed the United States would not oppose their action. The Eisenhower administration had repeatedly clashed with Nasser—they would be happy to see him defeated, the allies thought. They were dead wrong. Eisenhower and Dulles worried that the tripartite action would be seen as neo-imperialist aggression by the Arab world that would drive the Arabs into the Soviet camp. On the second day of the war, President Eisenhower himself called Ben-Gurion and told him to end all military action. Ben-Gurion refused. At a United Nations emergency session, Israel's UN representative Abba Eban eloquently explained his country's precarious position:

> If we have sometimes found it difficult to persuade even our friends in the international community to understand the motives for our action, this is because nobody in the world community is in Israel's position. How many other nations have had hundreds of their citizens killed over these years by the action of armies across their frontiers? How many nations have had their ships seized and their cargoes confiscated in international waterways? How many nations find the pursuit of their daily tasks to be a matter of daily and perpetual hazard? In how many countries does every

single citizen going about his duties feel the icy wind of his own vulnerability? . . . Surrounded by hostile armies on all its land frontiers, subjected to savage and relentless hostility, exposed to penetration raids and assaults by day and night, suffering constant toll of life among its citizens, bombarded by threats of neighboring governments to accomplish its extinction by armed force— embattled, blockaded, besieged, Israel alone among the nations faces a battle for its security anew with every approaching nightfall and every rising dawn.[15]

The speech became famous in Israel as a statement of the Jewish state's security nightmare. It had no such impact in the UN General Assembly. The UN voted sixty-four to five in favor of a resolution calling for Israel to withdraw from the Sinai.

But Israel refused. Then the Soviet Union stepped in. In a note on November 4, the Soviets warned that Israel's actions were putting "into jeopardy the very existence of Israel as a state," a thinly veiled nuclear threat.[16] Ben-Gurion again refused to end the war, perceiving the Soviet threat as a bluff. The Soviets issued similar warnings to Britain and France the next day. American pressure forced the European powers to withdraw their troops from the canal, but Israeli forces remained in place.

While the war was over, Israel still fought over the fate of the Sinai in the United Nations. Foreign Minister Golda Meir traveled to New York, where she told the General Assembly: "Israel's people went into the desert or struck roots in stony hillsides to establish new villages, to build roads, houses, schools and hospitals; while Arab terrorists, entering from Egypt and Jordan, were sent in to kill and destroy. Israel dug wells, brought water in pipes from great distances; Egypt sent in fedayeen to blow up the wells and the pipes. Jews from Yemen brought in sick, undernourished children, believing that two out of every five would die; we cut that number down to one out of twenty-five." Israel "fed those babies and cured their diseases; the fedayeen were sent in to throw bombs at children in synagogues and grenades into baby homes."[17]

Once again, the United Nations was unmoved by Israeli entreaties. The assembly passed another resolution, calling for Israel to withdraw from the Sinai, this time by a vote of seventy-four to two. Under international pressure, Israel withdrew from the majority of the Sinai, except for Gaza and Sharm el-Sheikh. Meir explained to the General Assembly: "It is inconceivable to my government that the nightmare of the previous eight years should be reestablished in Gaza with international sanction. Shall Egypt be allowed once more to organize murder and sabotage in this strip? Shall Egypt be allowed to condemn the local population to permanent impoverishment and to block any solution of the refugee problem?"[18]

As a result, the United Nations agreed to place forces in Gaza and Sharm el-Sheikh. This would end the fedayeen raids from Gaza and ensure that the Straits of Tiran would remain open to Israeli shipping. Moreover, the United States agreed to ensure free shipping for all nations into the Gulf of Aqaba. Israel accepted these terms and withdrew from the rest of the Sinai. Five months after the war began, the last Israeli soldiers departed the Sinai in March 1957. As they did, the Israeli government announced that any closure of the Straits of Tiran would be regarded as an act of war. Whether this statement would serve as a deterrent was unknown. But few expected that peace with Egypt would last.

-10-

Masada Shall Not Fall Again!

Years of Growth and Consolidation, 1957–1967

"Israel after the Sinai Campaign will never again be the Israel that existed prior to this great operation," Ben-Gurion declared.[1] He was right. With the fedayeen in Gaza eliminated, Egypt's military weakened, and the Straits of Tiran open, Israel was in a stronger position than ever before. Before the war Israel had been more of a besieged refugee camp than a state. It had spent the first years of independence gathering in as many people as possible, with an utter lack of resources, all while under constant harassment from nearly every border. After the Sinai Campaign, Israel's borders quieted down.

Israel's security situation had improved, but its long-term survival remained in doubt. Hostile Arab states continued to surround it and call regularly for its destruction. Few military and diplomatic leaders inside the country thought there would not be another round of fighting with the Arabs. Still, the next decade was one of growth and expansion. The economy grew and immigrants poured in from North Africa, Eastern Europe, and Iran, increasing the population by 50 percent. Farms and cultivated areas continued to expand, due in no small part to an impressive irrigation system, the Israel Water Carrier, which ran fresh water from the Sea of Galilee to the parched regions of the country. The cities and suburbs grew as well, and there were a few signs of affluence for the first time in the nation's history. It was also during this time that the Jewish state undertook an action that underscored its very purpose.

On the afternoon of May 23, 1960, anticipation permeated every corner of the packed Knesset auditorium. Although word had leaked out that Ben-Gurion was about to make an extraordinary statement, no one in the hall was ready when the prime minister took the podium and delivered his bombshell: "I have to inform the Knesset that a short while ago the Israeli Security Services captured one of the greatest Nazi criminals, Adolf Eichmann—who together with the Nazi leaders was responsible for what was termed 'The Final Solution to the Jewish Problem'—that is, the destruction of six million European Jews. Eichmann is already in detention in Israel and will soon be put on trial here."[2] According-ing to one witness, "The House was electrified. And for several seconds there was a stunned silence. Suddenly, from all parts of the Chamber, came a roar of applause. Rarely had the Knesset been so unanimous. Rarely had its members been so moved. The murderer of their people had been caught. He would be brought to justice."[3]

As the Knesset exploded into bedlam, its members swarmed to the rostrum to congratulate Ben-Gurion. The prime minister graciously replied that the praise should go to the security ser-vices that had captured Eichmann. He also insisted that Eich-mann must be tried in Israel as "historic justice and the honor of the Jewish people demand," that the "monster" be tried in the Jewish state.[4]

The trial was one of the most anticipated events in the Jew-ish state's history. The whole country listened as the prosecutor, Israel's attorney general Gideon Hausner, delivered his opening statement:

> As I stand before you, Judges of Israel, I do not stand alone. With me in this place and at this hour stand six million accusers. But they cannot rise to their feet and point an accusing finger toward him who sits in the dock and cry: "I accuse." For their ashes are

piled up on the hills of Auschwitz and the fields of Treblinka and the forests of Poland. Their graves are scattered throughout the length and breadth of Europe. Their blood cries out, but their voice is not heard. Therefore, I will be their spokesman and in their name I will unfold the awesome indictment. The history of the Jewish people is steeped in suffering and tears. . . . Yet never, down the entire blood-stained road traveled by this people, never since the first days of its nationhood, had any man arisen who succeeded in dealing it such grievous blows as did Hitler's iniquitous regime, and Adolf Eichmann as its executive arm for the extermination of the Jewish people.[5]

The prosecutor presented fifteen hundred documents and one hundred witnesses attesting to Eichmann's role in orchestrating the Holocaust. Many in the audience cried, and some fainted as the crimes were catalogued. From behind a bulletproof-glass prisoner's dock, Eichmann tried to minimize his role, claiming that "a line should be drawn between leaders and tools like me." Eichmann thus stated that he was guilty of arranging the transports that carried millions to their deaths, but he did not feel guilty for the consequences, as he did not know what their final destination was. The prosecution showed that he was not a victim of orders, but had actively conspired in crimes that resulted in the deaths of millions of Jews. Eichmann had been at the death camps at Chelmno and Auschwitz and was therefore aware of the final destination of the transports. He himself had overseen the construction of the first gas chambers at Auschwitz. He had also witnessed the massacre of Jews at Minsk and had seen several hangings inside the camps. Eichmann also tried to claim that he had no animus against the Jews, but the prosecutor produced a statement Eichmann had made in 1945 that the deaths of five million people were a source of great satisfaction for him. The act could no longer be maintained. Eichmann was exposed for what he was: an enthusiastic architect of genocide. Indeed, the commandant of Auschwitz, before being hanged for crimes against humanity in 1947, recalled that Eichmann "was completely obsessed with the idea of destroying every single Jew that he could lay his hands on. Without pity and in cold blood, we must complete this extermination as rapidly as possible. Any compromise, even the slightest, would have to be paid for bitterly at a later date."[6]

Eichmann was found guilty of crimes against humanity and sentenced to death, the only time the death penalty was ever carried out in Israel. Ben-Gurion explained the significance of the trial: "Here, for the first time in Jewish history, historical justice was being done by the sovereign Jewish people. For many generations it was we who suffered, who were tortured, were killed—and were judged. . . . For the first time Israel is judging the murderers of the Jewish people . . . and let us bear in mind that only the independence of Israel could create the necessary conditions for this historic act of justice."[7] The Zionist vision of a safe haven for Jews was being vindicated.

Ben-Gurion wanted more than a safe haven for the Jews, however. He wanted to ensure that no Holocaust could ever occur again. To this end, the governments of Israel and France had agreed to build a nuclear reactor in the Negev desert near the remote town of Dimona. Although the agreement was signed in 1958, its existence did not become public for another two years, and even then its true purpose was concealed. Speaking to the Knesset in December 1960, Ben-Gurion downplayed its significance, stating rather blandly: "We are presently engaged in building a research reactor with a 24,000 thermal kilowatt output, to serve the purposes of industry, medicine and science, and to train scientific and technical Israeli manpower."[8] Ben-Gurion stressed that the reactor was meant only for peace purposes and denied reports that Israel was making a bomb.

Despite his public denials, Israel's nuclear program was of paramount importance for Ben-Gurion. He had seen the death camps in Europe with his own eyes. By building the ultimate deterrent weapon, the Jewish state was taking steps to make sure that no other calamity would ever befall the Jewish people. Ben-Gurion acknowledged as much in a speech to the Armaments Developments Authority, although he still did not directly refer to atomic weapons:

I do not know of any other nations whose neighbors declare that they wish to terminate it, and not declare, but prepare for it by all means available to them. We must have no illusions that what are declared every day in Cairo, Damascus, and Iraq are just words. This is the thought that guides the Arab leaders. . . . Our numbers are small, and there is no chance that we could compare ourselves with America's 180 million, or with any Arab neighboring state. There is one thing, however, in which we are not inferior to any other people in the world—this is the Jewish brain. And science, if a lay person like myself could say, starts from the brain. And the Jewish brain does not disappoint; Jewish science does not disappoint. . . . I am confident, based not only on what I heard today, that our science can provide us with the weapons that are needed to deter our enemies from waging war against us. I am confident that science is able to provide us with the weapons that will secure the peace, and deter our enemies.[9]

Accounts differ, but by the late 1960s, Israel seemed to have had a nuclear weapons capability.[10] The Zionist vision of a safe haven for the Jews was now coupled with the ability to ensure no other Holocaust would ever occur. Meanwhile, other events were vindicating the vision of the Zionists of Israel as their historic homeland.

On May 11, 1960, the Israel Exploration Society called a meeting at the home of the president of Israel, Yitzchak Ben-Zvi. The society's archaeologists and volunteers had discovered a series of remote caves in the Judean desert dating from the time of the last rebellion against Rome (the Bar Kokhba revolt of 132–35 CE). The guests included David Ben-Gurion, several cabinet members, and journalists. The highlight of the evening was the presentation by former chief of staff Yigael Yadin, now retired from the army and the leader of the explorations to the remote caves. The caves, Yadin explained, were the last refuge of the remnants of the failed rebellion. Located high on a cliff side and nearly inaccessible, the caves were swelteringly hot and had no water and no sanitation. Yet the zealous Jewish rebels left unmistakable evidence of their time there: Roman-made bronze vessels with their graven, idolatrous images deliberately scratched off by the zealous Jews, cosmetic bottles, textiles, even human remains dressed in clothing from the Roman era. A master storyteller, Yadin transformed mere artifacts into the tale of a people whose determination to live as Jews led them to the deep, dark corners of caves in the most remote parts of the desert.

But the most important discovery was the papyrus letters found in the cave. Most of the letters dealt with the military issues the rebels faced. The letters painfully documented the failure of the rebellion and the terror felt by the people. But there was one letter than stood out above all the others. Yadin paused as he read the letter, for it was signed by the leader of the rebellion himself, Shimon Bar Kokhba. "Your Excellency," Yadin said and turned toward President Ben-Zvi, "I am honored to be able to tell you that we have discovered fifteen dispatches written or dictated by the *last* president of Israel eighteen hundred years ago."[11]

Yadin recalls:

> For a moment the audience appeared to be struck dumb. Then the silence was shattered with spontaneous cries of astonishment and joy. That evening, the national radio interrupted its scheduled program to broadcast news of the discovery. The next day, the newspapers came out with banner headlines over the announcement. Why was the whole nation elated over the discovery of a name on a fragment of papyrus? The answer lies in the magic of the name, a name treasured in folklore but almost lost to authenticated history, and the realization at this meeting that after nearly two thousand years, the desert had given up factual links with the man who led the last attempt of his people to overthrow their Roman masters.[12]

Yadin's father had set out to create a Jewish archaeology, tying the people to their ancient ancestors. Yadin was proceeding with Israeli archaeology, providing evidence of the ancient Israelites. In addition to the discoveries in the "cave of letters," Yadin had unearthed the biblical cities of Hazor and Megiddo. But in 1963 he set out on his greatest challenge: unearthing the fortress of Masada.

The account by Josephus of the Roman siege had gained some archaeological credibility over the years. The Roman camps at the base of the mountain had been discovered, along with the low wall around the mountain and the earthen ramp on the west side where the Romans had pushed the battering ram up the mountain and broken into the fortress. But proof of the dramatic tale of the 960 men, women, and children who had chosen suicide over slavery remained elusive. Yadin now set out to change that.

Unearthing Masada was a massive undertaking. Located in the remote desert wastes, the IDF assisted in the logistics of supporting two hundred workers and volunteers. Yadin's efforts quickly bore fruit. He uncovered the storerooms and western palace mentioned by Josephus. In addition, he discovered shekels minted during the rebellion, a Jewish ritual bath, and hundreds of potshards. One of the potshards contained the name Ben-Yair, the name of the rebel's leader. Yadin felt the potshard probably belonged to that very same man. More and more proof of the suicide story was coming to light. But what clinched it for Yadin was the discovery of human remains:

> When we came to clear the formidable pile of debris which covered the chambers of the small bathhouse, we were arrested by a find which it is difficult to consider in archaeological terms, for such an experience is not normal in archaeological excavations. Even the veterans and the more cynical among us stood frozen, gazing in awe at what had been uncovered; for as we gazed, we relived the final and most tragic moments of the drama of Masada. Upon the steps leading to the cold water pool and on the ground nearby were the remains of three skeletons. One was that of a man of about twenty—perhaps one of the commanders of Masada. Next to it, we found hundreds of scales of armor, scores of arrows, fragments of a prayer shawl and also an *ostracon* (an inscribed potshard) with Hebrew letters. Not far off, also on the steps, was the skeleton of a young woman, with her scalp preserved intact because of the

extreme dryness of the atmosphere. Her dark hair, beautifully plaited, looked as if it had been freshly coiffured. By her side were delicately fashioned ladies' sandals, styled in the traditional pattern of the period. The third skeleton was that of a child. There could be no doubt that what our eyes beheld were the remains of some of the defenders of Masada.[13]

The legend of Masada, already so important to the Israeli consciousness, now assumed mythic proportions, much like the Alamo for Texans. IDF recruits had been taking the pledge on the mountaintop since the 1950s, but now it took on even more significance. At one ceremony, Yadin told the recruits, "When Napoleon stood among his troops next to the pyramids of Egypt, he declared that 4,000 years of history look down upon you. But what would he not have given to be able to say to his men: 4,000 years of *your own* history look down upon you? The echo of your oath this night will resound throughout the encampments of our foes. Its significance is not less powerful than all our armaments!"[14]

Yadin himself summed up the meaning of Masada in his bestselling book on the excavation:

It is thanks to Ben-Yair and his comrades to their heroic stand, to their choice of death over slavery, and to the burning of their humble chattels as a final act of defiance to the enemy, that they elevated Masada to an undying symbol of desperate courage, a symbol which has stirred hearts throughout the last nineteen centuries. It is this which moved scholars and laymen to make the ascent to Masada. It is this which moved the modern Hebrew poet to cry: Masada shall not fall again! It is this which has drawn the Jewish youth of our generation in their thousands to climb to its summit in a solemn pilgrimage. And it is this which brings the recruits of the armored units of the Defense Forces of modern Israel to swear the oath of allegiance on Masada's heights: "Masada shall not fall again!"[15]

But even as Yadin wrote these words in 1966, Israel was under duress. The Arab states had not abandoned their goal of expelling the Jews and returning the land to the Palestinians. In February 1960 Egyptian president Gamal Abdul Nasser told a crowd in Syria, "Eleven years after this tragedy [the 1948 war], the people of Palestine have not changed. They, and we, are working for the restoration of their rights in their homeland. The rights of the people of Palestine are Arab rights above all. We feel it is our sacred duty to regain those rights for the people of Palestine."[16] A few months later, he spelled out his plan more clearly: "When we have brought our armed forces to full strength and made our own armaments, we will take another step forward toward the liberation of Palestine, and when we have manufactured jet aircraft and tanks, we will embark on the final stage of this liberation."[17]

But the next three years brought no such steps. Criticism within the Arab world increased on Nasser and the other leaders. He was a paper tiger, full of hot air but no real fight. Responding to such barbs, Nasser declared in July 1963, "It is not enough to deliver speeches declaring that we would liberate Palestine and liberate it just on paper for political consumption." But he explained, "We do not have any defined plan for the liberation of Palestine."[18]

The opportunity to devise such a plan came shortly. In August 1963 the Arab states learned that Israel would soon be completing a national water carrier, transporting fresh water from the Sea of Galilee in the north to the arid regions in the south. According to Abba Eban, "The enterprise was radiantly innocent. It caused no harm to anyone, and the threat to oppose it by force was regarded by most of mankind as senseless malice."[19] The Arabs disagreed. At a summit meeting in January 1964, the Arab states declared, "The establishment of Israel is the basic threat that the Arab nation in its entirety has agreed to forestall. And since the existence of Israel is a danger that threatens the Arab nation, the diversion of the Jordan waters by it multiplies the dangers to Arab existence. Accordingly, the Arab states have to prepare the plans necessary for dealing with the political, economic, and social aspects, so that if the necessary results are not achieved, collective Arab military preparations, when they are completed, will constitute the ultimate practical means for the final liquidation of Israel."[20]

The Arab League therefore agreed to support a Syrian initiative diverting the headwaters of the Jordan River, claiming the project would deprive Israel of water before Israel could deprive Syria of water. The IDF watched nervously as the project began. From their positions along the border they could clearly see the tractors, earth-moving equipment, and hundreds of trucks begin the massive construction job. The digging was successful, and in a few months' time it seemed as if the Arabs would succeed in their diversion project. Shortly afterward, the IDF drew up plans to destroy the equipment. However, the Syrian equipment was roughly thirteen hundred yards away. Chief of Staff Yitzchak Rabin and Northern Commander Ariel Sharon assigned their best gunners to the task. The tankers succeeded in destroying the earthmovers with direct hits. The Syrians renewed their effort, but the tankers blew up these vehicles as well. When the Syrians moved their digging operations further back, the IDF responded by extending the range of their tanks to two and a half miles. There was no restarting the project this time. The diversion scheme was abandoned. The water carrier was built, adding acres of farmland throughout the country.

The battle over water might have been over, but tensions with Syria remained high. The issue was border demarcations: the 1949 armistice agreements left the boundaries poorly defined and included three demilitarized zones (DMZs). Since these were west of the Jordan River, Israel claimed them as her sovereign territory. Syria insisted the DMZs remain unchanged until a final peace agreement was signed. In an attempt to exercise sovereignty over these areas, Israel sent farmers to cultivate these lands, build villages, and fortify the villages. Several parcels of land were also purchased from Syrian villagers. The Syrians resisted these efforts, sporadically firing down on the settlers from the Golan Heights with machine guns and mortars.

Several rounds of internationally brokered negotiations failed. Ariel Sharon, now in charge of the IDF's Northern Command, explained Israel's position:

Under constant harassment from the Syrians on the heights, we refused to back down from our claim to these disputed parcels. It was not so much that we needed the relatively few acres for agricultural production. It was rather that in those days, Israelis shared a nearly universal belief that the only possible way we could survive in the midst of our hostile neighbors was to stand firmly on our rights. The feeling was that we could not afford to back down an inch in the face of those who wanted to annihilate us. So ingrained was this approach that it would have been hard to find someone who opposed making the effort to farm this land. And it was not just a physical effort. It was a heavy economic burden, and it was costly in lives. The end result was that almost each day border clashes erupted over our attempts at farming and their attempts to stop us.[21]

Against this tempestuous background, the Syrians introduced another destabilizing element: Palestinian fedayeen. The Palestine Liberation Organization (PLO) had been established at an Arab League summit in 1964. Its charter declared that "Palestine is the homeland of the Arab Palestinian people" and that their goal was the "liberation of Palestine" and "the elimination of Zionism in Palestine." This would be achieved by "armed struggle as the only way to liberate Palestine." Specifically, "commando action constitutes the nucleus of the Palestinian popular liberation war." Therefore, the PLO set out on Syrian-sponsored missions into Israel beginning in 1965. The raids continued for the next two years and included sabotage and mine-laying operations. By the spring of 1967, the Israel-Syrian border was ripe for an eruption.

The eruption occurred on April 7. Syrian mortars lobbed two hundred shells at an Israeli farming community along the Sea of Galilee. Israeli tanks moved in and fired at the mortars. Syrian artillery opened up all along the border. The IDF responded by sending in the air force to silence the guns. The Syrians sent in their own planes. A massive dogfight ensued, as 130 planes battled for control of the skies. The skirmish ended in a decisive Israeli victory, with the Syrian air force chased from the skies.

The Israeli high command might have thought they gained some measure of security for the disputed border. But what they and nobody else knew was that the humiliating defeat the Syrians suffered would ultimately result in a crisis that would drag the entire region into another war.

-11-

To Live or Perish

The Jewish State Faces a Hostile Ring of Nations,
May–June 1967

On May 14, 1967, two hundred thousand Israelis gathered in Jerusalem to celebrate the state's nineteenth Independence Day underneath a massive Star of David hanging from Mount Scopus. In deference to high regional tensions, no tanks or planes participated in the parade. As the infantry marched past the government's ministers, reports came in of Egyptian troops moving into the Sinai. Israel's leaders received the information without panic. It was probably more hot air from Nasser. The ceremonies closed with songwriter Naomi Shemer's new ballad "Jerusalem of Gold," filled with mourning over the loss of the Jewish holy sites. But even as she sang of Jerusalem's Wailing Wall, events had already begun that would bring the Old City of Jerusalem under Jewish control within three weeks.

The same morning of Israel's Independence Day parade, the Soviet Union sent an intelligence report to the Syrians and Egyptians. It stated that Israel had mobilized its reserves and had deployed its forces to the Syrian border in preparation for a large-scale attack within the next week. None of the information was true. The Soviet's reason for tailoring a false report has baffled historians for decades. New research suggests that the Soviets were wary of Israel's nuclear program and hoped to goad Israel and the Arabs into war with the intention of destroying Israel's nuclear program.[1] If this was the case, then Egypt's reaction to the report was exactly what the Soviets wanted. Nasser and his top advisers met to discuss their response later that morning. They saw the situation as quite grave. If Syrian and Jordan fell, Egypt would be facing Israel alone. Chief of Staff Abdul Hakim Amer expressed confidence in the army's ability to repulse any Israeli attack. Amer suggested sending the infantry into the Sinai along three defensive lines. This would send a signal to Israel that if they attacked Syria, Egypt would not stand by. Nasser accepted this course of action—it would not provoke war, but it would also show that Egypt would not abandon its Syrian ally. That same afternoon thousands of troops began passing through Cairo's center on their way to the Sinai as crowds cheered them on. It seemed an unlikely road to war, but these first steps created a momentum of their own. Around the Arab world, these moves were applauded. Finally, someone was doing something for the Palestinian cause.

But even as Egyptian troops continued to move into the Sinai on May 15 and 16, Nasser learned that the Soviet report of a massive Israeli buildup along the Syrian border was false. Upon receiving this information, Nasser might have withdrawn the troops. However, he did not choose this course of action, not wanting to be seen as a coward. Rather, Nasser ordered the United Nations forces in Gaza and Sharm el-Sheikh, stationed there since 1957, to withdraw.

The UN had no choice in the matter. They could stay only with Egypt's consent. By May 19 the last UN soldier had been withdrawn. There was no longer a buffer force between Israel and Egypt. With eighty thousand Egyptian troops now in the Sinai, Israel mobilized its reserves. Doing so meant virtually shutting down the civilian economy. Army-age men left their homes and gathered in bases across the country before deploying to the Negev to face the Egyptians. As they did, Golda Meir recalled that "the overage men and women and children of Israel buckled down to clean out the basements and cellars for use as makeshift air raid shelters, to fill thousands of sandbags with which to line the pathetic homemade trenches that fathers and grandfathers dug in every garden and every schoolyard throughout the country, and to take over the essential chores of civilian life, while the troops waited, trained, and went on waiting. It was as though some gigantic clock were clicking away for all of us, though no one except Nasser knew when the zero hour would be."[2]

But war was not yet certain. Nasser hadn't closed the Straits of Tiran, which Israel had warned ten years earlier would be considered an act of war. Still, the tension in Israel was palpable. Would Nasser close the straits?

The answer came on May 22. Nasser declared that the Straits of Tiran would be closed to Israeli shipping. It was time to stand up for Arab and Palestinian rights, he explained. "No one is speaking in the Arabs' favor. How does the UN stand with regard to the Palestinian people? How does it stand with regard to the tragedy which has continued since 1948? Talk of peace is only heard when Israel is in danger. But when Arab rights and the rights of the Palestinian people are lost, no one speaks about peace, rights, or anything like this." Turning to the closure issue, he declared, "Under no circumstances will we allow the Israeli flag to pass through the Gulf of Aqaba. The Jews threaten war. We tell them you are welcome, we are ready for war. Our armed forces and all our people are ready for war, but under no circumstances will we abandon any of our right. This water is ours."[3]

Meanwhile, enormous throngs gathered throughout the cities of the Arab world. Huge crowds unfurled banners calling for the destruction of Israel and displayed the skull and crossbones of the PLO. Other placards showed bearded, hook-nosed Jews being trampled by Arabs.

"There was a hot crisis in the air," Foreign Minister Abba Eban recalled as the cabinet met on May 23. "There was no doubt that the howling mobs in Cairo, Damascus, and Baghdad were seeing savage visions of murder and booty. Israel, for its part, had learned from Jewish history that no outrage against its men, women, and children was inconceivable. Many things in Jewish history are too terrible to be believed, but nothing in that history is too terrible to have happened. Memories of the European slaughter were taking form and substance in countless Israeli hearts. They flowed into our room like turgid air and sat heavy on all our minds."[4]

Against this background, the cabinet reiterated that the Israeli government considered the closure of the Straits of Tiran to be an act of war. Although the port of Eilat was quite small, it loomed very large in Israel's strategic calculations. Nearly all of Israel's oil and fuel came in through Eilat. Moreover, a pipeline from Eilat to the Mediterranean made Israel a supplier of oil to Europe. The Negev could not develop if Eilat were closed. Most of all, Israel would lose its deterrent power if it allowed the port to be closed. Israel had stated, and the United States had accepted, after the 1956 war that a reimposition of a blockade on the Straits of Tiran would oblige Israel to act to protect its maritime port. A retreat from this position would potentially be disastrous when other issues arose. Thus the seemingly minor issue of a second-rate port became an issue of national interest, one that the state was willing to go to war over.

Several military commanders pressed for an immediate pre-emptive strike to break the blockade. Prime Minister Levi Eshkol responded that he had received a warning from President Lyndon Johnson not to fire the first shot. Moreover, the cabinet was almost entirely against a first strike. The IDF's chief of staff, Yitzchak Rabin, favored a preemptive strike but acknowledged that a forty-eight-hour postponement was acceptable. Rabin asked a cabinet member why he opposed a first strike. The response reflected the growing gap between the military and civilian leadership: "Politically we will be totally isolated, and we won't receive arms supplies if we run short during the fighting. If we're attacked, of course, we'll fight for our lives. But to take the initiative? To bring this curse down on us with our own hands? Do you want to bear the responsibility for endangering Israel? I shall resist it as long as I draw breath."

"Nasser has presented us with a grave provocation," Rabin replied. "If we don't face that challenge, the IDF's deterrent capacity will become worthless. Israel will be humiliated. Which power will support a small state that had ceased to be a military factor?

Why bother with a state whose neighbors are growing stronger and subjecting it to humiliating pinpricks? We're going to war over freedom of navigation. Nasser has threatened Israel's standing; later on his army will threaten Israel's very existence. I don't want to go to war either, but there's no way out if the American political efforts fail."

"Israel's existence will be endangered if we go to war," the minister retorted. "If we dig in we shall be strong. We'll dig in. We'll fortify ourselves. We can withstand any attack. But we won't fire the first shot!"[5]

With the top levels of the government divided, Eban departed to Paris, London, and Washington to search for a diplomatic solution. As he did, the tiny nation's nerves frayed with each passing day. At first Egypt had only sent its infantry into the Sinai. Now their armored divisions rolled in. On May 26 Nasser declared, "If Israel embarks on an aggression against Syria or Egypt, the battle against Israel will be a general one and not confined to one spot on the Syrian or Egyptian borders. The battle will be a general one and our basic objective will be to destroy Israel."[6] This last statement had a greater effect in Israel than any other of Nasser's pronouncements. Israel's leading newspaper printed a headline with Nasser stating, "Our objective will be to destroy Israel," alongside a statement by Hitler in 1939 declaring, "If world Jewry drags us into another war, they will be destroyed." The parallel between the two leaders seemed all too obvious to the many Holocaust survivors in the Jewish state.

Egypt's press backed their leaders' action. An editorial in Cairo's major daily titled "Why an Armed Clash with Israel Is Inevitable" read:

> This is the first time the Arabs have challenged Israel in an attempt
> to change an accomplished fact by force and to replace it by force
> with an alternative accomplished fact consistent with their rights
> and interests. The opening of the Gulf of Aqaba to Israel was an
> accomplished fact imposed by the force of imperialist arms. This
> week the closure of the Gulf of Aqaba to Israel was an alternative

accomplished fact imposed and now being protected by the force of Arab arms. To Israel, this is the most dangerous aspect of the situation. . . . Therefore, I say that an armed clash between UAR [Egypt] and the Israeli enemy is inevitable. . . . Let Israel begin. Let our second blow then be ready. Let it be a knockout.

Similarly, Cairo radio announced, "The Arab people is firmly resolved to wipe Israel off the map and to restore the honor of the Arabs of Palestine."[7]

The mood inside the Jewish state soured. Israelis called it "the Waiting Period," the tensest time in the country's stormy history. Golda Meir recalled:

> By the end of May, ordinary life—as we had known it in the previous months—came to an end. Each day seemed to contain double the normal number of hours, and the hours seemed endless. . . .
>
> There were also the grim preparations that had to be kept secret; the mass parks in each city that had been consecrated for possible use as mass cemeteries; the hotels cleared of guests so that they could be turned into huge emergency first aid stations; the iron rations stockpiled against the time when the population might have to be fed from some central source; the bandages, drugs, and stretchers obtained and distributed. And, of course, above all, there were the military preparations, because even though we had by now absorbed the fact that we were entirely on our own, there wasn't a single person in Israel, as far as I know, who had any illusions about the fact that there was no alternative whatsoever to winning the war that was being thrust upon us.
>
> When I think back to those days, what stands out in my mind is the miraculous sense of unity and purpose that transformed us within only a week or two from a small, rather claustrophobic community, coping—and not always well—with all sorts of economic, political, and social discontents into two and a half million Jews, each and every one of whom felt personally responsible for the survival of the State of Israel and each and every one of whom knew that the enemy we faced was committed to our annihilation.[8]

The streets of the tiny state were empty, save for a few military vehicles. All automobile headlights had to been painted blue to lower their chance of being a target for an aerial assault. Parents cemented their children's windows to protect against shrapnel. In anticipation of a massive death toll, the state undertook extraordinary measures, turning public parks into emergency cemeteries, stockpiling nylon sheeting for wrapping dead bodies, allocating funds for coffins and gravestones, and preparing instructions for identifying corpses and burials. Prime Minister Levi Eshkol addressed the nation on May 28, intending to boost morale. But he fumbled over his words, creating the impression that he was a weak leader during a major crisis. Eshkol had never been a popular figure; he came across as bland, distant, and unemotional, especially in comparison to Ben-Gurion, the fiery father of the state who had preceded him as prime minister. Eshkol's standing plummeted even further, adding to the general gloom hanging over the state.

Meanwhile, Israel's diplomatic efforts foundered. Eban's first stop was in Paris. The French had been Israel's main ally and arms supplier since 1956. But French troops had withdrawn from Algeria. France's policy now aimed at keeping a steady supply of Arab oil. There would be no replay of French intervention as in 1956. Eban then flew to London. His audience was more sympathetic, but Britain was in no position to break the Arab blockade.

That left the United States. Eban met with President Lyndon Johnson. Johnson advised Israel not to take any military action until a diplomatic solution could be arranged. Johnson's policy was in no small part influenced by the Central Intelligence Agency's assessment on the outcome of a possible war. Some senior U.S. policymakers feared the Arabs would win a war, dragging the United States into a conflict that would jeopardize its relations with the Arab world. They also worried that the Soviets would intervene on the Arabs' behalf, raising the prospect of a superpower confrontation. Finally, they were concerned that the Egyptian deployments were offensive and that the Egyptians were prepared to attack immediately.

However, newly declassified documents show that those fears were unfounded. The CIA assessed that Soviet intervention was unlikely and that the Soviets were simply trying to increase their stature in the Arab world; that the Egyptian and Arab troop deployments were defensive and for political effect; and above all, prophetically, that "Israel could hold the line on three fronts and simultaneously mount a successful offensive on the fourth front (the fronts include Sinai, Syria, Jordan, and Lebanon), could attain air superiority over Sinai in twenty-four hours, could regain the initiative on the ground in a few days, and, once fighting with Egypt had subsided, could occupy most of the West Bank in a few days."[9] Armed with this knowledge, Johnson determined there was time for diplomacy. Eban flew back to Israel, where he reported the details of the meeting to the cabinet. Acceding to America's request, the cabinet decided to postpone military action. Meanwhile, Johnson tried to put together an international regatta to open the Straits of Tiran.

As the diplomats and politicians debated, the noose tightened around the Jewish state. Nasser addressed the Egyptian National Assembly on May 29, declaring:

> We are ready for the confrontation. We are now ready to deal with the entire Palestine question. The issue now at hand is not the Gulf of Aqaba, the Straits of Tiran, or the withdrawal of the UNEF, but the rights of the Palestinian people. It is the aggression which took place in Palestine in 1948 with the collaboration of Britain and the United States. It is the expulsion of the Arabs from Palestine, the usurpation of their property. It is the disavowal of all the UN resolutions in favor of the Palestinian people. The issue today is far more serious than they say. They want to confine the issue to the Straits of Tiran, the UNEF, and rite of passage. We demand the full rights of Palestinian people.[10]

The speech had the effect Nasser desired. The very next day, Jordan's King Hussein, so often at odds with the radical Egyptian leader, flew to Cairo to meet Nasser. He was greeted by cheering throngs. The Arab world finally seemed to be coming together to restore the Palestinians' rights. Explaining the sudden turn of events, King Hussein said, "The desire to meet Nasser may seem strange when one remembers the insulting, defamatory words which for a whole year the Cairo radio had launched against the Hashemite monarchy. But from every point of view we had no right, nor could we decently justify a decision to stand aside in a cause in which the entire Arab world was determined unanimously to engage itself."[11]

In a highly publicized meeting, Hussein agreed to a defense pact with Egypt similar to the Syrian-Egyptian pact signed the month before. Israel now faced the possibility of war on three fronts. Iraqi forces arrived in Egypt the next day. Other Arab nations sent troops as well. Nasser announced, "The armies of Egypt, Jordan, Syria, and Lebanon are stationed on the borders of Israel in order to face the challenge. Behind them stand the armies of Kuwait, Sudan, and the whole of the Arab nation. This deed will astound the world. Today, they will know that the Arabs are ready for the fray. The hour of decision has arrived."[12] PLO leader Ahmed Shukeiry declared, "Those who survive will remain in Palestine, but I estimate that none of them will survive." Meanwhile, crowds chanted in the streets, "Nasser, Nasser, we are behind you. We will slaughter them; we will destroy them. Slaughter, slaughter, slaughter!"

But while these pronouncements sowed panic in the Israel public, the segment of society charged with dealing with the threat remained confident. Among the army commanders marshaling their forces in the Negev, there was unanimity that they would win a war, and win easily. Ariel Sharon, now leading a division in the Negev, recalled, "I trained the soldiers hard. And not only the soldiers: I trained the officers, too. Every morning they were all running and jumping and crawling, going through a rigorous course of physical conditioning. I did everything necessary to get all the reservists into shape, and they responded beautifully—physically and mentally. I had no question at all that if it came to a fight, we could handle the Egyptians in front of us."[13] Meeting with Eshkol and Rabin, Sharon pressed for an immediate attack, warning that they would win if they struck while the troops' morale was high, but if they waited, morale would drop and all could be lost. Eshkol sternly rebuffed him, calling him irresponsible. To Eshkol, force was the last option. The message was clear. Until the diplomats were done with their work, the IDF could not begin theirs.

The tide began to turn on June 1. American efforts to form an international regatta to open the Straits of Tiran had failed. Other nations did not want to risk their own ships for a cause that was not theirs. Secretary of State Dean Rusk declared it was "not our business to restrain anybody," meaning that Israel could initiate military action if it felt compelled to break the encirclement. The same day, the Israeli government formed a broad coalition, including opposition leader Menachem Begin. Eshkol appointed Moshe Dayan as minister of defense the next day. Dayan's confidence and enthusiasm lifted the country's spirit. The time for diplomacy was over. Foreign Minister Eban told Rabin that he no longer had any political objections to military action and that if Israel went to war, it would not face the same diplomatic backlash it had faced in 1956. Eban was correct. Whereas the world community had viewed Israel, along with Britain and France, as the aggressor in 1956, world opinion now cast the Arabs in that role. The daily images of throngs calling for the destruction of the Jewish state throughout the Arab world sickened most observers. Once viewed as the aggressor, Israel now seemed the victim. In the fickle realm of world opinion, sympathy for the Jewish state reached its zenith. Dayan spent most of the day on June 3 preparing his war plan. He knew the next day's meeting would be crucial. The cabinet met for the last prewar meeting on June 4. By this point reports had reached the cabinet that Egypt's generals were pushing Nasser for an immediate strike. Nasser's previous idea of absorbing a first blow by Israel and then knocking out Israel was being replaced by the notion that the Egyptians did not need to wait for an Israeli attack but should start the battle themselves and defeat Israel on their terms.

Dayan, therefore, emphasized the need to move quickly. Israel could win if they struck first. "It's our only chance to win, to wage this war our way," he declared. He was joined by an unlikely ally:

Prime Minister Eshkol, who had resisted all calls for war over the past three weeks. "I'm convinced that today we must give the order to the IDF to choose the time and the manner to act," Eshkol explained.[14]

The prime minister then called for a vote. It was unanimous. The war was on. Eban described the feeling inside the cabinet and the country: "The whole nation was convinced of a single stark certainty: The choice was to live or perish—to defend the national existence, or to forfeit it for all time."[15]

-12-

Israel's Golden Summer

The Six-Day War and Its Aftermath, 1967–1970

"A Mosaic of Destruction": The Egyptian Front

Just after 7:00 a.m. on June 5, Israel's French-built Mirage and
Mystere jets began taking off from their airfields. By launching
a preemptive airstrike, the Israel Air Force (IAF) hoped to destroy
most of the Egyptian air force on the ground. As the planes rose,
the IAF commander told the pilots, "The spirit of Israel's heroes
accompany us into battle . . . From Joshua Bin-Nun, King David,
the Maccabees and the fighters of 1948, 1956, we shall draw the
strength and courage to strike the Egyptians who threaten our
safety, our independence, and our future. Fly, soar at the enemy,
destroy him, and scatter him throughout the desert so that Israel
may live, secure in its land, for generations."[1]

Nearly two hundred planes—all but twelve of the IAF's entire
inventory—took part in the first strike. The jets flew low, under
fifty feet, to avoid radar detection. The path they took was over
the Mediterranean, before turning sharply south to Egypt. They
maintained strict radio silence. Their goal was surprise. As they
neared Egypt, the planes swooped up to nine thousand feet and
began their attack dive. An IAF pilot recalled the action:

We began to execute our mission with no interference. I focused
on my dive-angle, speed, altitude. The runway closed in. When the

precise moment arrived, I released my bombs. We rolled sharply and began a strafing run. In the midst of our turn, we could hear incredible explosions. The delay detonators of the bombs that we had sunk deep into the runways had awakened on time. Every shot was a wonderful bull's eye, and the field was littered with gaping holes. It would take hours to fill them, if there remained any reason to do so. The line of MIGS, our strafing target, came into focus. At full engine power and with clean wings (no bombs, no fuel tanks, no loads), our speed was tremendous.

I was amazed at the quiet. Why had we not heard any antiaircraft fire? It was hard to believe that they had really been caught with their pants so far down. The only panic could be heard on the communication network. Above a nearby airfield, our planes were dogfighting with MIGS. . . .

I placed the line of MIG-17s in my gun sights. Slightly before coming into range, I squeezed hard on the trigger. The 30-millimeter cannons roared, and their bullets plowed into the runway beneath the MIGS. The planes convulsed under the cannons and collapsed. An entire line of MIGS was wiped out before my eyes.

I turned again for a third run. This time we needed to hit only the planes that had not been struck in the previous runs. Only a few remained. A pull of the trigger, and the mosaic of destruction was complete.[2]

The surprise was total. Most of the Egyptian pilots were still at breakfast when the attack came. They ran to their planes, but few made it. Each Israeli jet made three passes. Several pilots reported no planes left to strafe by the third pass. An Egyptian pilot described the chaos:

Some thirty seconds from the end of the attack, a second wave of planes arrived. . . . We ran about the desert, looking for cover, but the planes didn't shoot. They merely circled, their pilots surprised that the base was completely destroyed and that no targets remained. We were the only targets . . . weak humans scurrying about the desert with handguns as our only means of self-defense. It was a sad comedy . . . pilots of the newest and best-equipped jets, fighting with handguns. Five minutes after the beginning of the attack, the planes disappeared and a silence prevailed that encompassed the desert, and the noise of the fire that destroyed our planes and the airbase and the squadron. They completed their assignment in the best way possible, with a ratio of losses—100 percent for us, zero for them.[3]

Back in Israel, IDF commanders waited with bated breath. "The suspense was incredible," recounted Ezer Weizman, the father of the IAF. "For five years, I had been talking of this operation, explaining it, hatching it, dreaming of it, manufacturing it link by link, training men to carry it out. Now in another quarter of an hour, we would know if it was only a dream, or whether it would come true."[4] Not only did Weizman's dream come true, but the extent of the attack exceeded everyone's expectations. Israeli commanders doubted the first airmen's reports about the attacks' success. But it was true. The IAF had destroyed two hundred Egyptian airplanes—roughly half of their air force's inventory—in one wave. They had also cratered the runways, preventing any counterattack. It had cost only eight planes, and the operation lasted a little over half an hour. Two more waves would destroy another one hundred Egyptian planes. The IAF then turned east and delivered similar blows to the Syrian and Jordanian air forces. Moshe Dayan described the feeling as a stone being rolled off his heart. With the Egyptian air force crippled, the ground forces could begin their assault free from the possibility of enemy air strikes.

The air strikes did more than change the military situation. It also brought salvation to a terrified public. Throughout the first day of the war, citizens waited for news in their blacked-out living rooms, their ears glued to transistor radios. They knew the war had started when they heard the air-raid sirens that morning, and now they longed to hear the latest from the battlefield. Instead of news of the war, however, all they heard for most of the day was music, Hebrew songs, and passwords to call up reserves. After a day of waiting, the official word finally came out after midnight with the incredible but true story that the Israel Air Force had destroyed the planes of Egypt, Jordan, and Syria that morning, a total of four hundred enemy planes. The skies now belonged to the Israelis. There would be no air raids over the country. The civilian population was safe. The war was not over, but the people of Israel had been delivered from destruction. All over the country, people who had been fearful that their families were about to be killed, relaxed and exhaled, their worries finally over. They opened up their doors, took in the pleasant night's air, and breathed for the first time in weeks.

After the first wave of planes returned, Dayan issued the order for the ground forces to attack. Along with the orders, he sent the following message:

> Soldiers of Israel, we have no aims of conquest. Our purpose is to bring to naught the attempts of the Arab armies to conquer our land, and break the ring of blockade and aggression which threatens us. Egypt has mobilized help from Syria, Jordan, and Iraq, and has received their forces under her command. She has also been reinforced by army units from Kuwait to Algeria. They are more numerous than we; but we shall overcome them. We are a small nation, but strong; peace-loving, yet ready to fight for our lives and our country. Our civilians in the rear will no doubt suffer. But the supreme effort will be demanded of you, the troops, fighting in the air, on land, and on sea. Soldiers of the Israel Defense Forces, on this day our hopes and our security rest with you.[5]

The supreme effort that Dayan spoke of was breaking the formidable Egyptian army in the Sinai. With 120,000 troops, 2,000 tanks, and 1,000 artillery pieces, the Egyptian forces were two to three times as large as the Israeli forces. Moreover, they held well-fortified defensive positions, including huge bases in the Sinai at Rafa, Jebel Libni, and Abu Agheila. The assault plan was in some ways similar to the 1956 war. An Israeli division would attack the northern positions at Rafa near Gaza and along the coastal highway, while another division attacked the Abu Agheila network further south, the same position the Israelis had failed to crack in 1956. This time, however, a third force would attack between the two divisions, over terrain the Egyptians considered impassable to armored vehicles. This division would aim to cut the north–south Sinai road—thus severing the Egyptians' supply lines—before attacking the base at Jebel Libni.

As in 1956, the key was Abu Agheila. Because it guarded the main Sinai highways, there was no way around it. Moreover, since the IDF's failure to take the position in 1956, the Egyptians had reinforced the area. The cornerstone of the Abu Agheila network was Um Cataf, a formidable series of fortresses, pillboxes, trenches, and natural ridges, surrounded by minefields and guarded by tanks. Inside the compound was the Egyptians' heavy artillery. The Egyptians' plan was to use the Um Cataf positions as an anvil on which to hammer the Israeli armor to death. They kept a tank division just south of Abu Agheila and another behind it to the west. They expected Israeli forces to batter themselves against the strong defenses at Um Cataf as they had done in 1956. Then the Egyptians would swing their tanks behind the already engaged and depleted Israelis and annihilate them.

But the commander tasked with taking Abu Agheila, Ariel Sharon, had no plans to throw his forces headlong at the strong defenses. Instead of launching his armor and infantry directly from the east as they had last time, Sharon would send out separate elements of his forces in complex, highly coordinated attacks from three sides, resulting in a series of surprises that would unbalance the defenders. To accomplish these surprises, Sharon would divide his tanks, sending them first to attack the Egyptian armor reserves west and south of Abu Agheila. This would isolate the main position of Um Cataf, the complex of trenches and pillboxes. With Um Cataf isolated, the main assault would shock the Egyptians.

The shock would begin with appearance of Israeli infantry from the north. The Egyptians would disregard any chance of attack from north of Um Cataf, since armor could not negotiate the heavy sand dunes there. But infantry could: the foot soldiers would be supported by Sharon's heaviest guns, which would pound the defenders as they attempted to repel the surprise attack from the north. The Egyptian artillery would be taken out by heliborne troops landing behind the Egyptian lines. At the same time, Israeli tanks would approach from the east, while other Israeli tanks would hit the rear of the trenches once they had defeated the Egyptian armor held in reserve behind the main lines. Moreover, the attack would take place at night, further disorienting the defenders. It was a complex, daring plan, but if it succeeded, the largest Egyptian base in the Sinai would fall, leaving the road open to the Suez Canal.

Sharon's attack began in the afternoon of the first day of the war, with the tanks swinging to the south and rear of the Egyptian positions, while the infantry began the long, painful slog through the northern dunes. As darkness fell, the infantry jumped out of the dunes and hit the Egyptian's flanks. Running along the lip of the trenches, they overwhelmed the defenders, who were expecting an assault from their front.

Meanwhile, the heliborne troops landed behind the front lines and attacked the defenders' artillery. A helicopter pilot described the ensuing firefight:

> The order to attack was given at a range of only fifty meters, and the artillery operators were completely surprised. Every Israeli squad decimated one cannon team with bursts from their Uzis and with hand grenades. Those Egyptians who survived jumped out of the trenches and ran for their lives. The work included the bunkers, as well, and from there, too, the Egyptians ran away. Several of the enemy had managed to return fire, and there were Israeli wounded. The battles were short. Suddenly, a large Egyptian convoy was seen approaching. It included seven trucks running with full lights and loaded with crates of shells. Sure of themselves in the heart of their own territory, the drivers of the trucks went up in flames with their loads. . . . The bodies of the dead and the skeletons of the trucks were all that remained of the full cannons and the incredible stocks of munitions.[6]

With the enemy's rear under attack, Sharon ordered his artillery to open up on the Egyptian's trenches. "Make it shake!" he ordered, as seventy-five of Israel's heaviest guns pounded the defenders. In the final assault, World War II–era Sherman tanks crashed through the narrow minefield in front of the trenches. Every one of Sharon's units had accomplished its objective. By dawn on the morning of the second day of the war, the entire Abu Agheila complex was in Israeli hands.

Other Israeli forces were successful as well. In the north, General Israel Tal's division encountered heavy resistance around the large fortifications in Rafa and Khan Yunis but managed to break through by the second day of the war. Between Sharon's and Tal's divisions, Avraham Yoffe—who had led the "Long Trek" to Sharm el-Sheikh in 1956—aimed to reach the north–south Sinai road. Although the road was only thirty-five miles from the border, Yoffe's division struggled. The soft sand ridges slowed the tanks and vehicles, while the men strained in the 130-degree heat.

But by the day's end, they had reached the vital crossroads. Once there, they defeated an Egyptian armor force, then headed south toward the large Egyptian base at Jebel Libni. Although it was a well-defended position, bristling with artillery and tanks, the skies belonged to the Israelis. With Israeli jets raining death from above, Yoffe's force attacked, shattering the defenders and sending them reeling west toward home. With their frontlines broken, the Egyptian high command ordered a retreat to the second line of defense. It was a reasonable order. The war was hardly over. The size of their forces remained enormous, and the second line was intact. But instead of an orderly withdrawal, the entire army raced home in an uncontrolled panic. From that point on, the Egyptian army in the Sinai could not offer any coordinated resistance to the IDF.

By the end of the second day of the war, the IDF had accomplished far more than they had thought possible. The air force had destroyed Egypt's air power in a single morning. All three IDF divisions had penetrated well into the Sinai, and the Egyptian army was in full retreat. The general staff had not planned for this contingency. Therefore, as the three division commanders met that night, they were forced to improvise a plan. They decided to prevent the Egyptians from stabilizing their lines and mounting a counterattack. Tal's and Yoffe's forces would race to the Mitla and Gidi Passes in the western Sinai, beating the retreating Egyptians to get there first. Once there, they would block the passes, while Sharon's forces would drive the remaining enemy tanks into the awaiting ambushes, destroying the last Egyptian forces in the Sinai. The race for the passes was on.

A tiny force of nine tanks headed the charge for the Mitla Pass. Four of the tanks ran out of fuel and had to be towed by the others. But they reached the pass and dug in. Scores of Egyptian vehicles approached the pass, only to be picked off by the entrenched Israelis. The battle continued throughout the night. The Israelis were nearly overwhelmed, but they picked up fuel and ammunition from the nearby Egyptian vehicles and held out through the night. Meanwhile, mass confusion reigned as the rest of Yoffe's tanks attempted to reach the pass ahead of the retreating Egyptians. At one point an Israeli tank company realized that they were in the middle of an Egyptian column; the commander ordered his unit to continue on as if all was well. Then they quickly veered off the road, turned on their searchlights, and opened fire on the column. It was utterly destroyed, and the company continued on the pass, joining the small force already there.

When the rest of Yoffe's tanks reached the Mitla Pass, the jaws of the ambush were shut. The Egyptian army was trapped. Egyptian tanks and armored personnel carriers continued to try to batter their way past the Israelis, but to no avail. The IDF tanks held the high ground and shot down, while the air force pummeled the Egyptians from the skies. Drivers panicked, running off the sides of roads, where their vehicles could not maneuver. Others tried to turn around, only to block the vehicles behind them. Many abandoned their vehicles and sought to reach home by foot, a dangerous prospect in the furnace-like desert.

The carnage was total. Israeli soldiers moving west through the pass drove by hundreds of destroyed tanks, artillery, trucks, and cars. Many of the vehicles were still smoking, sending up a black haze through the clear desert sky. Other chassis were no more than burned-out steel skeletons on the side of the road. Dead bodies lay strewn through the area. The scene of death continued for miles and miles, stretching up to the road to the pass. The number of prisoners was more than the IDF could handle. They released the enlisted men and kept only the officers. Some of the officers tore off their insignias to prevent capture. Thousands fled across the desert; many perished from exhaustion. At the Suez Canal's west bank, a massive throng of worried family members gathered to search for their loved ones staggering home after defeat and retreat across the burning desert. A short while later, Israeli units arrived and jubilantly cooled themselves off in the cold water. The war in the Sinai was over. It had lasted less than a hundred hours.

"We Have Returned to the Holiest of Our Sites": The Capture of Jerusalem

Egypt's Arab allies had not stood still in the meantime. On the morning of the first day of the war, Nasser telephoned Jordan's King Hussein and reported his armies had inflicted a severe defeat on the Israelis. He urged Hussein to take possession of as much land as possible. Israel had sent three messages earlier stating that if Jordan refrained from shelling Israel, Israel would honor the terms of the 1949 armistice. But shortly after 11:00 a.m., the Arab Legion launched a massive six-thousand-shell barrage on Jewish Jerusalem, wounding hundreds of civilians. Jordanian long-range artillery targeted airfields inside Israel. Jordan's prime minister announced, "We are today living in the holiest hours of our lives, united with all the other armies of the Arab nation, we are fighting the war of heroism and honor against our common enemy. We have waited years for this battle and to erase the stain of the past."[7]

With Jewish positions in Jerusalem and Tel Aviv threatened, the Israeli army began to move into the West Bank and Jerusalem. The key Jordanian position in Jerusalem was Ammunition Hill, a fortification of trenches, bunkers, and minefields where the British had stored their ordinance in World War I. Israeli

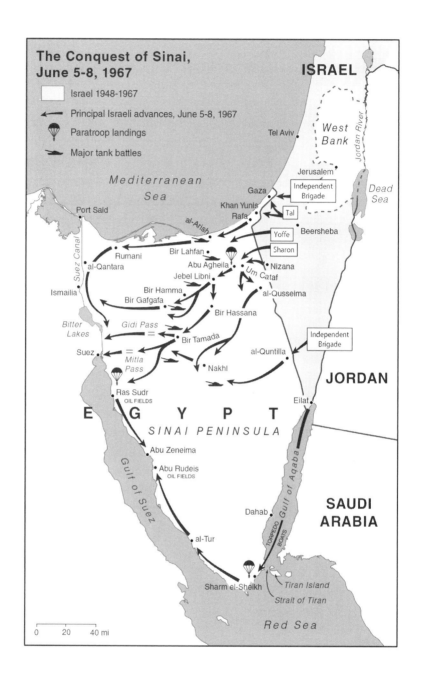

4. The Conquest of Sinai, June 5–8, 1967. Map adapted from Howard Sachar, *A History of Israel* (New York: Alfred E. Knopf, 1996). Erin Greb Cartography.

artillery opened up on the position but did little damage. As the soldiers moved in, they encountered fierce resistance. The lead squads were wiped out. The tanks proved unable to lower their guns far enough to fire at the dug-in Jordanian positions, and they could not call in artillery support without hitting their own soldiers. The soldiers had to advance over open ground without cover, and the lead infantry squads were wiped out. But the paratroopers did not quit. Upon reaching the Jordanian positions, the fighting degenerated into a vicious hand-to-hand battle. It raged on for four hours. But by dawn of the second day of the war, Ammunition Hill was in Israeli hands.

Daybreak brought more advantages to the Israelis. With the IDF in complete control of the skies, Israeli offensives succeeded in pushing back the Jordanians all along the West Bank. "For lack of air cover, our tanks are being disabled at a rate of one every ten minutes," King Hussein cabled Nasser. By that afternoon, Jordanian forces were in full retreat. King Hussein rushed from his palace in Amman and looked down at the remnants of his army in the Jordan Valley. He recalled, "I will never forget the hallucinating sight of that defeat. Roads clogged with trucks, jeeps, and all kinds of vehicles twisted, disemboweled, dented, still smoking, giving off that particular smell of metal and paint burned by exploding bombs—a stink that only powder can make. In the midst of this charnel house were men. In groups of thirty or two, wounded, exhausted, they were trying to clear a path under the monstrous coup de grace being dealt them by a horde of Israeli Mirages screaming in a cloudless blue sky seared with sun."[8]

Meanwhile, Israeli forces had encircled the Old City of Jerusalem. Judaism's holiest sites lay tantalizingly close. The cabinet was unanimous in wanting to take it, but Dayan demurred. He wanted to wait for the fighting in the Sinai to end before he committed Israeli forces to the possibility of another major battle. Early the next morning, however, Dayan had a change of mind. Rumors that a UN-imposed ceasefire might go into effect later that very day made Dayan fear Israel would never again have the chance to take the Holy City. He immediately gave the order to move ahead.

The brigade commander sent a message to his men: "We occupy the heights overlooking the Old City. In a little while, we will enter it. The ancient city of Jerusalem, which for generations we have dreamed of and striven for, we will be the first to enter it. The Jewish nation is awaiting our victory. Israel awaits this historic hour. Good luck."[9] The soldiers moved down from the heights and stood in front of the gates to the Old City. The assault began when tanks blasted a bus that had been placed to block the Lions Gate entrance. The men raced in through the narrow alleys of the Old City, past the shuttered houses and buildings. Only a few shots rang out from isolated Jordanian soldiers, who were quickly driven off. As the forward elements neared the Temple Mount, an Israeli soldier recalled, "There you are on a half-track after two days of fighting, with shots still filling the air, and suddenly you enter this wide open space that everyone has seen before in pictures, and though I'm not religious, I don't think there was a man who wasn't overwhelmed with emotion. Something special had happened." A few minutes later, the word went out: "The Temple Mount is in our hands!"[10]

Abba Eban wrote, "The Western Wall, the most sacred place in Judaism, was in Israeli hands. No man of historic imagination could fail to be awed at this reunion of a people with the relic of its ancient glory. Young Israeli soldiers, raised in the hard-headed secular mood of their generation, wept like children as they stood in silence before the massive scarred stones."[11]

As the paratroopers gazed up in awe at the wall, IDF leaders rushed in to see it for themselves. Chief of Staff Rabin and Minister of Defense Dayan, escorted by the area commander, raced toward the Temple Mount. Rabin recalled the overwhelming moment when Jewish dreams finally came true:

> As we made our way through the streets I remembered from childhood, pungent memories played on my emotions. The sheer excitement increased as we came closer to the Western Wall itself. The Wall was and is our national memento of the glories of Jewish independence in ancient times. Its stones have the power to speak

to the hearts of Jews the world over, as if the historical memory of the Jewish people dwelled in the cracks between those ancient ashlars. For years, I secretly harbored the dream that I might play a part not only in gaining Israel's independence but in restoring the Western Wall to the Jewish people, making it the focal point of our hard-won independence. Now that dream had come true, and suddenly I wondered why I, of all men, should be so privileged. I knew that never again in my life would I experience quite the same peak of elation.

When we reached the Western Wall, I was breathless. It seemed as though all the tears of the centuries were striving to break out of the men crowded into that narrow alley, while all the hopes of generations proclaimed, "This is no time for weeping! It is a moment of redemption, of hope." Following the ancient custom, Dayan scrawled a wish on a slip of paper and pushed it in between two of the stones. I felt truly shaken and stood there, murmuring a prayer for peace. Motta Gur's paratroopers were struggling to reach the Wall and touch it. We stood among a tangle of rugged, battle-weary men who were unable to believe their eyes or restrain their emotions. Their eyes were moist with tears, their speech incoherent. The overwhelming desire was to cling to the Wall, to hold on to that moment as long as possible.[12]

At the wall, Rabin announced, "The sacrifices of our comrades have not been in vain. The countless generations of Jews murdered, martyred, and massacred for the sake of Jerusalem say to you, 'Comfort ye, our people; console the mother and the fathers whose sacrifices have brought you redemption.'"[13] Dayan addressed the journalists who had already gathered at the wall, announcing Israeli policy: "We have returned to the holiest of our sites, and will never again be separated from it. To our Arab neighbors, Israel extends the hand of peace, and to the peoples of all faiths, we guarantee full freedom of worship and of religious rights. We have come not to conquer the holy places of others, nor to diminish by the slightest measure their religious rights, but to ensure the unity of the city and to live in it with others in harmony."[14]

It was the single greatest moment in Israel's history. But along with control of the holy sites came the dilemma of ruling over a hostile Arab population. Moreover, the refugee problem worsened as thousands of Palestinians fled in fear of the IDF. The Associated Press reported on their exodus:

> Jerusalem was falling, and now the movement of refugees was in the opposite direction, away from the advancing army. Arab metal smiths and tea merchants and souvenir sellers were shutting their shops in the winding, narrow bazaars of the Old City, loading up their donkeys and camels and streaming out of the Moslem quarter, through the Damascus Gate and Herod's Gate. They were leaving their tiny apartments and incredibly cramped little houses in the sloping arched streets and alleyways. They were fleeing the bombs that already were falling in the surrounding hills, the fire-belching tanks moving ponderously, unrelenting, over the highways to the north and south in a murderous pincer that would encircle the Old City in a few hours.
>
> Their movements was east—east on the main road to Amman, east through the Judean hills, east across the Jordan, east away from the thunder and the devastation, the night fires in the hills, the horror and the death, away from the Jews, away from the hated enemy. They took with them all that their wives and donkeys could carry, leaving behind food still warm on the table, pictures on the wall of bearded and robed ancestors, trunks full of the treasures and trivia of several lifetimes on those decaying cobblestone streets. . . .
>
> All day long, under the merciless sun, the Arab refugee families moved east along the road, war's river of sorrow, flowing toward the bombed out Allenby Bridge over the Jordan. At 6 AM, they suddenly appeared rising up from the robes in which they had wrapped themselves against the cold desert winds, like wraiths come to life from distant mirages over the sand.
>
> Rashid Areikat, deputy area officer for UNRWA, stood in the doorway of his office watching them stream by the gates of Aqabat Jaber, one of the four refugee camps he administered. The war

west of the Jordan was over, but for them the heartache had just begun. He saw whole Arab families, from feeble grandparents to tiny toddlers, moving in barefoot procession along the dusty road, erect, graceful people, toting all their belongings—bedding, gasoline stoves, pots and pans, enormous jars of water—on their heads. In that debilitating heat, with the Dead Sea shimmering in the distance like a burning blue coal in the yellow desert, some of the Bedouins had removed their *kefeyas* ("desert headdresses") to hold the white cloth aloft as a flag of surrender.

Many of the pilgrims on that burning road wore two or three overcoats, several dresses or an extra pair of trousers, as wearing their entire wardrobe was the best method of transporting it. Some of the women carried an infant in each arm, and were followed by a string of small children, each carrying a smaller one. Docile donkeys, swaying camels and an occasional broken-down draft horse trotted along in the pathetic parade, laboring under great burdens of furniture, mattresses, and wooden steamer trunks from voyages on ships long since scrapped. . . .

Rashid Areikat had seen at least 50,000 of them pass his doorstep. Two days prior, he had worried how he would set about feeding 60,000 Palestinian refugees in his four camps. Now he had less than 15,000 left and enough food on hand to last for six months. After years of yearning to go back to their ancient lands in old Palestine, they had suddenly left the camps to head even farther east across the Jordan.

The scene at the Allenby Bridge was as moving as any along the road. The Jordanians had blown up the bridge to keep the advancing Israeli army from crossing the river. The wrecked bridge's long concrete span dipped down from the high banks to the brackish green water in a perfect V. To negotiate the precipitous span, which fell away before them like a garish ski slide, the fleeing Arabs had to hold onto hastily-tied guy ropes, making their way across the stream on a few planks lashed together, the climb up on the other side of the span by pulling on the ropes.

For most, this meant selling their donkeys, camels and horses—which could not manage the perilous footing—and getting rid of much of the impediments that they had carried all the way from Jerusalem. At high noon, the west bank of the Jordan resembled an Arab bazaar, with the pilgrims arguing excitedly and angrily with buyers for a fair price for their animals. All around, there were donkeys and goats tied to every available tree, left behind by the fleeing Arab families, and the grassy shores were littered with piles of cast-off clothing, furniture, empty shoes, and rusting gasoline cans. Every now and then, to underline the horror of it all, a body bobbed up in the greenish water, bloated and black. It belonged to one of the fleeing pilgrims who had stubbornly insisted on crossing the bridge as the Legionaries were blowing it up. . . .

The Allenby Bridge was the point of no return. Some reached the river bank after days of walking, and suddenly turned back, as if deciding then and there to take their chances with their Israeli conquerors. Some sat for hours under the gnarled, silver-gray olive trees, praying to Allah for guidance. But for most, the Jordan was their Rubicon and they crossed over willingly, determinedly, going back to Hussein's kingdom, leaving behind—perhaps forever—their dreams of one day returning to Old Palestine.

Late in the afternoon, with a molten sun burning into the Dead Sea's lunar landscape, the great, sad, solemn river of humanity dwindled to a trickle, and by 4 PM—curfew time for the vanquished—the road to Jericho was empty.[15]

Roughly one hundred thousand civilians fled the fighting, adding to the larger Palestinian exodus that had occurred in 1948. Like their predecessors, they would mostly end up in miserable refugee camps, bent on returning home. In the days leading up to the war, the refugees had hoped that their hour of deliverance had finally arrived after nineteen years. Some had even started to move west, only to be caught in the crossfire of war.

As the refugees were fleeing, an incident occurred off the Sinai Peninsula. On the afternoon of June 8, the USS *Liberty*, an intelligence-gathering ship, was attacked by Israeli aircraft and torpedo boats. Earlier that morning, reports of a naval bombardment on El-Arish reached IDF General Staff Headquarters in Tel

Aviv. Chief of Staff Rabin took the reports seriously, concerned that the shelling was a prelude to an amphibious landing that could outflank advancing Israeli troops. He reiterated the standing order to sink any unidentified ships in the war area. As the *Liberty* sailed toward Egypt, an Israeli naval ensign estimated the ship was traveling at thirty knots. It was a crucial error. As the *Liberty*'s top speed was eighteen knots, the estimate meant that the ship in question could not be the *Liberty*.[16] Moreover, the Israelis had standing orders to fire on any unknown vessel in the area sailing at over twenty knots, a speed that could be attained only by fighting ships. Subsequent Israeli overflights failed to identify the ship as American, according to radio transmissions.

As a result, Israeli planes and torpedo boats bombed and strafed the ship, inflicting severe damage. Thirty-four U.S. servicemen were killed, and 171 were wounded by napalm, shrapnel, and bombs. The deck was torn apart, and a hole could be seen in the ship's side. Survivors and those ill-disposed toward Israel have claimed the attack was deliberate, an Israeli attempt to deny the United States information about an upcoming attack on Syria. The notion that a tiny country would intentionally attack a naval vessel belonging to the most powerful nation on earth has always been problematic, especially considering that Israel needed the United States as an ally. Numerous U.S. and Israeli investigations all concluded that the attack was a mistake. Nevertheless, conspiracy theories have continued to flourish.

More evidence surfaced in 2006, with the declassification of two CIA reports on the incident. According to a CIA memorandum from June 13, 1967:

> Intercepted conversations between the helicopter pilots and the control tower at Hatzor (near Tel Aviv) leave little doubt that the Israelis failed to identify the *Liberty* as a U.S. ship before or during the crisis. . . . A subsequent message from the control tower to the helicopter identified the ship as Egyptian and told the pilot to return home. Although the *Liberty* is some 200 feet longer than the Egyptian transport El Quesir, it could easily be mistaken for

the latter vessel by an overzealous pilot. Both ships have similar hull and arrangements of masts and stacks.[17]

Another CIA report, dated June 21, 1967, was in response to the official Israeli investigation. The Israeli report pointed to three separate mistakes and found that the "attack on the USS *Liberty* was not in malice; there was no criminal negligence and the attack was made by innocent mistake." The CIA concluded that "the attack was not made in malice toward the U.S. and was by mistake, but the failure of the IDF Headquarters and the attacking aircraft to identify the *Liberty* and the subsequent attack by the torpedo boats were both incongruous and indicative of gross negligence."[18] Like the CIA, American officials were angry, but they understood the realities of war. Johnson accepted Israel's apology, and Israel paid $12 million in compensation for the victims.

Additional declassified documents discredit the idea that Israel attacked the ship in order to deny the United States information about their plans to attack Syria. These declassified cables show that the U.S. government was quite aware of Israel's plans regarding Syria. On June 8 the American consulate in Jerusalem reported that Israel was retaliating for Syria's bombardment of Israeli villages "in an apparent prelude to large-scale attack in effort to seize Heights overlooking border kibbutzim." That same day U.S. Ambassador Walworth Barbour in Tel Aviv reported that "I would not, repeat not, be surprised if the reported Israeli attack [on the Golan] does take place or has already done so," and IDF Intelligence Chief Aharon Yariv told Harry McPherson, a senior White House aide who was visiting Israel at the time, that "there still remained the Syria problem and perhaps it would be necessary to give Syria a blow."[19] Although the final decision to attack Syria had not been made at the time of the attack on the *Liberty*, it was clear to American officials that Israel was leaning in that direction.

Moreover, there was the question of what the *Liberty* was doing so close to an active war zone. In his memoirs, Rabin related that several years later, while serving as Israel's ambassador to the United States, he learned what happened:

With the outbreak of fighting on June 5, we notified the American naval attaché in Israel that we intended to protect our shores from Egyptian naval attacks by employing a combination of naval and air units. In the event that Egyptian vessels approached our shores, we would not be able to delay our response. We therefore asked that American ships be removed from the vicinity of the Israeli shore, or that the Americans notify us of their precise location in the area near our coast. In the storm of battle, there was no time to check whether or not our request had been fulfilled. During my term as ambassador, however, I learned that Washington had indeed instructed the Sixth Fleet to move its vessels away from the Israeli coastline, but due to a bureaucratic blunder the order failed to reach the *Liberty*.[20]

Subsequent U.S. Navy revelations show that this was indeed correct. The *Liberty* was ordered to return to a safe distance from the war zone on the night of June 7, but due to the navy's complex and overloaded communications system, the order didn't arrive until June 9, the day after the attack.[21] While no amount of evidence can ever ease the pain, objective observers should be able to accurately judge what really happened.

A few hours after the *Liberty* incident, the cabinet met to discuss the situation on the Syrian front. Syrian forces had not joined the war, although their artillery continued to shell Israeli settlements in the northern Galilee. Chief of Staff Rabin spoke first, noting that with the collapse of Egypt and Jordan, the IDF had the forces ready to eliminate the Syrian guns before any UN-imposed ceasefire went into effect. Next, the cabinet heard from representatives of the settlers in the northern Galilee. It was an unprecedented move, perhaps part of Eshkol's plan to try to persuade wavering ministers to support taking the Golan. "If the State of Israel is incapable of defending us, we're entitled to know it!" the settlers declared. "We should be told outright that we are not part of this state, not entitled to protection of the IDF. We should be told to leave our homes and flee this nightmare!"[22]

Yet these impassioned pleas failed to persuade the man who

mattered most, Moshe Dayan: "Why, in the throes of this struggle, would we want to take on yet another state with different international borders? That's a little too much." Later that night, the IDF's Northern Command chief, David Elazar, phoned Dayan and Rabin, venting his frustration at the decision. "If we don't do something on this border now, it will be a curse for generations to come," he told Dayan. Then to Rabin: "What has happened to this country? How will we ever be able to face ourselves, the people, the settlements? After all the trouble they caused, after the shellings and harassment, are those arrogant bastards going to be left on top of the hills riding on our backs?"[23] Still, Dayan was not ready to order an attack.

But as with the decision to take Jerusalem a few days earlier, external events would change Dayan's mind. In the early morning hours, Dayan received two reports: one was an intelligence estimate stating that the Syrian positions on the Golan were collapsing even before the IDF launched an attack; the second was an intercept from Nasser to the Syrian president, urging him to accept a ceasefire before it was too late. "This compels us to take the maximum lines," Dayan told Eshkol. "Last night, I had no idea that the leadership of Egypt and Syria would crumble like this and give up the battle. In any event, we must exploit this opportunity to the utmost."[24] At 6:00 a.m. he ordered Elazar to take the Golan Heights.

Once again the air force led the way. But over nineteen years, the Syrians had dug into the Heights's forts and concrete pillboxes, which withstood the air barrage. It would be up to the infantry to take the positions. It was a formidable task: they had to charge uphill against the overlapping forts and their guns, protected by minefields and barbed wire. To break through the defenses, the IDF specially outfitted bulldozers for the task. A tanker recalled the action as the attack began: "At first, we weren't afraid at all. Bulldozers ran in front of us, clearing the wire and mines. But then the sky opened up. The bulldozers were knocked out." All of the bulldozers were hit, and their wrecked hulks were shoved aside by the onrushing tanks. The attack continued. "Half-tracks were blown up into the air. Suddenly, we were hit! I went up to the turret hatch and saw that the tank was ablaze and that I was burning with it. I heard shots, heard someone on the radio calling for air cover. I decided it was better to be shot than burned to death, and I threw myself from the turret. They picked me up and put me on the deck of another tank. I was still on fire."[25]

Moving slowly across rough terrain littered with barbed wire and mines, the Israelis took heavy casualties. But they kept going until they were face-to-face with the Syrian tanks. Shooting at close range, the IDF tanks got the better of it, knocking out the Syrian armor. The tanks then crushed the remaining Syrian positions under their treads. The infantrymen entered the pillboxes and bunkers, engaging the Syrians in furious hand-to-hand combat. As the fighting intensified, panic and confusion began to overtake the defenders. By the end of the first day's fighting, the Israelis had taken the first line of the Syrian positions on the Golan, but the defenses behind the first line remained intact.

David Elazar expected the lines to stabilize on the second day, due to a Syrian counterattack or a UN ceasefire. But the Israeli government stalled for time, and the IDF had until evening to take the Heights. Instead of another bloody day of fighting, the Syrians panicked and retreated on the morning of the second day. The IDF pushed the lines forward for the rest of the day, completing the conquest of the Golan before the ceasefire went into effect at 6:30 p.m. The Six-Day War was over.

From Darkness to Light: After the War

"The Israeli people stepped from darkness into light," one author wrote.[26] Abba Eban called it "Israel's golden summer" and recounted how "Israelis thronged by the tens of thousands to the Western Wall and Temple Mount to gaze incredulously on the stones that symbolized their ancient glory."[27] Nor was Jerusalem the only site important in Jewish history that had fallen under Israeli control. Much of the Hebrew Bible took place in the West Bank, including Abraham's burial place at the Cave of the Patriarchs in Hebron, Rachel's Tomb in Bethlehem, and the site of Joshua's conquest of

Jericho. Israelis flocked to visit these places. The whole of Eretz Yisrael was under Jewish control. If the 1948 war had created the Jewish state, the Six-Day War had made it whole.

But Israel now controlled millions of Palestinian Arabs, people who viewed the Jews as their mortal enemies. At first the Palestinians seemed in a state of shock. They did not offer any organized resistance. Meanwhile, curious about their new neighbors, Israelis, Abba Eban wrote, "moved awkwardly into Arab towns and villages, absorbed by the swift color and variety of their movement, listened to the cacophony of their market places and inhaled the characteristic smells of strong coffee, donkey's dung, nargileh smoke, and Arab bread. They were somewhat alien and remote to all of this, yet they responded with respect to the evidence of a solid, earthy way of life."[28]

For their part, the Palestinians were surprised to find that the Jews were not quite the demons they had been made out to be. An Arab resident of Ramallah wrote:

> I had been brought up to think of Jews as monstrous and Israel as an artificial creation that was doomed to perish. I had just been through a war that I had expected would bring victory and the fulfillment of all our dreams. Instead, it brought defeat and all the consequent fears. On a warm Thursday afternoon on June 9—just three days after the start of the war—two young Israeli army reservists accompanied by the Palestinian editor of an Arabic daily appeared at our door. Their appearance and manner violated everything I had been taught to expect of Jews. They spoke good English, they were polite, gentle, and civilized, and they asked to see my father. What was I to make of them? Were these the monsters I had expected in some disguise? Or was I to believe in their politeness and conviviality?[29]

It was clear that the region had undergone a monumental change, affecting both Arab and Jew. But the question remained: would there be peace? The answer came sooner than most expected.

On July 23, 1967, President Nasser spoke to his people on the anniversary of the coup that had brought him to power. Judging by his appearance, it was hard to believe he was the same man who stood at the head of the united Arab coalition in early June. In the few weeks since then, he had aged terribly. His hair had grayed, and his heart started giving out. The Egyptian nation was badly shaken as well. They had lost the war, most of their army, and the entire Sinai Peninsula.

But Nasser would not concede to the Zionists. Nasser had used this date once before to announce momentous events. In 1956 he had chosen the anniversary to pronounce his nationalization of the Suez Canal, an event that led to war later that year. Nasser's pronouncement eleven years later would have the same effect: "We shall never surrender and shall not accept any peace that means surrender. We shall preserve the rights of the Palestinians."[30] Arab policy was set. There would be no peace, no recognition of Israel, no negotiation until the "rights of the Palestinian people" were returned. Israel's military triumph had not translated into a political victory. There would be more bloodshed; the only questions were when and how. For even as Nasser spoke these defiant words, eight hundred tanks, hundreds of artillery pieces, and over ten thousand vehicles—the pride of the Egyptian army—lay smoldering in the Sinai desert's unforgiving wastes.

Nonetheless, Nasser found a way to reequip his forces, and this time they would be better than before. The Soviet Union, humiliated by the destruction of its Arab clients in the Six-Day War, immediately agreed to rearm them. The loss of Egypt and Syria would mean the end of Soviet influence in the region. The Soviets therefore poured their best tanks, planes, and surface-to-air missiles (SAMS) into Egypt and Syria, along with military and technical advisors. The Arabs would have better equipment and would be better trained this time. In a mere eighteen months, the Egyptian army reached the same size it had been before the Six-Day War. Nasser knew that his forces were not yet ready for a full-scale war with Israel, however. With the Suez Canal separating the two forces, any Egyptian attempt to cross would lead to massive casualties. He therefore settled on a different strategy: if he could not kill the Israelis, he would bleed them to death.

To this end, Egypt built up a massive number of artillery guns along the Suez Canal, far more than the Israelis could deploy. The guns would shell the Israeli forts on the other side of the canal, known as the Bar-Lev Line. In this manner, Nasser hoped to wear down the Israeli forces and morale, inflicting a high cost on them. But the IDF was just as determined not to crack. The Egyptians knew that the Israelis had a low tolerance for casualties. Therefore, IDF commanders struck back hard to show the Egyptians that they were more vulnerable than the Israelis and that continued attacks would hurt them more than Israel. The War of Attrition began in March 1969, with an ever-spiraling cycle of violence. Egyptian guns would shell Israeli positions. Israel would respond with commando raids on the Egyptian side of the canal, blowing up enemy forts and capturing equipment. When this failed to stop the artillery attacks, Israel responded by using their planes as flying artillery. These attacks caused considerable damage to the Egyptian artillery forts, as well as the cities on the Egyptian side of the canal. A massive flight of civilians from the Egyptian Canal Zone ensued.

But Nasser would not relent. Israel switched tactics and began attacking targets deep inside Egypt, blowing up ammunition depots, headquarters, and training bases around Cairo. These attacks humiliated Nasser. He demanded action from his Russian patrons. The Russians brought in their newest anti-aircraft weapon, the SAM-3. Israeli fliers responded by taking out the SAM-3 sites. With Egypt's air force unable to stop the IAF, Russian pilots themselves began flying the missions. Dogfights raged over the Canal Zone, and possibility of a confrontation with one of the superpowers loomed. But before the situation spiraled out of control, Nasser backed down and accepted a ceasefire in August 1970.

He may have been playing for time before launching a new initiative, but Nasser's heart gave out in September. Huge throngs lined the streets of Cairo along his funeral procession. His death was mourned throughout the Arab world. To make matters worse for the Arabs, Anwar Sadat—Nasser's successor—was viewed as a weak leader, lacking in stature, particularly compared to his charismatic predecessor.

Most Israelis shared this assessment of the new Egyptian leader. Ezer Weizman wrote:

> Nasser always came across as a monarch of a great Arab empire; his mistakes were always on a grand scale, as befitted a man of his stature. In comparison with him, Sadat resembled a Saul who set out to look for his asses and chanced to find a kingdom. From the very first, it was hard to take him seriously. His faulty English, his oft-repeated vows to regain Sinai, "using force to restore that which was taken by force," his bombastic proclamations about the impending showdown with Israel—all these reinforced our negative view. Sadat appeared to be unsophisticated and undemocratic, a fanatical Muslim nationalist who could be toppled by the slightest shove.[31]

Nobody suspected that Sadat would prove to be the most formidable foe Israel ever faced. In the end it would be he, not Nasser, who would permanently transform the region.

-13-

We May Be in Trouble

Buildup to Surprise, 1970–1973

On the morning of October 6, 1973, America's ambassador to Israel sent a flash message to Secretary of State Henry Kissinger. According to the ambassador's memo, "At the Prime Minister's urgent request, I met with her at her Tel Aviv office this morning at 10:15." The ambassador must have known something was terribly amiss: October 6 was Yom Kippur, the Day of Atonement and the holiest day of the Jewish year. For Prime Minister Golda Meir to summon the U.S. ambassador with an "urgent request" on this day was more than a bit unusual.

Nonetheless, the ambassador could not have been prepared for what happened next:

> Mrs. Meir initiated conversation by noting "we may be in trouble," and then gave me a review of the situation regarding reported Syrian and Egyptian build-ups during the past few weeks. I noted that we had taken the initiative to discuss this matter with the IDF on several occasions and we were told the situation was not dangerous. Mrs. Meir said that this was an accurate evaluation at the time, but that within the last twelve hours the situation had become very serious. Israel had information from a number of totally reliable sources that Syria and Egypt were planning a coordinated attack against Israel today in the late afternoon.[1]

Meir then asked for American help in averting a war. Kissinger furiously manned the phones for the next ninety minutes, with calls to the Soviet ambassador asking him to restrain his Arab clients, to the Israeli ambassador warning against a preemptive strike, to the Egyptian foreign minister urging that they not attack, and to King Hussein of Jordan and King Faisal of Saudi Arabia, urging them to restrain Sadat and Assad.[2]

But it was too late. The war began that afternoon. Israel was completely unprepared. As a result, it would face its greatest crisis since 1948, surpassing the threats it endured in 1956 and 1967.

Egypt Prepares for War

The surprise attack Israel endured was due in large part to Egyptian president Anwar Sadat's determination to gain back the Sinai. Sadat had tried to negotiate for the return of the Sinai in 1971, but Golda Meirs's cabinet found his terms unacceptable. Moreover, Sadat did not receive any help from the Americans. Henry Kissinger told an Egyptian ambassador:

> My advice to Sadat is to be realistic. The fact is that you have been defeated, so don't ask for the victor's spoils. Either you can change the facts and consequently our perceptions will naturally change with regard to a solution, or you can't change the facts, in which case solutions other than the ones you are offering will have to be found. I hope that what I am saying is clear. I am certainly not asking Sadat to change the military situation. If he tries that, Israel will win once again—and more so than in 1967. In such a situation, it would be very difficult for us to do anything.[3]

Sadat took the advice to heart. "It was impossible for the United States or—indeed, any other power—to make a move if we ourselves didn't take any military action to break the deadlock," he wrote in his memoirs. At a meeting of the Armed Forces Supreme Council in October 1972, Sadat told his generals, "I will not sit at a table with Israel while I am in such a humiliating position, because that means surrender. In the face of our people, our enemies, and our friends, we must prove unemotionally and with careful planning that we are capable of sacrifice and can stand up and fight and can change the situation with whatever means are at our disposal. . . . The time for words is over . . . we have to follow this plan to change the situation and set fire to the region. Then words will have real meaning and value."[4]

Everyone assembled knew that going to war with Israel would be difficult. Several generals objected due to Israel's greater air superiority. But Sadat responded, "We will simply have to use our planning and our talents to compensate for our lack of certain kinds of equipment."[5] When the minister of war expressed reservations about fighting, Sadat dismissed him, along with two other generals and an admiral who had voiced similar views. The message to the army was clear: Egypt was going to war. Sadat saw no other option.

The three years since Sadat had come to power were among the most humiliating in Egyptian history. The War of Attrition had presented the possibility of retaking the Sinai, but the state of no war, no peace that had existed since then offered no chance of regaining lost Arab land. The country lay prostrate and helpless before a seemingly unbeatable foe. The Egyptian president aimed to change all that.

The method he chose was neither an all-out war designed to take the entire Sinai nor another war of attrition. Egypt could not win the former, while the latter did not offer Israel enough incentive to return the Sinai. Sadat and his planners therefore decided on a limited war. Egypt's forces would cross the Suez Canal and stay there, not pressing forward as Israel expected. Egyptian planners called for a "local" war whose goal was not the conquest of the entire Sinai but aimed at upsetting the security balance in the region and force Israel to the negotiating table by inflicting heavy losses on them. Egyptian leaders were convinced that such a strategy would make Israel realize it could not continue to occupy the Sinai.

Yet even this limited-war plan faced major obstacles. Egypt's war planners identified three major problems: crossing the Suez Canal, Israel's superior air force, and Israel's superior tank force.

Crossing the canal would be a complicated operation, requiring rubber boats, pontoon bridges, and a massive number of infantrymen. Egypt purchased all the necessary equipment for the crossing. In addition, Israel had built massive earthen ramparts on their side of the canal.

The Egyptian solution to earthen ramparts was simple but effective: they purchased high-powered hoses capable of breaching the barriers. Egypt's planners also had to contend with the limited capabilities of their infantrymen. The typical Egyptian conscript was illiterate and performed complicated tasks poorly. Egypt's planners were aware of this. They therefore scripted the entire crossing plan down to the last detail, so that each soldier knew his role. There would be no room for mistake in their planning.

In the Six-Day War and the War of Attrition, Egyptian pilots had proved completely unable to match their Israeli counterparts. The army's chief of staff, Saad Shazly, however, believed he had found a way to challenge Israel's air superiority with ground-based surface-to-air missiles (SAMS). By building an enormous missile network on their side of the canal, they would nullify Israel's air advantage, allowing the infantry to cross the canal unharassed by the IAF. In addition, Egypt purchased mobile SAM systems that they would take across the canal when the war began. Since the war plan did not call for an advance into the Sinai, the army would be safe from air attacks.

Finally, there was the pride of the Israeli army, the tank corps, to contend with. Egyptian tankers had proved unable to match them. Shazly decided upon a newly developed Soviet weapon: the Sagger anti-tank guided missile (ATGM). The ATGM was the perfect weapon for the Egyptian army. They were easy to use and lightweight, requiring only two-man teams to carry and operate. This would allow the Egyptians to bring them across in large numbers in the opening hours of the attack across the Suez Canal. Once across the canal, the Egyptian infantry could dig in and prepare for the expected Israeli tank-led counterassault.

There was one more element to Egypt's war plan: surprise. To compensate for Israel's qualitative military advantage, Egypt's generals sought to exploit Israel's disadvantage in manpower. With its small population, Israel's military depended on its reservists. By launching a surprise attack, the Arabs hoped to hit the Israelis before the reserves could be called up. Israel's expanded borders meant that it would take longer for the reserves to reach the front than in the past. Therefore, the Egyptians executed a deception campaign—so secret that only the very top echelon of Egyptian commanders knew when and where the attack would take place. The Egyptian army built sand ramparts along the canal to disguise their activity and built secret bunkers to store men and equipment beneath the ramparts. They tried to move the equipment at night and bury it before dawn. The Egyptians assembled the troops for a final offensive slowly, over a period of four months.

The Egyptians took special care with the canal-crossing equipment, as they realized the forward placement of this equipment would tip off the Israelis to an attack. Therefore, they moved this equipment from rear to front (as well as laterally) repeatedly, to give an impression of training. The Egyptians constantly held exercises along the canal to lull the Israelis into a false sense of security. From January to October in 1973, the Egyptian army mobilized its reserves and practiced maneuvers twenty-six times, including a major mobilization in May. Nonetheless, Egypt's planners predicted the Israelis would have a five-day warning before the war began, and that would mean heavy casualties during the canal crossing. But it was a price Sadat was willing to pay.

Israel Ignores Signs of War

As events transpired, the IDF did not have a five-day warning, but a five-hour warning before the war began. And if Sadat was the driving force in making it happen on the Egyptian side, the key figure who let the surprise happen on the Israeli side was none other than Israel's director of military intelligence, Eliahu "Eli" Zeira. The man who was responsible for warning the IDF of pending war not only failed to do so, but in fact lied and deceived his superiors about the nature of the Egyptian buildup. Zeira was so convinced that Egypt would not attack, he went so far as to alter key facts, omit others, and refuse to even consider the possibility of war.

Zeira's confidence was rooted in the protocols of meetings at the highest levels of the Egyptian government. The protocols were provided by Dr. Ashraf Marwan, Nasser's son-in-law. Marwan had approached Israeli intelligence after the Six-Day War and offered his services. He provided Israel with a large number of internal Egyptian documents. Two documents in particular stood out to Israeli intelligence analysts. The first was a transcript from a meeting held in Moscow on January 22, 1970, between Nasser and the Russian general staff. Nasser explained that to regain the Sinai, two preconditions must be met. First, he needed Scud missiles to attack Israel's cities. Second, his air force needed long-range fighter bombers capable of striking deep into enemy territory and destroying their fortified command centers. The second document was a letter written by Sadat to the Soviet premier on August 30, 1972, reiterating Nasser's position that without bombers and missiles, Egypt could not retake the Sinai.

When these requests were denied, Israeli intelligence concluded that the possibility of an Egyptian attack was close to zero. Intelligence also concluded that Syria would not go to war without Egypt. Zeira maintained that war was not to be expected because the Arabs did not have enough air power to allow them to strike deep into Israel and challenge the Israel Air Force and did not possess long-range ground-to-ground missiles to deter—by threat of retaliation—deep Israeli air strikes. It was a position that Zeira would stick to unflinchingly. But unbeknownst to Israeli intelligence, Sadat and his planners had chosen to use surface-to-air missiles instead of planes and long-range missiles to counter the vaunted Israel Air Force. Israeli intelligence based their estimate of war on a false conception.

In late August and early September 1973, intelligence reported a buildup of Egyptian and Syrian arms along the borders. Most intelligence analysts viewed the buildups as defensive in nature. As the deployments grew, General Israel Tal, who had led successful attacks against Egypt in both the 1956 and 1967 wars and was considered the IDF's foremost authority on tank warfare, expressed his concern over the Syrian buildup to Zeira. He told Zeira that the Syrian military posture pointed toward war. The Syrians had forward deployed bridging tanks, which could span the anti-tank ditches Israel had constructed on the Golan Heights, the infantry were in emergency positions that would allow them to attack without further warning, and the SAM system covered Syria. However, Intelligence Chief Zeira rejected Tal's assertions, noting that he—not Tal—was the expert concerning enemy intentions. Tal replied that he—not Zeira—was the expert on tank warfare, and if the Syrians launched a surprise attack, the forces on the Golan stood no chance. He also told Zeira that the only thing preventing Chief of Staff David Elazar from mobilizing the reserves was intelligence's low estimate of war. But Zeira remained unimpressed.

A short while later, one of the most extraordinary meetings in Israel's history took place. A helicopter from Jordan arrived at an intelligence facility near Tel Aviv. The passengers were Jordan's King Hussein and his prime minister. The two visitors were taken to meet Israel's prime minister, Golda Meir. Jordan had been working with Israel since the Six-Day War to prevent another round of violence. Hussein had lost half his kingdom in 1967. He knew Jordan would inevitably be dragged into the fighting if another war broke. He did not want this, and that was the reason for his clandestine meeting with his Israeli counterpart.

Meir warmly greeted her guest and shook his hand. They sat down and sipped hot drinks leisurely before Hussein came to the point:

> From a very, very sensitive source in Syria that we have had information from the past and passed it on . . . all the units that were meant to be in training and were prepared to take part in this Syria action are now, as of the last two days or so, in position of pre-attack. That includes their aircraft, their missiles, and everything else that is out on the front at this stage. Now this had all come under the guise of training, but in accordance with the infor-

mation we had previously, these are the pre-jump positions, and the units are now in these positions.

This was potentially devastating news. Israeli intelligence was aware of the buildup but viewed it as defensive. Now the leader of an Arab state was telling them that the buildup was actually offensive in nature.

Meir asked if the Syrians would start something without Egypt, to which Hussein replied, "I don't think so. I think they are cooperating."[6] Another piece of the puzzle fell into place. Israel had assessed that Syria would not attack without Egypt, but now the Arab monarch suggested Syria and Egypt were working together on a war plan. The news electrified one of the intelligence officers at the meeting. He immediately phoned his follow officers and explained, "The bottom line of what Hussein had to say was that there will be a war with Egypt and Syria."[7]

But at a meeting the next morning to discuss the King's message, Zeira maintained that the "very, very sensitive source" Hussein described was of low quality. It would later transpire that the source was, in fact, a Syrian major general and therefore of impeccable quality. The officer who had warned of war was called an alarmist, and business went on as usual before the Jordanian monarch's clandestine warning.

If it was incredible that an Arab leader would cross into Israel to warn of a pending Arab attack, it was even more astounding that Israeli intelligence would disregard the warning. On September 30 Israel's Egypt desk learned a large-scale military exercise in the Suez Canal Zone would take place from October 1 through October 7. The Egypt desk expected that all branches would participate and raise their state of alert. They also expected the call-up of reserves, additional preparations including completion of fortifications along the canal, and checking the readiness of the units. The Egypt desk head then assessed that these signs, "which allegedly can be seen as alert signals, are, in actuality, solely connected with the exercise."[8] This definitive assessment overstepped the bounds of intelligence reporting by predicting future events regardless of any possible changes, making any future reports irrelevant: it was an exercise, no matter what happened. The Egyptians could not, and would not, cross the Suez Canal without air support.

The next day, Israel received a report that the Egyptian crossing exercise would end in a real crossing and that the Syrians would join the war. The report also detailed the Egyptian war strategy as a limited plan to take only part of the Sinai. The goal of the war was to force Israel to negotiate withdrawal from the Sinai. In addition, Egypt was moving forward armored units and bridging equipment. All the information in the report was correct, as Israel later found out. The report also explained the motivation for a war that seemed unwinnable: to restart negotiations through a limited conflict. It was not Egypt's intent to conquer the entire Sinai. This information should have undermined the Israeli concept and explained the Syrian and Egyptian buildups. The only missing piece was when the exercise would end and the real crossing would commence. A second report came in that evening reiterating the information from that morning, adding that while the exercise was a cover for war, the date of the operation was not yet set.

But neither of these reports swayed Zeira. At a meeting with the general staff, Zeira noted that Egyptian mechanized divisions, airborne troops, and bridging troops had advanced to the canal. The Syrian deployment was the largest that had been seen in a year. "There are several sources saying the exercise is not an exercise but is leading toward war," Zeira said. "This definitely does not seem likely to us, even though these are good sources."[9]

Others within the intelligence services disagreed. One officer warned the Northern Command intelligence officer that war could break out that very day. When war did not break out the next morning, the officer was reprimanded. Another intelligence officer was shaken by the report and demanded that Zeira activate a collection of sensitive listening posts in Egypt, known as the "special means." These listening posts were of vital importance to Israel's warning system due to their great capabilities.

When operated by a signal, "operators in Israel could hear not only what was said over the telephone and cable lines, but could also eavesdrop on conversations in the rooms where the telephone and the telex consoles were located."[10] But activation of the "special means" would risk their detection, and because Zeira was convinced the situation didn't merit their activation, he refused. "What do these sources exist for if not for situations like the one we're facing?" the exasperated officer asked. "The situations you see are not the ones I see," Zeira replied coolly.[11]

The next day another IDF officer asked Zeira about the "special means." Chief of Staff David Elazar, on whose head lay the primary responsibility for mobilizing the army for war, was suspicious about a new report that Syria had moved its air force forward. He therefore asked Zeira if the "special means" had been turned on. Zeira replied that they had, when in fact they had not been activated. This answer mollified Elazar, who later explained that he "knew their capability and if there was no war information from them, it was a sign that all was in order."[12] This was a devastating blow to the IDF's intelligence warning capabilities. According to Israeli documents declassified in 2012, Elazar had placed a premium on the special means' ability to collect information on an Egyptian attack. In testimony given after the war, Elazar explained, "There could not be a situation where we would be completely surprised [because] I count on the intelligence system, I count on the 'means.'" In another part of his testimony Elazar added, "When I assumed that we would have a warning, I relied mainly on those means that I knew that we have and they would provide us with the information [needed for] action."[13] Like many other army officers, intelligence personnel, and policymakers, Elazar considered the special means "Israel's national insurance policy" and based much of his estimate of war on those capabilities. It was not the last time Zeira would lie to key policymakers about the true warning situation. With the joint Egyptian-Syrian attack nearing, Zeira's misinformation was crippling the policymaker's ability to make sound decisions.

On October 4—only two days before the attack was to begin—
the IDF remained in no position to go to war. Information began
pouring in about the possibility of hostile enemy action in the
near future. First, Israel intercepted a transmission from Moscow ordering an immediate evacuation of the families of Soviet
military advisers from Syria and Egypt. The Soviets were flying
eleven massive cargo planes to Damascus and then to Cairo to
remove their citizens. In addition, Soviet warships began departing Egyptian ports. The intelligence officer responsible for the
signal's interception phoned Zeira at home. "This can't mean anything but war," he told Zeira, noting that the advisers hadn't left,
meaning that they were staying to help their clients in a war.[14] But
Zeira remained nonplussed. He simply replied that there might
have been a falling out between the Soviet and their clients; after
all, Egypt had expelled their Soviet advisers in 1972, only to have
them return later that year. Why the women and children and
not the advisers left remained unexplained by Zeira. The first
opportunity to mobilize for war thus passed. With a forty-eight-
hour warning, the IDF might have been prepared for the massive
assault that began two days later.

October 5 dawned and the IDF had not begun to prepare for
war. The window was closing rapidly, but it was still not too
late. The director of military intelligence, however, would ensure
that no effective warning would reach the top-level policymakers. Early in the morning, Dr. Ashraf Marwan, a top source who
had provided intelligence in the past, warned of war. An intelligence official flew to London to meet with Marwan. Zeira mentioned in a morning meeting with the chief of staff that a source
had given a warning but did not specify if it was a war warning. He added they would know more from the source later that
evening. Next, Israeli photo interpreters released the finding of
aerial reconnaissance photographs taken the day before. The
summary stated, "In the canal area, the Egyptians have taken
up an emergency deployment larger than any deployment previously known to us."[15]

Since the last aerial photographs on September 25, the Egyptians had added 308 artillery guns, brought bridging equipment to the crossing revetments along the canal, moved tanks into the marshaling yards of their firing ramps, brought forward a large number of armored fighting vehicles, and forward deployed a tank brigade. These new dispositions reflected an immediate capability to attack across the canal.

Defense Minister Moshe Dayan was struck by the vast amount of equipment. "You could get a stroke just reading the numbers."[16] Dayan then asked Zeira if the "special means" had been activated. Zeira responded by saying that everything was quiet. For the second time, Zeira lied to a superior about their status. After the war, Dayan would explain that it was his confidence in the special means that affected his perception of the likelihood of war more than any other factor. Had Dayan known that they had not in fact been turned on, he may have acted differently. Of all of Zeira's many sins, this was probably the worst; based on the false information provided to him, Dayan took no action. Chief of Staff Elazar, however, was alarmed by the size of the Egyptian deployment along the canal. He therefore ordered the highest state of alert for the standing army, canceled leaves, and put the emergency mobilization network on standby. But as Elazar, Dayan, and Zeira knew, the standing army was not large enough to halt a full-scale enemy attack. Only mobilizing the reserves could achieve this. But due in large part to Zeira's incorrect information, the reserves remained at home.

Zeira continued to wreak a path of destruction for the rest of that critical day. He met with Prime Minister Golda Meir and assured that no Arab attack was pending, despite the massive buildup along the borders. He then reiterated this message to the cabinet. Yet others within the intelligence community felt that the scope of the Egyptian buildup along the canal was too large to ignore. That afternoon, the General Headquarters convened an emergency meeting. Zeira began the meeting by summing up three major developments: the Egyptian exercise and deployment along the canal, the Syrian buildup, and the Soviet evacuation. Zeira then gave his assessment:

Everything I counted so far does not change our basic estimate that the probability of war initiated by Egypt and Syria is still very low. The Syrian action could be a small-scale attack in the Golan Heights, and if this succeeds, they might go deeper. As for Egypt—either opening fire or helicopter-borne raid. . . . The lowest probability—a large-scale attempt of crossing the Canal, aiming at taking over both banks, and trying to reach the Passes. . . . In summary, I don't think that we go for war, but today we have more question marks than, I would say, 24 hours ago.[17]

Zeira discounted the possibility of a coordinated Egyptian-Syrian attack as "low probability—even lower than low."

Chief of Staff Elazar spoke next. He was not as confident as Zeira. He noted that if a large-scale attack occurred without warning, they would have to block it with the standing army, which he saw as catastrophic. However, if he had a twenty-four-hour warning, he believed they could manage. Yet when intelligence did receive a warning that would have given Elazar his twenty-four-hour warning, Zeira did not pass it on.

At 5:00 p.m. that evening, intelligence intercepted a message stating that the reason for the Soviet evacuation from Syria and Egypt was their intention to launch a war against Israel. "A reliable source gave a message, according to which the regime in Damascus decided to expel by air the Soviet military experts, including their families, from Syria. According to these sources, the Syrians explained their move by claiming that they and Egypt intend to launch a war against Israel." It was the piece of information Elazar was waiting for. He would later testify that if he had received this information Friday evening, he would have issued the orders to mobilize the reserves. With enough warning, he claimed the army would have been able to stop the Syrians on the northern front and slow down the Egyptians in the south. But Zeira decided not to tell the chief of staff, because the source was not reliable enough. It was a poor reason, as the source was a Syrian intercept and thus highly reliable. An unambiguous warning of war had finally come in, but the chief of staff and minister of defense did not receive it on time. If they had, the war might have turned out differently.

In the early-morning hours of October 6, Israel's top policy-makers received a warning from Ashraf Marwan that war would break out on both fronts that very evening. At 6:00 a.m. Dayan and Elazar met to discuss their options. They could not agree on the size of a reserves force to mobilize.

But even at that late hour, Zeira continued to foul their decision-making process. Zeira came in with an updated assessment. The Soviets were accelerating their evacuation, and the Syrian layout was more offensive than defensive. He also finally mentioned the signals intercept from the night before explaining the Soviet evacuation in terms of an Arab attack. Despite this, he offered three explanations: separate Egyptian and Syrian exercises, a coordinated Syrian and Egyptian exercise, and a coordinated war. Zeira estimated the last option was unlikely, since Sadat had no political reason to go to war. Yet Zeira admitted that he could not bridge the gap between the incoming information and his estimate. Had Zeira strongly warned of war, the reserves might have been mobilized at that point. But Dayan and Elazar could not agree and left the matter for the prime minister. More precious time was wasted.

At the meeting with Golda Meir, Zeira explained that "technically, the Egyptians and Syrians are ready, prepared, and able to start a war at any time."[18] He told Meir that Egypt was not in a position where they had to start a war, and if they did, Sadat knew Egypt would lose. Zeira could not believe Sadat would start a war with inferior capability, despite the overwhelming evidence that pointed to war. Therefore, it wasn't until after 9:00 a.m. that the order went out to mobilize the reserves, and only a portion of them.

By then, it was too late. The war would begin in less than five hours. Israel's warning system had failed miserably. After the war, Zeira, along with three other intelligence officers, would be fired. He should have been court-martialed. His decision to lie to top policymakers, delay passing on critical pieces of intelligence, and ignore evidence were not only professional errors but ethical ones that extended far beyond his mandate as director of military intelligence. More than any single person, Zeira was responsible for the surprise attack that the Jewish state suffered. Zeira would later claim that Marwan was a double agent who fed Israel false information that crippled its warning system. In fact, it was only Marwan's warning that finally persuaded policymakers to begin mobilizing the reserves. If the Egyptians had planted a double agent, they could not have asked for a better one than Eli Zeira.

America Ignores Signs of War

Israel's was not the only intelligence service that failed, however. The United States failed to accurately read the situation as well. Newly declassified documents explain how America's warning system failed to detect the signs of war. In April 1973 the National Photographic Interpretation Center (NPIC) noted a large Egyptian exercise in the desert, including a mock-up of the Suez Canal and Israeli defenses along the Bar-Lev Line and SA-6 missiles with armored units to provide air protection. A CIA analyst who specialized in the region warned that an Egyptian attack was imminent. When the attack failed to materialize, the analyst was transferred.

After the spring exercise, the Washington Special Actions Group (WSAG), the CIA's estimative body, reviewed the possibility of war and concluded, "There is a low probability that Sadat will renew fighting to break the deadlock—not because Sadat would not want to go to war, but because he is conscious of the severe results of such a step in view of the balance of power in the area, the relative weakness of Egypt and the current international circumstances."[19] The report also regarded joint Egyptian-Syrian operations as out of the question.

This view prevailed for the next few months. From June to September, U.S. diplomatic and intelligence reported that war was improbable, despite the ongoing deadlock in negotiations.

On September 28 Sadat delivered a speech that he called a "finishing touch" in his deception campaign.[20] As a CIA-issued Central Intelligence Bulletin (CIB) from September 29 shows, he succeeded more than he could have hoped: "President Sadat's address to the nation last night was primarily a fence-mending effort to designed to mollify and undercut domestic and foreign opponents. . . . Although generally circumspect toward the U.S., Sadat made some uncharacteristically benevolent statements, reflecting a guarded optimism that Washington intends some action to break the Middle East impasse." The bulletin noted the dramatic gesture of granting of amnesty to student protesters as "designed to head off the possibility of further student disturbances."[21]

This is exactly what Sadat had in mind: "This move was interpreted as an attempt at domestic reconciliation. Nobody realized it was part of my war plan."[22] The CIB also noted that Sadat was pleased that Secretary of State Henry Kissinger met with Arab representatives at the UN and claimed that Sadat's "approach reflects a sense of expectation toward possible U.S. moves on the Arab-Israeli conflict and a desire to avoid dampening prospect for movement. He made a point of noting at the end of his speech that he had deliberately avoided rhetoric on 'the battle.'" It is clear that Sadat deceived CIA analysts with his speech. The CIA believed that Sadat was more concerned with domestic priorities and diplomacy than with making war on the Israelis. This analysis colored the CIA reports on the Egyptian exercise the next week.

American intelligence services noted the massive Egyptian exercise in the Suez area and Syrian buildup in the Golan. On September 30 Secretary of State Kissinger asked for an intelligence review of the situation. The State Department's intelligence bureau (INR) responded with the following assessment: "In our view, the political climate in the Arab states argues against a major Syrian military move against Israel at this time. The possibility of a more limited Syrian strike—perhaps one designed to retaliate for the pounding the Syrian air force took from the Israelis on September 13—cannot, of course, be ruled out." Similarly, the Defense Intelligence Agency reported on October 3 that "the movement of Syrian troops and Egyptian military readiness is considered to be coincidental and not designed to lead to major hostilities," since the DIA assessed Israel's military capability was greater than that of the Arabs.[23]

The NPIC also observed irregularities. The NPIC's executive officer Dino Brugioni wrote, "While no photographic evidence pointed to a specific start date for a war, imagery began to show that serious preparations for an attack were underway. Crack Egyptian armored divisions from the Cairo and Dashur areas were being deployed along the Suez Canal, along with hundreds of artillery pieces, bridging equipment, and SAM batteries. There was more than ordinary activity at ammunition dumps and at logistics sites. In the north, the Syrians had brought tanks and artillery from the rear close to the Purple Line. The all-important battalion of FROG tactical missiles disappeared from known locations."[24] On October 4 the NPIC passed this information along to the defense attachés, who briefed the Israelis in Tel Aviv. The Israelis were aware of the buildup and believed it to be an exercise.

On the morning of October 5 the CIA released a CIB on the Egyptian exercises in the Suez area. The CIB summarized the activity as nonthreatening: "The exercise and alert activities under way in Egypt may be on a somewhat larger scale and more realistic than previous exercises, but they do not appear to be preparations for a military offensive against Israel." The CIA's assessment that the exercise was not a preparation for war was based on the fact that the earlier exercises did not break out into war. "Cairo usually conducts such exercises in the fall and spring. The scenario usually involves defending against an Israeli assault across the Suez Canal, and then launching a counterattack." The exercise was routine; there was no cause for alarm. The CIB noted the difference between this exercise and other ones: "Previous Egyptian exercises have been more paper and communications than the current one, which evidently involves the mobilization of larger numbers of personnel"; and it stated that "it is unusual, but not without precedent, for Egyptian forces to exercise during Ramadan, the Moslem month of religious fasting." As for the irregularities in the size and scope of the exercise, this was explained as additional rigor to make the exercise seem more real: "The movement of commando units and the use of a more secure means of communication make the exercise more realistic. Because of this realism, Cairo may have put its air defense and air forces on alert in preparation for the exercise and as a precaution against an Israeli reaction. The call-up of air force reservists is on a larger scale than that which occurred in the last major exercise in March, but this may be necessary because of the length of the alert."[25]

The CIB does not explain why the Egyptians had taken so many steps to make the exercise more "realistic." The measures detailed in the report—switching from radio transmissions to landlines, putting air defense and air forces on alert, and calling up air force reservists—are major steps and should not have been seen as simply increasing realism. The CIA was lulled to sleep by the repeated exercises, just as Sadat planned. Another reason for complacency was that the Israelis did not view it as a threat. "Tel Aviv assesses the Egyptian activity as normal, large-scale maneuvers and has not alerted its forces." But the size and scale of the Egyptian exercise should have raised some alarm bells.

Later that day, news came in of the departure of Soviet dependents from Egypt and Syria. The fact that the technical and military advisers stayed caused some concern among policymakers. National Security Council (NSC) deputy director Brent Scrowcroft called the CIA and asked for an updated assessment. The new report essentially restated what was in the morning's CIB: "It appears that both sides are becoming increasingly concerned about the activities of the other. Rumors and agent reports may be feeding the uneasiness that appears to be developing. The military preparations that have occurred do not indicate that any party intends to initiate hostilities."[26] The same afternoon, Israel delivered its latest estimate to the United States: "Our assessment is that the alert measures being taken by Egypt and Syria are in part connected with maneuvers (as regards Egypt) and in part due to fears of offensive actions by Israel. We consider the opening of military operations against Israel by the two armies as of low probability."[27] The signs of war grew stronger, and the next day the CIA released its last CIB prior to the outbreak of war. The CIB summarized the situation by stating, "Both the Israelis and the Arabs are becoming increasingly concerned about the military activity of the other, although neither side appears to be bent on initiating hostilities."

The CIB began by reporting on the departure of Soviet dependents from Egypt and Syria via transport planes and noted that "Soviet attention to the Middle East has risen sharply in the last few days," although the CIA did not draw any larger conclusions about these hasty departures, nor did they offer any explanation for the Soviet evacuation. Turning to the exercise in Egypt, the CIB noted that the training was continuing and repeated its assessment from the day before that the Egyptians normally conduct such exercises, and the only difference was that these were more realistic. The CIB stated, "While the Israelis have reported a build-up of tanks and artillery along the Canal, this cannot be confirmed." This statement shows a disconnect between the CIA and the NPIC, since the NPIC was aware of the artillery along the canal by October 4. It is not clear why the CIA analysts did not have this information by October 6. As for Syria, the CIB stated, "Syrian air activity appears to be normal, but there have been a number of reports that Damascus is redeploying some of its ground forces to the Golan Heights area."

Finally, the CIB noted that "the Israeli attitude toward these developments has changed considerably since October 1, when they viewed the activity in Egypt as normal and that in Syria as defensive in nature. During the past few days, the Israelis have conducted air reconnaissance of both the Suez Canal and Golan Heights areas."

The CIB reported on three events—the departure of Soviet personnel, a massive Egyptian exercise along the canal, and a deployment of Syrian ground forces to the Israeli border—but did not view them as related. None of this activity caused the analysts concern, since they based their assessment of war on their view of Arab political calculations:

> For Egypt, a military initiative makes little sense at this critical juncture of President Sadat's reorientation of domestic and foreign policies. Another round of hostilities would almost certainly destroy Sadat's painstaking efforts to invigorate the economy and would run counter to his current efforts to build a united Arab

political front, particularly among the less militant, oil-rich states. For the normally cautious Syrian President, a military adventure now would be suicidal, and he has said so. Far from seeking revenge for the loss of their MIG-21s to the Israeli air force, the Syrians appear to be bracing for a possible second blow from Israel.[28]

After the war, CIA director William Colby criticized the intelligence community for "focusing on what the Arabs . . . *should* do rather than what they *were* doing."[29] Nowhere is this critique more relevant than in the two concluding paragraphs from the October 6 CIB. Apparently, CIA analysts believed they could read Sadat's mind and took Assad's remarks at face value. The information staring them in the face about the massive Arab deployments and Soviet evacuation were relegated to secondary roles by the CIA's analysts, since they believed they knew what the Arabs intended to do. More than anything else, it was this assessment that let down American policymakers, just at the time when the Arabs were preparing to attack.

As for the possibility of hostilities, the CIB assessed that "Syrian fear, now being reflected in Damascus radio broadcasts, could lead to a mobilization of their defenses, which in turn could alarm and galvanize the Israelis. Such a cycle of actions and reactions increases the risk of military clashes which neither side originally intended." Any violence that occurred would therefore be accidental, not intentional.

Nor was the CIA alone in their analysis. The same day, the DIA reported essentially the identical analysis: "The current large-scale mobilization exercise may be an effort to soothe internal problems. As much as to improve military capabilities . . . mobilization of some personnel, increased readiness of isolated units, and greater communication security are all assessed as parts of the exercise routine. There are still no military or political indicators of Egyptian intentions or preparations to resume hostilities with Israel."[30]

Amazingly, the intelligence community continued to assess that Syria and Egypt were not attacking together, even after the war began. At 9:00 a.m. on October 6 the WSAG met to gather the views of the intelligence community on the possibility of war, in light of an Israeli report that Egypt and Syria would attack later that day. The war had, in fact, started a few minutes before the meeting began. Yet the WSAG released the following estimate:

> We can find no hard evidence of a major, coordinated Egyptian/ Syrian offensive across the Canal and in the Golan Heights area. Rather, the weight of evidence indicates an action-reaction situation where a series of responses by each side to perceived threats created an increasingly dangerous potential for confrontation. The current hostilities are apparently a result of that situation, although we are not in a position to clarify the sequence of events. It is possible that Egyptians or Syrians, particularly the latter, may have been preparing a raid or other small-scale action.[31]

This rather stunning report shows that even once the war began, the intelligence agencies remained convinced that it was an accident, despite the fact than an "action-reaction cycle" could hardly occur at the same time nearly two hundred miles apart. Only when the hostilities continued did it become clear what had happened.

With no warning from their own intelligence services, American policymakers were caught by surprise on the morning of October 6. Kissinger had only ninety frantic minutes to try and head off the war. A memo from that morning gives a picture of what American policymakers could have done had they been given more warning time by the intelligence agencies. At 7:00 a.m. National Security Council Middle East desk chair William B. Quandt sent a memo to NSC deputy director General Brent Scowcroft. The memo mentioned the warning Meir passed to the U.S. ambassador about a pending attack. Quandt summarized the evacuation of Soviet personnel from Egypt and Syria, the Egyptian exercise, and the deployment of Syrian forces. Quandt then offered two interpretations of the evidence:

> Egypt and Syria, despite the military odds against success, do intend to initiate hostilities as a way of forcing international atten-

tion to the Middle East and activating the use of oil as a political weapon against the United States. The Soviets have gotten wind of this and are evacuating dependents and some advisors.

A major crisis is under way in Arab-Soviet relations and under the cover of a war scare, Soviet advisors are being expelled from both Egypt and Syria. There have been numerous strains in Arab-Soviet relations recently, and King Faisal has been pressing hard to convince Sadat and Assad to cut their ties to Moscow.[32]

Quandt noted that the intelligence services favored the second interpretation. Despite this, Quandt had the presence of mind to offer suggestions for action if hostilities were to erupt. These steps included démarches to the Soviets and Egyptians, evacuating the U.S. citizens from the region, asking the shah of Iran to use his influence with Sadat to discourage force, and—perhaps most importantly—alerting U.S. forces in the Mediterranean and Europe for possible action in the Middle East. As it was, Quandt's memo went out only one hour before the war began.

Taken together, Kissinger's phone calls and Quandt's memo suggest a range of diplomatic, political, and military actions the United States could have taken to prevent an attack on its ally had they been given more lead time. But it was not to be. Israel's frontline troops stood alone as the war erupted on the afternoon of October 6, 1973. Egypt would send 100,000 men and 1,550 tanks against 436 Israeli soldiers with 3 tanks manning the Bar-Lev Line, while Syrian deployed 1,500 tanks and 942 artillery guns against 177 tanks in the Golan Heights. The latest battle for the Jewish state's survival had begun.

-14-

The Destruction of the Third Temple
Yom Kippur War and Its Consequences, 1973–1977

"We Have No More Force to Stop Them": The Opening Hours of the War

At 2:00 p.m. on the afternoon of October 6, 1973, Israel's borders exploded. After three years of silence, the Bar-Lev Line descended into the fury of an assault on a scale previously unknown in the Middle East, as two thousand Egyptian guns and heavy mortars opened fire on the Bar-Lev line. An estimated ten thousand shells fell on the Israeli lines in the first minute alone. The lookout towers on the Israeli forts were blown away immediately, and the defenders quickly retreated into their forts. With no way to shoot back, the defenders hid and prayed. Egyptian mortars pounded their fortifications, causing many to be destroyed. The forts that were not destroyed were isolated and cut off, unable to offer any real resistance to the attacking army. After the shellings, thousands of Egyptian commandos and infantrymen descended down the ramps to the canal, where they boarded rubber boats and began crossing. Shielded by smoke shells and chanting *Alahu Akbar* (God is great!), they paddled across unmolested. Once across, they fanned out and dug in. Within a mere two hours, nearly twenty-five thousand men had crossed and established five bridgeheads on the Israeli side, each a mile deep and five miles wide. On the Egyptian side, engineers began assembling bridges capable of carrying tanks and heavy trucks across the canal. Other tanks were transported across on large ferries. Next, the Egyptian turned their water hoses on the sand barrier the Israelis had been convinced would make the landing of tanks impossible. But the hoses effectively wore down the dirt, opening breach after breach into the barrier. That evening, all eight heavy bridges were completed. Egyptian tanks, men, and materiel poured across the canal. "Not since the construction of the Pyramids had Egypt seen such a massive and well-executed enterprise," journalist Abraham Rabinovich wrote.[1] The Egyptians had expected up to ten thousand casualties during the crossing. With almost complete surprise, they barely suffered two hundred. The crossing had succeeded, but the Egyptian army was hardly out of danger. The IDF stationed a large number of tanks behind the Bar-Lev Line. The plan was for these tanks to launch a counterassault against the units that had crossed the canal while the air force pounded the units that were still crossing. The tankers began their attack, surprised at the Egyptian crossing, but nonetheless confident in their mission—after all, what good were lowly infantrymen against modern battle tanks? But as the tanks neared the Egyptian lines and began firing their machine guns, they were ambushed. The dug-in Egyptians stood their ground, their wire-guided Sagger anti-tank missiles aimed right at the charging tanks. When the tanks were in range, they fired. Up and down the line, Israeli tanks exploded on impact. Two-thirds of the tanks in the Sinai sector were disabled by the day's end.

The first counterattack had failed, but there was still the air force. They had almost no time to prepare and went hastily into battle. Although they managed to shoot down a fair number of Egyptian planes and helicopters, the air attacks made little difference. Several of the IAF's new American-built Phantom jets went down to surface-to-air missiles, as Shazly planned. The crossing continued unabated. The first day of the war went to the attackers. It was the greatest feat of Arab arms in centuries. Egyptian honor had been restored, regardless of the outcome of the war. Although the first day's crossing had been successful, the IDF was not defeated. Soon, the reserves would arrive with additional tanks. Moreover, the air force would regroup and—with more time—could launch a better coordinated attack. But events on the Syrian front disrupted these plans.

Like the Egyptian attack, the Syrian assault began with a massive artillery barrage at 2:00 p.m. For forty-five minutes Syrian guns shelled the Golan Heights. As they did, the 177 IDF tanks stationed there divided into two groups: one went to the northern section of the Heights, the other to the southern section. When the smoke finally cleared from the barrage, the IDF tankers looked down into the valley before them and saw hundreds of tanks, armored personnel carriers (APCs), and vehicles filled with jubilant soldiers moving toward them. The huge columns were led by bridging vehicles capable of throwing spans across the anti-tank ditches. In both the northern and southern sectors, the defenders were greatly outnumbered. But the IDF tankers in the north mounted large, earthen ramps that provided them with a high vantage point. From their ramps, the tankers waited. The Syrians did not advance until dark, and then only slowly. They were waiting for the rest of their units before attacking the Israeli positions en masse. This proved fortunate for the defenders, for whereas the Syrian tanks were equipped with night-vision capabilities, the IDF tanks were not. The Syrians would have had an advantage in night fighting but did not exploit it. The defenders in the north experienced a tense but relatively quiet night. In the southern sector, however, the Syrians quickly penetrated the IDF's front lines and began driving across the Golan. There was almost no resistance.

Around the same time the Syrians were driving across the southern Golan, the general staff was preparing for the second day of war in the IDF headquarters' bunker beneath Tel Aviv, known as "the Pit." Minister of Defense Dayan had been briefed about the IAF's plan for the southern front. Instead of attacking the Egyptian tank columns, they would first attack the SAM sites. It would take four waves, and in the meantime, the Egyptians would continue crossing unmolested. When the SAM sites were disabled, the IAF would be able to pound the Egyptian ground units mercilessly, much as they had in 1967.

After hearing this plan, Dayan tried to get a few hours' sleep on an improvised bed. An aide roused him from his slumber at 4:00 a.m. with a report. A message had been intercepted from a Syrian tank commander: "I see the whole Galilee in front of me. Request permission to proceed."[2] Dayan was stunned, but it was true: the southern Golan was falling.

Dayan immediately boarded a helicopter and flew to the Northern Command's headquarters to ascertain the situation himself. The commanders bluntly explained the situation to Dayan: "The fighting in the southern part of the Golan Heights is finished, and we have lost. We have no more force to stop them. Additional armor forces from the reserve will not be ready to move against the Syrians before noon." The commanders told Dayan that only the air force could stop the Syrians until the reserves arrived.

Dayan was struck by the gravity of the situation. He immediately phoned Benny Peled, the IAF commander. Peled's planes were in the midst of the first of the planned four-wave attack on the Egyptian SAM sites. The first wave succeeded in taking out several anti-aircraft batteries and four airfields and had downed four MIGS at the loss of two Phantoms. His planes were returning and would be refueled for the second phase. For the first time, things seemed to be going in the right direction.

But the phone call from Dayan changed everything. Dayan told Peled that the southern Golan had fallen and the Syrians would cross the Jordan River by noon unless the air force attacked. Dayan reminded Peled that 150 miles of unforgiving desert terrain lay between the Suez Canal and Israel, but if the Syrians crossed the Jordan River, they would be inside the civilian areas. Therefore it was up to the IAF. "I want them to be able to swoop down without stop so the Syrian tank crews won't be able to lift their heads," Dayan said. To underline how grave the situation was, Dayan told Peled, "Benny, unless we stop their tanks, this is the destruction of the Third Temple."[3] The Third Temple was a metaphor for the State of Israel. By appealing to Peled so emotionally, Dayan in effect placed the survival of the state in Peled's hands.

Back at the Pit, Peled gathered the senior IAF staff and told them the Syrian front was critical and the air force would have to be rushed north. Nearly the entire staff disagreed. There were enough planes in the north to accomplish the task, one officer argued. Another said the narrow Golan comportment was too small for the entire air force to maneuver effectively. But Peled had been ordered to break off the Sinai attacks by the chief of staff and the minister of defense, who claimed Israel's survival was in danger. "I understand you all," he told the senior staff as he smacked the table. "The air force goes north!"

As IAF pilots returned from their first bombing run, they were informed that they would be flying north to attack Syrian SAM sites instead of Egyptian SAM sites. It was a complete surprise. A Phantom squadron leader related his feelings:

> To Syria! And with such urgency! What the hell was going on up there in the North? . . . Scrambling to a missile attack? No! This is too wild. Have the generals at HQ thought this through? No one pounces onto missile batteries just like that, out of the blue. SAMs have proven to be a terrible enemy in the years since the Six Day War. . . . A great effort was made over the years to develop methods to fight the missiles—secret methods, complex and sophisticated. The fighter squadrons were trained with new tactics that were polished down to the finest details. . . . Now that the hour has come, for some reason the entire plan lies shattered. . . . Has headquarters completely lost its mind?[4]

The Phantom pilot's instincts were correct. Without a clear plan, the IAF ran into a storm of anti-aircraft missiles that brought down ten more planes, without accomplishing any of its objectives. A total of thirty-five planes had been lost in the first two days alone, a significant percentage of the IAF's limited inventory. After this colossal failure, Elazar ordered a halt to all IAF attacks on SAM sites in the north and south.

Error had compounded error. The total surprise Israel suffered led to the successful Syrian and Egyptian advances on the first day. With Syria seemingly at Israel's doorstep, the general staff had panicked and ordered a hasty air operation. But in fact, even as the intercepted Syrian message about seeing the whole Galilee came in, the Syrian advance had halted. The forward Syrian forces reached their maximum penetration at 4:00 a.m. and then stopped. At dawn, they did not continue their advance, seeking to consolidate their position.

Meanwhile, the IDF reserves began to arrive and ascend the southern Golan. The tanks began to wind their way up the mountain road and approached the Syrians. They opened fire, and the Israelis' more-accurate gunners began picking off the Syrian tanks one by one. More reserve units arrived, and soon the IDF began pushing the invaders east, back toward the border. The farthest penetration of the Syrians had been checked. By the time the air force went into action in the north around midday, the situation had improved. Even though this was known, the operation was not called off. But calling off the attack on the Egyptian missile sites in favor of an attack that had never been rehearsed was a mistake that should not have been made. By doing so, the IAF lost planes in a fruitless attack that could not have succeeded in the narrow Golan comportment. These losses led Elazar to cancel the resumption of the attacks on the Egyptian sites that had succeeded in the first wave. Had these attacks continued, Egypt might have been deprived of its air cover, and the massive army gathering on the east bank of the Suez Canal could have been bombed into submission from the air. But it was not to be. In sharp contrast to the Six-Day War, the IDF's ground forces were alone. And it would be a desperate battle.

Black Days on Both Fronts

As the reserves made their way toward the Syrian forces in the southern Golan, the outnumbered IDF tanks in the northern Golan of the Seventh Brigade took their positions on and around the earthen ramps. IDF general-turned-historian Chaim Herzog described the scene at the start of the second day of the war:

> As Sunday morning, October 7, dawned on the 7th Brigade, the sight of devastation and war unfolded itself before the weary eyes

of the troops. An armada of burning tanks and destroyed vehicles lay strewn across the valley. Crew members were rushing around between the flames; turrets blown off their chassis lay near the decapitated tanks; red and purple flames licked around the ammunition trucks and armored personnel carriers, as from time to time one of the vehicles exploded and disintegrated. Mushrooms of white smoke gathered over the tanks. The accurate Syrian fire had forced the tank commanders to take cover and close down the hatches in the turrets. As they emerged again and surveyed the scene, a fresh Syrian column advanced under cover of the heavy artillery fire, ready to do battle a second time.[5]

Shortly after dawn, the massive Syrian artillery barrage descended on the defenders, followed by a full-scale tank assault. As the Syrian tanks neared, the men of the Seventh Brigade opened fire, scoring several direct hits. Battalion commander Colonel Avigdor Kahalani recalled, "The Syrians were still coming, apparently determined to get our vantage point. Burning Syrian tanks were exploding and showering chunks of steel across the valley. A turret shot into the air, landing upside down. 'All stations, this is the battalion commander. You're doing a fine job. This valley looks like a bonfire holiday. It's up to us to stop them.'"[6] The Syrian advance halted later in the morning. The men of the Seventh Brigade estimated they had knocked out eighty to ninety enemy vehicles.

The battle raged on and off. Syrian armor advanced behind artillery fire, crawling up the valley toward the IDF positions. At no point did the Syrians try to maneuver or avoid enemy fire. Israeli gunners were therefore able to knock out many tanks at long range, but they could not prevent some enemy units from reaching their positions. The fight became a close-range duel, with Israeli and Syrian tanks mixed together, while the smoke from the burned-out vehicles filled the air and choked the men's nostrils. The battle continued throughout the night, and even though the Syrians had superior night-fighting equipment, they could not dislodge the Seventh Brigade.

While the Syrians regrouped for another assault, Colonel Avigdor's men refueled and reloaded the tanks, while engineers repaired the damaged ones. Darkness lifted on the morning of October 8 to reveal over 130 knocked-out, abandoned, smoking Syrian tanks in the valley in front of the Israeli defenders. Many of the destroyed Syrian tanks were actually between the Israeli positions or even behind them. The men of the Seventh Brigade, having fought through the night, now realized they had halted a major advance. But the battle was far from over.

As Avigdor's units readied for the Syrian attack on October 8, Israeli forces in the Sinai prepared for a counterattack against the Egyptian lines. The general staff had been briefed on the attack the night before. Six hundred tanks led by three of the IDF's best commanders were poised to throw back the Egyptians, finally turning the tide of war. Even Dayan, who had been so distraught earlier in the day, was caught up in the moment: "From tomorrow, we would begin to lift our heads out of the water. The initiative was ours and we could pick the battleground and assemble our forces accordingly. Why shouldn't we win? The divisional and brigade commanders were the best of our soldiers: [Arik] Sharon, [Bren] Adan, [Albert] Mendler—the major league of the IDF. The entire chain of command, up to the chief of staff, was from the armored corps. All of them are experienced in combat, all of them know the Sinai well. Tomorrow will be the day of armor."[7]

But if the divisional commanders were the best and most experienced IDF leaders, the regional commander who oversaw them was relatively new. Shmuel Gonen had performed well as an officer in the Sinai in 1967. He had just taken over the Sinai command from Ariel Sharon, however, and as events would prove, he was not up to the task. As the three divisions moved forward, Gonen continually changed their orders, sending them back and forth across the desert in disorderly, uncoordinated movements. When IDF forces did engage the Egyptians, it was in piecemeal attacks that were repelled by ATGM rockets. At the day's end, the IDF had gained no ground and lost roughly seventy-five tanks.

Gonen had first ordered Ariel Sharon's division south, but when

Adan's forces took heavy losses, Gonen ordered Sharon back to where he had started. Sharon was furious:

> My feelings at that point were simply not describable. If on the surface I appeared normal, it was because I was numbed with rage. It was now October 8. Two days earlier, the entire division had been called out of their homes and synagogues. In less than twenty-four hours, they had been fully mobilized and had driven 200 miles to the battlefield. It was a remarkable performance, one that no other army in the world could have matched. The previous night they had received their orders and deployed before dawn, ready to fight. And now, on this absolutely crucial day of battle, they had spent their time driving around the desert like idiots.

Sharon called October 8 "the black day of the Israeli Defense Forces, a day that traumatized the army."[8]

Dayan and Elazar shared similar views. Upon learning of the failure of the Sinai counterattack, they assembled the general staff in the Pit. Dayan recommended preparing fallback positions in the Sinai and even suggested arming civilians with anti-tank weapons. Elazar was not quite as pessimistic, but both men would not let the armor on the Golan retreat even "a centimeter." Several sources claim Dayan asked and received approval from Golda Meir to prepare "the Temple" weapons, meaning nuclear arms. Apparently, eight planes were loaded with nuclear bombs at an IAF airfield, and nuclear-armed missiles were raised onto launch pads at another location.[9] Whether or not this happened remains an official state secret, but assuming these accounts are correct, it underlines the gravity of the military situation.

October 8 was another difficult day for the Seventh Brigade, fighting numerically superior forces on the Golan Heights. For the third day, the Syrians continued their attack. This time it was led by better-trained troops with the latest-model Soviet tanks. But Colonel Avigdor's tanks continued to destroy the forces coming their way, even as their numbers and energy dwindled. With no time to sleep or eat, the brigade's fighting skill declined. More men were killed and more tanks put out of action. Behind the front lines, the ordinance crews worked feverishly to keep the few remaining tanks operable. The brigade was now down to fewer than fifty tanks. The men began to despair. The Syrians kept on coming. If reinforcements did not arrive soon, they would be overwhelmed. Miles behind the embattled Seventh Brigade the reserves, called to join their units when the war broke out, were making their way forward, but it was a slow process. They got there however they could. In cars, in buses, or hitchhiking, individuals arrived to find their bases nearly empty, the ammunition still locked up, their vehicles parked in storage. In small units they moved toward the fighting. It wasn't how it was supposed to be. They were to have been given the order to mobilize well before the fighting broke out, gathered at their bases, and left as whole battalions and brigades in good order with a clear plan of deployment. Instead they improvised, arriving piecemeal rather than in units. But their presence at the front was welcomed by the few already there.

The Seventh Brigade had been born in desperation, created to take Latrun in 1948. Since then, it had played key roles in 1956 at Abu Agheila, and in 1967 under Shmuel Gonen it had broken the Egyptian lines at Rafa. Considered the elite of the armored corps, it seemed to be at the end of its line. The next morning the few remaining Israeli tanks awoke to a massive artillery barrage, larger than any of the previous ones. Planes joined in the frenzy, and soon thousands of explosions around the tanks kicked up a dust storm filled with lead fragments and deadly shrapnel. The roar was deafening. Blinded by the dust, the tank commanders closed their hatches and waited for the barrage to end. Colonel Avigdor realized that this was the final Syrian push, a concerted effort to finally break the stubborn defenders in this zone. When the shelling stopped, hundreds of top-line Syrian tanks, backed by armored personnel carriers, began the ascent toward the Seventh Brigade's position.

Avigdor's men opened fire at their maximum range and began putting Syrian tanks out of action. They exploded in a massive fireball, their turrets blown off from the hull. The massive column continued to roll on, however. They intended to use their sheer numbers to overwhelm the embattled defenders. As they neared the ramps, the Israelis continued to hold the high ground, but there were only about fifteen operable tanks remaining. At last some Syrian tanks moved past the ramps and began firing from behind, neutralizing the IDF's advantage. In addition to the Syrian tanks behind the ramps, other tanks attacked the Israelis from the front and sides. It was an all-out frenzy of a battle. There was no coordination anymore. Each tank was its own unit. They fought and fought, firing until they were numb. The heat from the burning tanks around the battlefield began wilting the men inside their cramped quarters. Their nostrils were choked by the smell of gunpowder and burning cordite. The men fought on, but the end was near.

Avigdor was sure it was his last battle. But at that moment, eleven reservist tanks arrived. Their commander had been on his honeymoon in Nepal when the war broke out. He rushed back to Israel and immediately reported for duty. His timely arrival saved the Seventh Brigade, which was now down to seven tanks. The battle continued as the fresh tanks fired on the tiring attackers.

The Syrians began to waver. Their assault ground to a halt. Then Syrian armor and vehicles turned around and retreated across the valley they had fought so hard to win. Some of their crews abandoned their vehicles and ran home on foot, leaving behind their once-formidable army. The remaining IDF tanks pursued them before stopping at the anti-tank ditch. Over the radio net, headquarters told the survivors, "You have saved the people of Israel." In the southern Golan, the IDF had also defeated the Syrians forces. They began pursuing the enemy across the border into Syrian territory. The tide had turned in the north, but the Egyptians remained firmly entrenched in the south.

Stouthearted Men

Buoyed by his army's successful canal crossing and holding actions, Anwar Sadat's popularity skyrocketed. He had orchestrated the first major Arab victory over the Zionists. Cheering throngs mobbed him in Cairo as he addressed the National Assembly. He had done the impossible: recapture Arab land. Moreover, his huge army seemed in no immediate danger from the Israelis, but at this point, Sadat's ally begged for his aid. With Syrian forces in full retreat, President Hafez al-Assad requested that Sadat retake the offensive to relieve the pressure on his defeated army. In their prewar planning sessions, Egyptian generals had shown their Syrian counterparts plans to take the Sinai up to the passes east of the Suez Canal. This was never the Egyptian intention, but Sadat felt he could not be seen abandoning his Arab brothers. His army's excellent performance may have also convinced him that they could beat the Israelis, who had already taken heavy losses. Chief of Staff Shazly was firmly opposed, arguing that if the armor moved beyond the SAM shield, they would be vulnerable to air attacks. But it was Sadat's war, and it was his decision. The army would attack.

Back at the Pit, intelligence came in on Egypt's upcoming attack. The assault presented the IDF with a huge opportunity. If they could break the Egyptian assault, they could then use the momentum to follow up the victory by moving bridging equipment through a gap between the Egyptian armies along the Suez Canal. They could then cross the canal, cut off the enemy supply lines, and trap the Egyptian armies on the east side of the canal. It all depended on an Egyptian assault, but when the Egyptian armies began to move into attack position, the general staff realized their wish was coming true.

After a week of disasters on the southern front, there was finally a ray of light. Chief of Staff Elazar helicoptered to the Sinai to prepare his troops. As he flew over the Israeli lines, he viewed an impressive sight. The IDF had gathered in large numbers in desert dunes, their tanks being refurbished, fueled, armed, and readied for battle. When he landed, he felt the confidence brimming among the men whose morale had been shattered after days of setbacks on the southern front. Both divisions under Bren Adan and Ariel Sharon were ready to deal the Egyptians a crushing blow. Elazar was hopeful: "It's about time. We need a big, beautiful offensive with lots of Egyptian tanks—to wipe them out east of the canal and then to cross. That's today's program." He got his wish. At 6:00 a.m. on the morning of October 14, six hundred Egyptian tanks rolled out from the canal toward the Israeli positions to the east. The IDF had deployed their armor on high ground with good visibility. As the Egyptian tanks approached, the Israelis prepared to break the attack. At three thousand yards, they opened fire on the exposed columns.

An Egyptian colonel named Mahmoud was leading his armored brigade:

> Suddenly, all hell broke loose around him. His tanks, which only minutes ago had been quietly rolling up the gradual slope, seemed to fly into the air and disintegrate before his eyes. The plain shook with the crash and thunder of hundreds of Israeli shells pouring high explosive torment on the Egyptians. Tortured screams burst forth over the radio channel. Tanks were exploding all around. Infantry carriers trying to turn and retreat capsized, and spilled their troops on the already body-filled sand. As dazed foot soldiers and tank crews scurried for cover, many were mowed down by machine gun and mortar fire.
>
> Colonel Mahmoud was dumfounded by shock: he could not believe the horror unfolding before his eyes. The unearthly battle din was overwhelming and made it impossible to reach his battalion commanders by radio. Finally, he managed to get his command group under cover. Too late: the Israelis were already outflanking his force from the north, blocking his retreat. The Egyptians did not seem to realize their colonel's plight and hardly maneuvered in response. A command car exploded near the colonel's carrier, his artillery commander had just been killed. All attempts at orderly retreat now turned into a rout. . . . The remnants of the lst Armored Brigade fled in disarray, leaving behind the charred skeletons of tanks and their fallen comrades.[10]

Egyptian tanks began burning all across the desert floor. Some managed to reach the ridges below the IDF positions, giving them temporary protection. From there, they attacked uphill and closed the distance with the Israeli tanks. They were met with a hail of tank and artillery fire. Another Egyptian unit was wiped out as they advanced into a wadi and IDF armor caught them in a trap on high ground from three sides. By late afternoon the entire offensive had been halted. American photo interpreters counted 264 destroyed Egyptian tanks, against only 6 for Israel. The IDF was finally beginning to recover some of its swagger.

With the Egyptian attack broken, it was time to strike across the canal. The plan called for a crossing between the two entrenched Egyptian armies. Known as "Operation Stouthearted Men," it required Ariel Sharon to establish a crossing area at a pre-prepared position along the canal known as "the Yard." From there, the IDF would prepare two bridges: one was a pontoon bridge whose sections would have to be floated into place by engineers; the other was a massive four-hundred-ton roller bridge that had to be pulled across the desert dunes by tanks. The advantage of the roller bridge was that it was a single unit that did not have to be assembled. But due to the Egyptian's unexpected success, it would have to be towed three times the planned distance, a difficult task for such an unwieldy structure. As the bridges were being assembled, paratroopers would cross the canal in rubber boats. If all went well, they would catch the Egyptians by surprise, cross en masse, and trap the enemy army.

But there were serious dangers with the plan, dangers the IDF staff was aware of. Bridgeheads are not considered safe unless they are out of range of enemy artillery. The Yard would be well within the Egyptian's crosshairs. Even worse, one Egyptian unit was only eight hundred yards from the Yard, at a position known as the "Chinese Farm." The Chinese Farm was actually a Japanese irrigation project, and its ditches made excellent defensive positions. The general staff therefore ordered an attack on the Chinese Farm to push the enemy back from the crossing site at the Yard. Despite the anticipated difficulties, the general staff saw no other option. There was no other way to dislodge the Egyptians from the east side of the canal. Stouthearted Men was appropriately named.

The operation began at 5:00 p.m. on October 15. It immediately ran into difficulties. With only a narrow corridor to the canal open, a massive traffic jam delayed the arrival of the pontoon sections. Even the small rubber boats the paratroopers would use were delayed. The general staff had hoped to complete both bridges by dawn, but that was clearly not going to happen. Meanwhile the massive roller bridge was slowly pushed and pulled along the dunes by tanks harnessed with cables, a monstrous mirage that seemed out of place in the desert. Suddenly, the bridge fell over. It needed to be repaired, and that would take days, not hours.

When the rubber boats finally arrived at the Yard, the paratroopers crossed into the African side of the canal. It seemed like a different world. A freshwater canal had created a green, vibrant area that stood in stark contrast to the harsh desert wastes around it. With the pontoon bridge pieces stuck in the massive traffic jam, the tanks remained stranded. Instead the commanders ordered that the inflatable rafts be used to ferry the tanks across. The flimsy rafts were not built to move heavy vehicles, but they were the IDF's only hope of making an armored crossing that night. The rafts managed to carry one tank each. By morning, the tiny crafts had ferried twenty-seven tanks across, far fewer than the general staff had hoped for.

But if the bridging operation was struggling, it paled in comparison to the task of clearing out the Chinese Farm. At nightfall, the tank brigade moved down toward the farm. They were outnumbered five to one, but they had surprise on their side. The tank column moved into the farm unmolested. They continued to drive in. About half of the column was inside the enemy position when all hell broke out, as Egyptian tanks shells and rocket-propelled grenades (RPGs) descended on the attackers. The rear of the brigade took heavy losses, but the forward elements found themselves in the midst of a massive logistics center. Spread out in front of them in neat rows was the Egyptians' ammunition dumps, fuel tankers, artillery, and SAM batteries. Scores of parked tanks, armored personnel carriers, trucks, jeeps, and supply vehicles lay gleaming in the moonlight. It was an enormous bonanza for the attackers. The tanks opened fire on all sides and scored direct hits at the close range. Ammunition dumps exploded in enormous blasts, enemy vehicles went up in flames, SAM missiles went up in wild gyrations as they were hit. The entire area was lit up by the flames from the blasts. As Egyptian troops rushed out of their foxholes to see what caused the commotion, they became easy targets for the machine gunners. The element of surprise had favored the IDF.

The sheer number of Egyptians began to tell, however, as the defenders recovered from their initial surprise. RPG teams and infantrymen fired on the attackers. Egyptian tank crews mounted their steel beasts and began firing on the Israelis. In the darkness it was hard to distinguish friend from foe. Tanks crashed against each other, soldiers mistook enemies for allies. But the light from the explosions favored the Egyptian RPG teams, who began destroying IDF tanks. To limit the amount of light, the Israeli tank crews began crushing ammunition crates under their treads instead of blowing them up with cannon fire. Despite heavy losses, the Egyptians clung stubbornly to their defensive positions. At 3:00 a.m. the Israeli commander threw in his remaining two companies. Another ferocious battle erupted, but the area remained in Egyptian hands, save for a small intersection at the southern end of the Chinese Farm.

The frenzied fighting continued throughout that horrible night. After ten hours of combat, the sun rose over the desert to reveal an incredible sight. In the area in and around the Chinese Farm, hundreds of burning and destroyed vehicles lay strewn in the sand. Jeeps and trucks were scattered around the battlefield. Huge tanks lay with their turrets blown off, the gun barrels buried in the sand. It was a poignant reminder that even the largest vehicles were not immune to the carnage of war. Charred corpses of Israeli and Egyptian soldiers lay only a few feet from each other; the darkness had made it nearly impossible to fight at long distances. The air was suffused with the smell of cordite and smoke. Orange glows from the burning hulks made the entire scene appear ghastly and surrealistic. The whole area was a mass graveyard. It had been the fiercest battle of the war, if not all of the Arab-Israel wars.

Sharon recorded his impressions as he moved from headquarters to the canal:

> The morning of October 16 dawned on the most terrible sight I had ever seen. I had listened intently to their reports over the radio net, and the conflagration of the battle had lit up the sky just to the north of us. But each of us in the headquarters unit had been directly involved in action, so busy that we had not fully grasped the immensity of the struggle or its destructiveness. But as the sky brightened, I looked around and saw hundreds and hundreds of burned and twisted vehicles. . . . No picture could capture the horror of the scene, none could encompass what had happened here.[11]

The lead brigade had lost 56 of its 97 tanks, with over 100 killed. Egyptian losses were perhaps twice as much.

Despite the carnage, the fight for the Chinese Farm was not over. The Egyptians had not been pushed back far enough from the crossing site. The crossing remained stalled on the morning of October 16. The pontoon pieces had not yet arrived. The paratroopers who had crossed set off with their tanks that morning. Catching the Egyptians by surprise, they destroyed tanks, vehicles, and several SAM sites. By dawn, they had opened a small hole in the skies free from SAMs. It would allow the IAF to begin to operate again over the crossing area. Meanwhile, engineers rushed about inside the Yard, directing traffic and loading men and supplies onto the rafts before the Egyptians caught onto what they were doing. Overseeing the operation was Ariel Sharon. Sharon was convinced that the momentum was with them. If they could move as much material across the canal as possible, they would catch the Egyptians by surprise. He was therefore stunned when he was ordered by Southern Command to halt all crossing activity. He was warned that his forces were cut off and surrounded by the Egyptians.

Sharon responded that it was the Egyptians who were surrounded. But Southern Command did not want to risk floating more tanks over before the bridgehead was secure and before the pontoon bridge was finished. The force on the other side would remain small. Sharon fumed at the order. He was convinced that if more tanks had been allowed to cross, that very day would have seen the IDF triumphant. Instead, he was forced to wait.

As Sharon impatiently waited for the order to cross, the battle for the Chinese Farm renewed. General Bren Adan decided that the only way to get into the irrigation ditches and clear out the Egyptians was with infantry, not armor. A paratroop IDF battalion went in that night, but they were caught on open terrain and pinned down. By morning, they had lost a third of their men. When they pulled out of the farm on the afternoon of October 17, they thought they had failed. But the Egyptians had been pushed back far enough to allow for vehicles to move forward. With the road to the Yard finally clear, the pontoon pieces rolled forward. But the attack to clear the Chinese Farm had also alerted the Egyptians of what the IDF was attempting. The crossing's success remained very much in doubt.

An extremely agitated Ariel Sharon recorded what happened next:

> All of October 16, we were forbidden to reinforce the west bank bridgehead. That night, exhausted and morose, I went to sleep on the warm engine cover of a tank. Early in the morning of the seventeenth, I was awakened by the sound of more self-propelled rafts being towed into the yard. They were a welcome sight. With enough of these rafts on hand, we would now be able to assemble the bridge. Once that was done, we might finally be able to change some minds about getting our forces across fast, even though by this time surprise was no longer with us.
>
> The rafts rumbled slowly into the yard and down toward the rampart opening, where the engineers' already frantic pace began to pick up even more. But just at that moment a tremendous Egyptian artillery barrage brought a curtain of shells crashing down on us. Almost simultaneously, MIG fighters swarmed over the yard in an attack that turned the compound into an inferno.

With incredible courage, soldiers were standing outside in this storm of fire directing traffic. Columns of vehicles were entering the yard, some of which exploded in the bombardment and had to be pushed out of the way, although with all the tanks and trucks already crowded in, there was hardly room to push them anywhere. Officers from command APCs were constantly jumping out to help with traffic control. Others worked with the engineers, who were assembling and launching the rafts under the same deadly hail. Hundreds of shells seemed to be hitting the area. The chaos was mindboggling.[12]

At that point, the MIGs made another run at the Yard. Sharon jumped into his M-113 command APC. As he did, a shell exploded behind him, leaving a crater where he had been standing. He ordered the APCs to the other side of the yard. "As we negotiated our way slowly through the yard, the M-113 was rocked by bomb concussions. Suddenly, I felt a smashing pain on my forehead. I had a moment to see blood splattering all over and I heard someone way, 'Our friend just bought it.' But an instant later, my eyes opened and I realized that whatever had hit me was just a glancing blow."

Sharon was dazed, but intact. Shortly afterward, engineers began assembling the pontoon bridge, floating each section into place. By the evening of October 17 it was ready. Israeli armor began lumbering across the bridge, still under Egyptian artillery fire. The rafts began to ferry tanks across as well. One raft was hit by a shell, and the tank crew was lost with its vehicle. The armor assembled on the west bank and began moving out, taking out more SAM sites. As they did, the IAF began to control the skies again. Meanwhile, the Egyptians launched tank attacks toward the crossing area from the north and south. Israeli intelligence warned of the attacks, and IDF armor rolled into ambush positions. Both offensives were crushed. In the south, Bren Adan laid an ambush, destroying fifty enemy tanks to only four Israeli tanks lost. The bridgehead remained secure.

With the bridgehead secure and the roads to the canal open,

it was time to put the massive roller bridge into place. The tank crews put the harnesses back on and began pulling the huge structure toward the canal. In front of them, bulldozers cleared out a thirty-yard-wide path, pushing destroyed tanks and vehicles aside and leveling out the terrain. All the while, the Egyptians attacked the massive object, impossible as it was to conceal in the open desert. Their air force led the assault, but seven state-of-the-art MIG fighters went down in flames. The bridge continued to crawl forward. Then the Egyptians tried to take it out with artillery. A direct hit might well have put the bridge out of commission, but the shells fell harmlessly in the desert dunes. The bridge arrived at the canal at sunset on October 18. It took Israeli engineers twenty-four hours to attach the steel beast to both sides of the canal. Finally, late on October 19, it was completed, allowing more IDF units to cross the canal into Africa.

For the first time in the war Israeli armor was operating on flat, open terrain, allowing them the maneuverability they had been expecting and preparing for since 1967. Their sprits rose and they fanned out, destroying more SAM sites and infantry companies and silencing the Egyptian guns that had made the crossing so hellish. Several Egyptian counterattacks failed. Bren Adan's units raced to cut the supply lines to the Egyptian army on the east side of the canal. Trapping the Egyptian army would give Israel the upper hand in any postwar negotiations. It would also ensure that the enemy would not use a cease-fire to restock their forces for another round of fighting. Adan's forces swung into action, moving as fast as they could, not even halting to take prisoners. The Egyptian air force threw all they had into stopping the assault, but Israeli tanks cut off all routes across the canal to the Egyptian Third Army. An entire Egyptian division was now trapped on the east side of the canal and completely at the mercy of the IDF. Several generals pressed to annihilate the entire enemy force. Bren Adan believed the IDF could destroy the entire division in one night.

But it would be the superpowers, not the Israeli generals or politicians, who would decide the fate of the trapped Egyptian army.

The Soviets feared that the Israelis would destroy the trapped army and then march onto Cairo, an unacceptable outcome for them. Soviet premier Leonid Brezhnev wrote a strongly worded message to President Richard Nixon calling for an immediate cease-fire and the dispatch of American and Soviet forces to ensure compliance: "As you know, the Israeli forces have already fought their way into Suez. It is impossible to allow such to continue." Brezhnev then warned, "I will say it straight that if you find it impossible to act jointly with us in this matter, we should be faced with the necessity urgently to consider taking appropriate steps unilaterally. We cannot allow arbitrariness on the part of Israel."[13]

Secretary of State Kissinger received this message with alarm. The goal of his Middle Eastern policy had been to reduce the Soviets' presence there. He would resist the introduction of Soviet troops by force if necessary. To underline the seriousness of their message, the Joint Chiefs of Staff raised the start of alert of the armed forces from Defcon 4 to Defcon 3, the highest state of readiness in peacetime. In addition, the Joint Chiefs alerted the Eighty-Second Airborne Division for possible movement, moved a carrier group from the Atlantic to the Mediterranean, and even flew B-52 bombers capable of carrying nuclear weapons from Guam to the United States. Knowing that the Soviets would pick up on all of these actions, Kissinger then sent a reply, written in Nixon's name, to the Kremlin. The memo stated that sending Soviet and American military forces was inappropriate under the circumstances. The memo then warned, "We must view your suggestion of unilateral action as a matter of the gravest concern involving incalculable consequences. It is clear that the force necessary to impose the ceasefire terms on the two sides would be massive and would require closest coordination to avoid bloodshed. This is not only clearly unfeasible but is not appropriate to the situation."[14] Kissinger ended the memo by reiterating that Soviet unilateral military action would produce "incalculable consequences," which the Soviet leaders understood to be the threat of nuclear war.

The Soviets realized how serious the Americans were and quickly backed down on their call for unilateral action or the introduction of Soviet military forces. In a conciliatory letter sent the same day as Kissinger's nuclear threat, the Soviets declared they would cooperate with the United States on sending Soviet and American "observers" to the region.[15] In return, Kissinger forced Israel to accept the cease-fire and allow supplies to reach the surrounded Egyptian army. Israel's military men bristled at the prospect, but the tiny state could not afford to alienate its super-power patron. Moreover, Kissinger was thinking ahead: he knew that if an entire Egyptian division were wiped out, Sadat would never negotiate for a permanent peace with Israel. The Israeli government accepted the deal, and the war was finally over. It had cost the Jewish state 2,800 dead and 8,800 wounded, but a complete disaster had been avoided. The IDF had crawled back from the dead.

After the War

The postwar negotiations began. It was the first time the Israelis and a delegation from an Arab state negotiated face-to-face. That in itself was a notable achievement, but the two sides remained far apart in their positions. The Egyptians wanted the Israelis to withdraw to the Sinai passes. The Israelis, still capable of destroying the Egyptian army on the east side of the canal at a moment's notice, found this unacceptable. After six weeks of talks, Kissinger brokered an agreement. The IDF would withdraw from the west side of the canal to a position five kilometers east of the canal. The Egyptians would remain on the eastern side of the canal, a tangible achievement for the success in the first days of the war. The agreement did not seem fair to Israelis, who felt the Egyptian should also be compelled to withdraw to their side of the canal. But by allowing Egyptian forces to stay on the east bank, Kissinger let Sadat maintain the appearance that he had won the war, a necessary precondition for a future peace deal. This Disengagement of Forces Treaty was viewed by all as a temporary measure. On the Syrian front, Israel agreed to withdraw from territory it had captured during the war and return to the lines from the end of the Six-Day War, vacating only the Syrian town of Quneitra. There were no face-to-face meetings with the Syrians however. Both treaties were monitored by U.S. reconnaissance missions, known as "Olive Harvest," whose findings were relayed to the opposing sides.

The war had been traumatic for Israel, and the aftermath was difficult as well. After the war, the Arab states unleashed a new weapon in the form of an oil boycott. The Western world's need for fuel drove the Europeans away from Israel. Developing nations broke their ties with the Jewish state, seeing it as an imperialist oppressor of the Palestinians. The economy was hamstrung from the call-up of reservists; Israel spent an enormous sum on arms in 1974, fearful of a replay of the previous year's war. The government was forced to implement austerity measures that citizens chafed at.

Violence continued to be directed at the Jewish state. In one notorious incident in the northern town of Ma'alot, PLO gunmen murdered twenty-two schoolchildren. A year after the war ended, one citizen summed up the nation's mood:

> The holidays are drawing to a close this year. They passed peacefully but somberly. Memories of last Yom Kippur are still too ripe and, when coupled with the rather murky prospects for the immediate future, did not combine to make a very happy New Year season. Israel today is plagued by many of the same maladies that afflict other countries—a deteriorating economic situation, poor and lack-luster leadership—and in addition, a disturbing internal social situation readying itself for eruption. Superimposing upon this unstable defense and foreign conditions certainly does not make the best combination for a happy year.[16]

Israel's trials continued in 1975. Backed by the Arab nations, the oil-dependent Europeans, and many of the newly independent states of Africa and Asia, the PLO was granted observer status at the UN, and Chairman Yasir Arafat addressed the UN General Assembly. Only days before his address, he had declared, "We shall never stop until we can go back home and Israel is destroyed. The goal of our struggle is the end of Israel, and there can be no compromise or mediations. We don't want peace—we want victory. Peace for us means Israel's destruction, and nothing else."[17] Arafat toned down his rhetoric at the UN, but Israelis felt his mere presence there gave legitimacy to calls for the destruction of the Jewish state.

Even more disheartening was when later that year the UN passed a resolution equating Zionism as a form of racism. "A great evil has been loosed upon the world," the U.S. delegate thundered, calling the resolution an "infamous act."[18] The cumulative effect was that the Jewish state was more isolated than at any time in its history before the 1956 war.

There was one bright spot that year, as Israel and Egypt agreed to another treaty after a strenuous round of shuttle diplomacy by Henry Kissinger. The negotiations had been quite difficult. At one point, a frustrated Kissinger abruptly changed his plans and visited Masada. Afterward he told Prime Minister Yitzchak Rabin, "It's tragic to see people dooming themselves to a course of unbelievable peril."[19] The message was clear. If Israel did not agree to the treaty, Masada was in danger of falling again. Kissinger's tactic worked. Rabin relented and agreed to the so-called Sinai II treaty. The IDF withdrew to the eastern passes of the Sinai, with the area between the two armies becoming a UN buffer zone. American-manned early-warning stations would be set up near the passes. Egypt agreed to refrain from the use of force or the threat of blockade. Commercial Israeli ships would be allowed through the Suez Canal.

It was an important agreement, but it would pale in comparison to what came next.

-15-

Nation Shall Not Lift Up Sword Against Nation

The Camp David Accords, 1977–1981

"Sanctified in Jewish Blood": The New Government's Approach

June 20, 1977, was a watershed in Israel's political history. On that day Menachem Begin's right-wing Likud Party assumed power after defeating the Labor Party in the general elections. For the first time the government was not run by the Labor Party, the party of David Ben-Gurion, which had led the state since its inception in 1948. The new government came in with a very different outlook on territorial issues from its predecessor. The Likud championed retention of the West Bank, which it referred to by its biblical names, Judea and Samaria, whereas Labor advocated turning over some of the area to Jordan as part of a peace treaty. By using the names Judea and Samaria, the Likud emphasized the biblical link with the land. In their platform, they stated, "The right of the Jewish people to the land of Israel is eternal and indisputable and linked with the right to security and peace; therefore Judea and Samaria will not be handed over to any foreign administration." Moreover, the Begin-led government planned not only to retain the territory, but to greatly increase the number of Jewish inhabitants there through the introduction of settlements. It was a major part of their ideology: "Settlement, both urban and rural, in all parts of the Land of Israel is the focal point of the Zionist effort to redeem the country, to maintain vital security areas, and serves as a reservoir of strength and inspiration for the renewal of the pioneering spirit."[1] Likud leaders referred to the building of settlements as "the creation of facts," which would prevent any withdrawal from the West Bank in the future.

The Likud was backed in its settlement venture by Gush Emunim (Block of the Faithful), a religious group founded to promote Jewish settlements in the West Bank. The group itself was formed three years earlier at a new settlement on the site of Kush Etzion, where four Jewish settlements had been destroyed in 1948. Claiming that the Labor government had abandoned Zionism, Gush leaders declared, "The Gush see themselves as a spiritual elite forced into politics by the urgency of the hour in which the Israeli Government strayed from Zionism."[2] Gush Emunim members would be key in the Likud government's program of settling more Jews in the West Bank.

The rise of Gush Emunim and the victory of Likud underscored a basic division that was taking place in Israel. Since 1967 the question of the territories had taken an increasing role in Israeli politics, religion, and ideology. The country was divided over the future of the West Bank. Those on the left favored withdrawal from the territory in the framework of a larger peace deal. Those on the right favored its retention for security and religious reasons. That fundamental question has divided the country ever since. It continues to hang over life in Israel, the great unanswered question of Israeli life.

Although Begin refused to negotiate over the future of the West Bank, he nonetheless wanted to pursue peace, as he made clear in his first address to the Knesset as prime minister. In a speech that was defiant but hopeful, Begin invoked the themes of Jewish history, suffering, and right to the land that he would so often return to while prime minister:

> We were granted our right to exist by the God of our fathers at the glimmer of the dawn of human civilization nearly four thousand years ago. For that right, which has been sanctified in Jewish blood from generation to generation, we have paid a price unexampled

in the annals of the nations. Certainly, this fact does not diminish or enfeeble our right. On the contrary. Therefore, I re-emphasize that we do not expect anyone to request, on our behalf, that our right to exist in the land of our fathers be recognized. It is a different recognition which is required between ourselves and our neighbors; recognition of sovereignty and of the common need for a life of peace and understanding. It is this mutual recognition that we look forward to. For it we shall make every possible effort.[3]

Nonetheless, Begin's policies immediately raised tensions with the United States. Although Begin signaled a willingness to withdraw from large parts of the Sinai, it did not seem a propitious time for peace with Israel's Arab neighbors—but that is exactly what happened.

"The End of the Earth": Sadat's Quest for Peace

On November 9, 1977, President Anwar Sadat addressed the Egyptian Parliament's opening session. PLO chairman Yasir Arafat, the very symbol of Palestinian resistance, was in attendance. Neither Arafat nor anyone else in the chamber was ready for what Sadat would say. Departing from his prepared text, the Egyptian president suddenly declared, "I am prepared to go to the end of the earth, and Israel will be surprised to hear me say to you: I am ready to go to their home, to the Knesset itself and to argue with them there. We have no time to waste."

A hush fell over the hall. It was several seconds before the assembly applauded, including Arafat. The PLO leader and the delegates probably believed that Sadat was only using a figure of speech. Few thought he really intended to go to the Zionist enemy's seat of government. But the Egyptian leader meant every word. In his memoirs, Sadat explained his thinking: "Egypt has become a backward country because of the slogan 'war is supreme.' Without peace, Egypt will revert to the old attitudes. It is important that we create an atmosphere that fosters development, if Egypt is to survive and become a partner in the twenty-first century, before it is too late."

Moreover, there was the exorbitant cost of the wars with Israel. Sadat made a simple calculation:

> How much have these wars cost Egypt and the Arab world since 1948? Until the October War, 99% of the economic burden was born by Egypt. Even after the October War—when the entire Arab world made a lot of money out of oil and added to their wealth— Egypt, by contrast, was drained of its resources. We did not even achieve much during the October War. We regained a very small portion of the Sinai, and we managed to reopen the Suez Canal. Against this the cost to Egypt was 14 billion pounds, plus all the losses in men and equipment. The October War also made it clear that we can gain less by war than by peace, since the United States sided with Israel during the war, and we cannot fight the United States. And the Soviet Union will never side with an Arab country as the United States did with Israel.

The only question left in Sadat's mind was how to pursue a peace initiative with Israel. Even as he met with his Saudi counterparts, King Khaled and Prince Fahd, these thoughts occupied his mind, but he did not inform them of his idea of ending hostilities with Israel. Upon returning to Egypt, he set upon a bold plan to finally end the conflict with Israel. "Why should I go round in circles to reach my target?" he thought. "Peace cannot be achieved under any circumstances. It can be achieved only through direct meetings between the parties to the conflict. Why shouldn't I go to the Israelis directly? Why shouldn't I stand before the Knesset and address the Israelis themselves as well as the whole world, putting forward the Arab cause and stating its dimensions?"

Moreover, the Egyptian leader was sure that going to Israel would have a tremendous impact on the Israeli people:

> The effect of this initiative will be to show the Israelis that they would now be dealing with a new style of Arab leadership. The Israeli leadership has been able to persuade the people that there was no hope for peace between Israel and the Arabs, and they have portrayed the Arabs as monsters who wanted only to drive

Israel into the sea. All the slogans ever written in the Egyptian and Arab press have been used by the Israelis to perpetuate the idea that there is no hope of security with the Arab world. The Israelis will not believe it when I say I will come to Israel, but I will come and they will start to believe in peace.[4]

Sadat was correct. The stunning declaration was greeted by skepticism in Israel. The head of intelligence even warned it was preparation for a surprise attack. Minister of Defense Ezer Weizman recalled, "I didn't believe a word of it! I thought his statement about coming to Jerusalem was no more than meaningless lip service, and I utterly mistrusted it."[5] Prime Minister Menachem Begin, however, decided to take Sadat's declaration at face value. In an ironic turn of events, Begin had been elected prime minister a few months earlier, ending Labor's thirty years at the head of the government. The hawkish leader had always taken a hard line toward the Arabs, favoring the establishment of a "Greater Israel," encompassing the Golan Heights, West Bank, and Gaza Strip. He had only recently renounced claims on the east bank of the Jordan River.

But the Egyptian president began his quest to regain the Sinai through negotiations. In response to Sadat's declaration, Begin announced that he "extends, on behalf of the Israeli Government, an official invitation to the President of Egypt, Anwar Sadat, to come to Jerusalem to conduct talks for a permanent peace between Israel and Egypt."[6] He could not resist adding, "I will also be happy to visit Cairo and look at the pyramids," because "after all, our forefathers helped build them."[7]

Sadat responded that he would accept Begin's invitation. Most Israelis still refused to believe it, and the director of military intelligence called it a trap. The IDF's chief of staff publicly warned of a pending Egyptian attack. But only ten days after his announcement at the National Assembly, Sadat was scheduled to land at Ben-Gurion International Airport. As the hour approached, many residents of the Jewish state doubted if he would actually show up. Israelis around the nation watched incredulously on their televisions as the plane landed. The door opened and out came Sadat himself, elegantly dressed in a blue suit, beaming with a wide grin. He was greeted with a formal welcome. A band played the national anthems of both countries, and a military honor guard lined the sides of the red carpet leading down from the airplane. Over a thousand journalists captured the moment. Applause rang from the tarmac.

Sadat was first greeted by Menachem Begin, who led him to the awaiting dignitaries. To former prime minister Golda Meir, Sadat said, "For a long time, I have looked forward to meeting you."

"But you never came," Meir responded.

"But I'm here now," Sadat replied.

He then greeted Ariel Sharon, Begin's minister of agriculture, best known to Sadat as the general who led the IDF across the Suez Canal in the war. "If you attempt to cross the west bank again, I will have you arrested," he joked, showing his disarming sense of humor.[8]

Sadat explained to the IDF chief of staff, who had warned the announced visit was merely a prelude to an attack, "I wasn't deceiving you," as his arrival clearly showed. The next day Sadat visited Jerusalem, including the Dome of the Rock and the Holocaust Museum at Yad Vashem.

The highlight of the trip, however, was Sadat's speech to the Knesset that afternoon. Would Sadat's proposal match his dramatic gestures? The packed chamber gathered, hoping to hear conciliatory words from the Egyptian president. Instead, Sadat told them, "I have not come here for a separate peace treaty. A peace agreement should be based on the following points: ending the occupation of the Arab territories occupied in 1967; achievement of the fundamental rights of the Palestinian people; and their right to self-determination, including the right to establish their own state."

The chamber began to sink into disappointment. These terms were not acceptable to the majority of the members. Then came the clincher: "I have not come here to submit a request that you evacuate from the occupied lands. Total withdrawal from Arab land occupied after 1967 is self-evident. We shall not countenance any arguments about it, nor will we go begging to anyone." Weizman scribbled to Begin and Dayan that they needed to prepare for war. They nodded in agreement. But Sadat continued, "What is peace for Israel? It means that Israel lives in the region, with her Arab neighbors in security and safety? Is that logical? I say yes. It means that Israel lives within its borders, secure against any aggression. Is that logical? I say yes. It means that Israel obtains all kinds of guarantees that will ensure these two factors. To this demand, I say yes."[9] This was more pleasing to his listeners, particularly the part about living in security and safety.

There was a method to Sadat's madness. During the course of negotiations that followed, Sadat would point out that he was not raising new demands, just restating what he had told the Knesset. Moreover, Sadat's demands—however difficult they may have been for Israel—were in return for full peace, something that had never been proposed before. Weizman noted, "As Sadat came to the end of his address, I felt that he had sprung the surprise of a political Yom Kippur (war) upon us. Leading off with a stunning piece of exhibitionism, he had taken the war out of the deserts of Sinai and carried it into the debating chamber of Israel's Knesset. In view of the whole world, he had forced us into a corner."[10]

In his reply, Begin refrained from laying out his negotiating positions and focused on the trip's importance: "I greet and welcome the President of Egypt for coming to our country and on his participating in the Knesset session. The flight time between Cairo and Jerusalem is short, but the distance between Cairo and Jerusalem was until last night almost endless. President Sadat crossed this distance courageously. We, the Jews, know how to appreciate such courage, and we know how to appreciate it in our guest, because it is with courage that we are here, and this is how we continue to exist, and shall continue to exist."[11]

That night, the two delegations assembled for dinner at the King David Hotel. Weizman recalled the tension: "Everyone seated at the table—Egyptians no less than Israelis—looked as though they had just returned from a funeral. President Sadat's speech to the Knesset had cast a gloomy spell over the first encounter around a table between the leaders of Egypt and Israel. They were staring into their soup plates, as though the only reason for coming together after all these years of enmity was to test the skills of the chef." It was bound to be awkward, the two sides having fought so many wars against each other. At times they barely seemed to recognize the other's humanity. An Israeli delegate recalled, "I realized that I was staring at the Egyptians as though they were from outer space. What had I thought previously? Had I expected their way of eating and drinking to be unlike that of ordinary mortals? I found myself waiting to see whether they'd wipe their mouths on the tablecloth. What strange thoughts can run through a man's mind after so many years of hostility!"

"Your prime minister's speech was disappointing," an Egyptian delegate told the Israelis, breaking the tense silence. Weizman replied that Sadat's speech hadn't made him dance for joy. So ended the first attempt at conversation. Then an Egyptian began talking about the reconstruction of cities along the Suez Canal that Israel had destroyed during the War of Attrition. It was an uncomfortable topic, as Weizman pointed out in his memoirs: "There were two other generals seated at the table: Dayan and Yadin, men whose orders at various times had wreaked havoc in Egypt and inflicted losses upon its people. What was going on in the minds of the Egyptians sitting beside them? Did Sadat know of my part in the order that had sent the Suez refinery up in flames? I recalled the Phantoms I had sent to set off supersonic booms over Cairo. Did the Egyptians have the same memories when they addressed me?"

"I know the Suez Canal well," Weizman told his Egyptian counterpart. "One of your snipers shot my son in the head." Another awkward silence fell. The Egyptians responded by mentioning Sadat's brother had been killed in 1973. Begin noted that Dayan and Yadin lost brothers in 1948. "The awkward silence was breaking down, but our conversation was confining itself almost exclusively to the bloodshed of the past," Weizman wrote. "Perhaps it was unavoidable. After so many years of antagonism, it would have been impossible to begin anywhere but in the past."[12] Mercifully for the delegates, the dinner finally ended.

Sadat and Begin then met privately, but the talks went nowhere. Sadat wanted a full withdrawal from the Sinai and West Bank in return for full peace. These terms were unacceptable to Begin. Realizing that Begin was intransigent on these points, Sadat decided to try talking to other cabinet members, including Defense Minister Weizman.

The two men sat down on a sofa. Both were nervous. But both were equally determined to bring peace to their long-suffering people. "Mr. President," Weizman said, "your speech in the Knesset yesterday was very harsh. There isn't a government in Israel that could accept what you said and remain in office as long as thirty seconds."

"Arab soil is sacred, and we cannot let you keep our land. But we do understand you have a security problem," Sadat replied. "It's time for us to stop killing one another," he said, reiterating his earnestness in pursuing a full peace in exchange for a full withdrawal.

"Seated at his side, I still regarded him as an enemy," Weizman recalled. "It never occurred to me that he intended to propose a full peace treaty with everything that entailed: embassies, airlines, and the lot. For my part, I hoped for nothing more than some agreement that would prevent a new war."[13] Sadat had come for full peace treaty, but the two sides remained far apart on its terms.

Despite the gaps between the two sides' positions, Sadat's trip was nonetheless of monumental importance. For the first time, Israelis saw an Arab leader who was charming, well dressed, soft-spoken, clearly wanted peace, and was willing to risk life and limb for it. Perceptions in Egypt changed as well. The people had been impressed by the welcome extended their leader by the Israelis. The Arab press refrained from traditional demonizations of the Zionist enemy and began analyzing the situation with a cooler head.

With the formalities over, bargaining now began in earnest. The two sides remained far apart. On the first official visit by an Israeli cabinet member, Weizman flew to Egypt in December 1977 to meet with Sadat. The Egyptian president reiterated his position: "I just want you to tell Begin that for things to move quickly, he must proclaim his agreement in principle to withdrawal from all the occupied territories and a solution of the Palestinian problem."

"Mr. President, that's not so easy," Weizman replied. "The Prime Minister has difficulties of his own. You can't change everything so quickly, after so many years."

"I have changed things quickly! I want you to understand: something fundamental has changed. I suggest you start regarding my people not as enemies, but as allies."

Begin's top military advisers, Moshe Dayan and Ezer Weizman, saw a full withdrawal as out of the question. "I thought we could give up Sharm el Sheikh at the tip of the Sinai and extensive portions of the Sinai, as well. On the other hand, pulling back as far as the old international frontier was out of the question. We had not constructed the Rafah settlement on the border between Egypt and the Gaza Strip and Israel and our two big airfields in the Sinai for the purpose of handing them over to the Egyptians," Weizman wrote.[14]

But Begin surprised his own military men by agreeing to a withdrawal back to the old border. His stance on the airfields and the settlements remained the same, however. He reiterated these positions in his first meeting in Egypt with Sadat. Sadat would accept the airfields, so long as they were converted from military to civilian use and were under Egyptian sovereignty. Sadat viewed any Jewish settlement in the Sinai unacceptable. Begin would not relent on either of these points. The Egyptians also demanded a withdrawal from the Palestinian territories, a demand Begin would not consider, viewing the West Bank as an integral part of the Land of Israel. Deadlock ensued for months on end. After the dramatic visit to Jerusalem, Sadat's gambit seemed to have failed. He had paid a high price in the Arab world. Demonstrations had broken out against him, and the PLO had severed its relations. Egypt would eventually be expelled from the Arab League.

Against this gloomy background, President Jimmy Carter invited the two sides to the Presidential Retreat at Camp David, Maryland. Carter and his advisers did not view the chances of success as very high, but Carter would commit an enormous personal effort in pushing the talks forward. As the two sides arrived in the Maryland mountains in September 1978, their basic positions remained unchanged. The Israelis were adamant about maintaining the Sinai settlements and air bases. They also refused to countenance Palestinian self-determination. The Egyptians remained set on obtaining the entire Sinai, with no Jewish settlers or air bases, and Israel's withdrawal from the Palestinian territories.

For ten days, the talks went nowhere. Sadat was adamant about removing the Sinai settlements. "Neither I nor my people can accept them" he told Begin.

"We will not agree to the dismantling of the settlements," Begin retorted.

"We give you peace and you want land. You do not want peace!" Sadat shouted, pounding the table. "The land is not negotiable!"[15] But Begin would not budge.

The Egyptian delegation began to pack its bags. Only Carter's personal intervention prevented them from leaving. Carter warned Sadat that leaving would endanger the U.S.-Egypt relationship. Sadat agreed to stay, provided his next concession would be his last. That concession was backing down from his demand on Israeli withdrawal from the Palestinian territories, instead accepting a formula calling for recognition of the Palestinians' "legitimate rights."

Then the Israelis made a major concession. Defense Minister Weizman explained, "I reached my decision to concede the Sinai airfields—whose military importance I rated above that of the Rafah settlements—after realizing that there was no prospect of successfully concluding the conference without such a concession on our part."[16] Weizman therefore asked if the United

States would build substitute airfields in the Negev. The Americans agreed to loan Israel $3 billion for this purpose. Another major obstacle had been cleared.

That still left the issue of the settlements. On this issue, Begin was unwavering. "My right eye will fall out, my right hand will fall off, before I ever agree to the dismantling of a Jewish settlement," Begin declared.[17] For the heir of Vladimir Jabotinsky's Revisionist Party, settlements were the very meaning of the Jewish enterprise in the Holy Land. In Zionism's early years the settlements had marked the borders of the future state, while the settlers had built up a new breed of Jew, one that farmed the land and fought to keep it, rather than the landless city dwellers of Europe, who had always been at the mercy of others. During the War of Independence they had enabled the state to withstand the Arab invasion. The battles at the settlements of Degania and Yad Mordechai had become part of Israeli lore. Where a Jew had put down a settlement, Begin would not and could not order him to withdraw.

The other delegate members, however, came to an inescapable truth. "We have to choose between a peace agreement and the Israeli settlements in the Sinai," Weizman told Begin. Moshe Dayan agreed, but Begin would not budge. As a desperate gamble, one aide suggested calling Agriculture Minister Ariel Sharon to persuade Begin to remove the settlements. Sharon was an unlikely choice: he was the driving force behind the settlement project, in the West Bank and Gaza, as well as the Sinai. "We've got nothing to lose," Weizman said. "Call him!"

Sharon was at his home when he spoke with Begin. Much to the prime minister's surprise, Sharon said, "I see no military objections to their evacuation." Begin was deeply moved. The negotiation's outcome now lay in his hands.

It was the greatest dilemma of Menachem Begin's life, and one of the most important moments in Israel's history. Begin's own advisers favored the proposal, and the United States put great pressure on Begin to accept. Begin himself wanted to be remembered as the man who brought peace to his people. Yet standing in the way was his ingrained philosophy that Jewish settlements were untouchable. Begin was a man of principle, as even his greatest foes would acknowledge. He had launched a war of terror to drive the British out of Palestine after World War II and had never backed down from his cherished principles.

The stakes could not have been higher. Israel's destruction without the aid of the largest Arab state was not possible. Egypt had fielded the largest armies in the wars between the two sides. It had led all the war efforts, and it had sustained the largest casualties. The other Arab states could not defeat the Jews without it. But would Begin be able to make the concessions that were necessary for Israel's survival? At the eleventh hour, Carter and Begin met privately. Begin told Carter that if the settlements were the only obstacle to peace, he would submit the issue to the Knesset for them to decide. Begin would honor the Knesset's decision, even if they voted to dismantle the settlements. Begin was no longer standing in the way of peace. It was the breakthrough Carter had been seeking. Sadat agreed and a treaty of peace between the two countries was signed by the two leaders that very night. In agreeing to dismantle the settlements, the hawkish Begin had not only secured peace with Egypt, he had assured that Masada would not fall again. And although a regional peace remained elusive and the Palestinian question came no closer to being resolved, for the first time in its history, residents of the Jewish state could go about their daily lives without wondering if that day would be their last.

On March 26, 1979, the Israel-Egypt Peace Treaty was formalized in a signing ceremony at the White House. In the interim, the Knesset had overwhelmingly approved of the treaty, including the dismantling of the Sinai settlements. Hundreds of journalists were at the scene, capturing every moment of what was truly a historic event, as Begin, Sadat, and Carter shook hands and congratulated each other. After the signing ceremonies, Begin gave his address:

> I have come from the Land of Israel, the Land of Zion and Jerusalem, and I stand in humility and with pride, as a son of the

Jewish people, as one of the generation of the Holocaust and the Redemption.

The ancient Jewish people gave the world the vision of eternal peace, of universal disarmament, of abolishing the teaching and learning of war. Two prophets, Yeshayahu Ben Amotz and Micha HaMorashti, having foreseen the spiritual unity of man under God—with His word coming forth from Jerusalem—gave the nations of the world the following vision expressed in identical terms: And they shall beat their swords into ploughshares and their spears into pruning hooks, Nation shall not lift up sword against nation; neither shall they know war anymore.[18]

Begin called it one of the happiest days of his life.

Israel completed its withdrawal from the Sinai in 1981—exactly one hundred years after the pogroms in Russia had spurred the first wave of Zionists to return to the Land of Israel. Masada had not fallen.

Yet even as Israel withdrew from the Sinai, a new threat arose from another quarter. Iraqi president Saddam Hussein reached a deal with the French to construct a nuclear reactor at Osirak, near Baghdad. Israeli intelligence reported that Saddam intended to use the nuclear material to build a bomb. It also estimated that an attack on Tel Aviv with such a weapon could lead to three hundred thousand casualties. Prime Minister Begin therefore authorized an air strike on the Iraqi reactor. It was a risky move. No one had ever attempted to destroy a nuclear facility before. But Begin was convinced that the possibility of a nuclear-armed Iraq represented a threat Israel could not tolerate. The mission set out on June 7, 1981. An American newspaper recorded the result:

> Like a bolt out of the Old Testament, they hurtled at Baghdad out of the setting sun. Nearing their target, six F-15 interceptors camouflaged with the desert mottle of the Israeli air force peeled off to keep guard overhead. Eight F-16 fighter-bombers roared down on the concrete dome of the Osirak nuclear reactor. In a single series of lightning passes, the little fighters dropped their payload of 2,000 [pound] bombs. Within two minutes they disappeared

cleanly into the gathering darkness, leaving behind a few puffs of flak and a fearsome new turn in a dangerous nuclear game.[19]

The attack on the Osirak reactor was a complete success. The reactor was demolished with no Israeli casualties. "There won't be another Holocaust in History," Menachem Begin declared at a press conference afterwards. "We shall defend our people with all the means at our disposal."[20] It was a pledge he would follow unerringly in his second term, with devastating and often unexpected results.

-16-

The Most Televised War in History

The Lebanon War and the Intifada, 1982–1992

A New Strategic Environment

With the Egyptian peace treaty completed and Iraq's nuclear reactor disabled, Israel entered a new period in its history. The Jewish state's focus turned from survival to security, for while no existential threats to the Jewish state existed in early 1982, the security of its citizens remained threatened: the Camp David Accords had made no progress on the Palestinian issue, and the Palestinians under Israeli control in the West Bank and Gaza remained hostile to their occupiers and loyal to the PLO. The PLO itself had reconstituted itself into a formidable opponent. After expulsions from the West Bank and then Jordan, the PLO had taken advantage of the chaos in Lebanon. As a bloody civil war raged between Christian Maronites and Muslims, the PLO aligned itself with the Muslims and took over much of the southern part of the war-torn country. Ruling as a de facto government, the PLO had built a quasi-army of roughly six thousand fighters that was stockpiled with weapons, ammunitions, and rockets, the equivalent of one infantry division. They regularly subjected northern Israel to rocket attacks and occasional infiltration raids. The IDF responded with counterattacks but failed to cripple the PLO.

One man was determined to change that. In 1981, Ariel Sharon, one of Israel's greatest generals, became minister of defense.

He viewed the situation in Lebanon as a grave threat to the Jewish state. "There was no doubt in my mind that we could not afford the paralysis of life in northern Israel and the contraction of is population that the PLO's artillery terror was bringing about," Sharon explained.[1] It was his grand design to drive the PLO entirely from Lebanon. He hoped that by eliminating the PLO, a more malleable Palestinian leadership would emerge in the occupied territories.

But that was not all. He also wanted to eject the forty thousand Syrian troops in eastern Lebanon, ostensibly there to keep the peace. Finally, he sought to install a Christian-dominated government that would be friendly to the Jewish state. These were audacious goals, but Sharon would not be dissuaded. Sharon had been nicknamed "the Bulldozer" for his single-mindedness and dogged determination to complete whatever objective he set out to achieve, no matter how far-fetched and regardless if he had been given permission. These tendencies had landed him in hot water in the 1956 war; history would now repeat itself on a larger scale. With Begin's consent, he put into a motion a series of events that would change the face of the Middle East. How much he succeeded remains debatable.

Into Lebanon

On June 6, 1982, a massive force of eighty thousand IDF troops rolled across the Lebanese border. They were backed by tanks, artillery, and warplanes. They far outnumbered their PLO foes, and their advantage in weaponry was even greater. The PLO fighters seemed completely overmatched in the initial firefights on the roads into Lebanon. PLO squads would pop up behind a tree to fire on the Israeli columns. But the poorly trained fighters were usually cut down before they could get off a shot. Another PLO squad would then emerge a short way down and suffer the same fate. The Palestinians were unable to stop the IDF in the battles along the roads, and Israeli forces advanced seventeen miles on the first day alone. The IDF encountered a tougher battle at a Crusader fort known as Beaufort, but the rout of the PLO seemed well under way.

The second day of the war, however, brought unexpected difficulties. Defeating PLO fighters required the IDF to enter the Palestinian refugee camps in southern Lebanon. This was a type of warfare for which their tanks were not well suited. The tight, narrow alleyways of the camps allowed the PLO fighters to fire on the invading forces with anti-tank weapons from short ranges and throw hand grenades into the armored vehicles. The PLO had built an impressive network of bunkers and shelters in the camps in anticipation of an Israeli attack. Worst of all, the camps were residential neighborhoods, making it easy for the resistance fighters to blend into the general population. The IDF attempted to persuade the civilians to leave the camps for their own safety, but not all heeded the call. As a result, the commanders faced a difficult decision. They could bomb the camps into submission, causing scores of civilian causalities, or they could continue to fight slowly, street by street, which would undoubtedly lead to higher Israeli casualties.

This quandary quickly reached the highest levels of the chain of command. Late in the evening on the second day of the war, the IDF's field commanders gathered to discuss their options. Sharon recalled the meeting:

> This meeting started about 1:00 a.m. All the divisional commanders were there as well as many of the staff officers. In my military experience—perhaps in anyone's military experience—this was a highly unusual meeting, one in which moral issues, not tactical or strategic ones, dominated the discussion. As the night wore on, the small room we were meeting in became shrouded with cigarette smoke. Despite the crowded discomfort of the place, the discussion was intense and quiet, at times almost whispered. I had known most of these people for years; there was hardly one I hadn't been in battle with. I knew them as professional officers, men who had war in their blood. They knew precisely the price we would pay the next day if we decided not to blast the road open from the air—their soldiers' lives, perhaps their own lives.
>
> As we talked, messages came in the next room from the front

announcing new developments, adding to the tension. The Israeli army had never consciously and unnecessarily caused civilian casualties—that was a value built into its ethos. What should we do now? Should we pay the price to keep this value, should we make the sacrifices? When we finally finished early in the morning, every single one of the officers present had expressed himself. To a man they recommended that we not use the air force but instead continue house-to-house as we had done that day, in order to harm the Palestinian and Lebanese civilians as little as possible. And after listening to the soul-searching that had gone on for hours, that was the decision I took. I don't know if any other army in the world would have spent a night in the middle of a war, with all the war's problems, discussing such an issue, let alone making such a decision.[2]

The pledge not to use the air force in residential neighborhoods, however, proved harder to keep than the IDF commanders imagined. Nowhere was this more apparent than at a fierce battle in a refugee camp known as Ein Hilweh. Prior to the assault, IAF planes were sent in, but their payloads were leaflets warning civilians to leave. Many fled. The assault on the camp began as Israeli tanks and infantry moved into the camp. They were quickly met by a murderous hail of fire. With their casualties mounting, Israeli commanders concluded they had no choice but to call in heavy air and artillery strikes to root out the entrenched fighters. As bombs exploded in the refugee camp for the next few days, the stench of gunpowder, overflowing sewage, and rotting corpses permeated the thick summer air. The blasts reverberated around the camp, shaking the rickety buildings to their very foundations. The tactic worked, albeit not as quickly as the IDF commanders would have liked or were expecting. Infantry and tanks advanced into the bombed-out rubble, slowly but surely defeating the staunch resistance. The Israeli soldiers become numbed to the carnage and destruction around them but pressed on. The PLO fighters' last stand at Ein Hilweh took place in a mosque. Although they were completely surrounded and grenades were exploding all around them, the remnant refused to surrender. The bombing continued until the mosque collapsed on the defenders, suddenly ending the ferocious battle of Ein Hilweh.

Israeli forces continued to press north. With the IDF skirting the Syrian army's positions in eastern Lebanon, Syria reinforced its forces. Begin and Sharon viewed this as a provocation. Negotiations brokered by the United States failed, and Israeli and Syrian forces clashed. A bloody battle took place at a village called Ain Dara, where IDF units had hoped to break through the Syrian lines. But Syrian forces, having fared so poorly in the 1967 and 1973 wars, held off the IDF for two days. British journalist Robert Fisk described the destruction as he arrived at the scene shortly after the battle ended:

> The Syrian tanks were still burning fiercely beside the narrow village road, their wounded and dead crews lying in the fields, soaked in blood. Ain Dara itself had been wrecked, its houses smashed open by Israeli shellfire: many were still on fire. Down the road, the occupants of a lunatic asylum, long deserted by their nurses, wailed from the roof of their shattered home. When we first arrived, a Syrian soldier walked up to my driver holding the headless body of his officer. He was crying, choking on his tears, pleading with us to put the corpse in the truck of our car and take it to Damascus. Four tanks in the main street had been hit from the air; flames were still licking around their tracks and ammunition lockers, scoring the rocks black around them. A lorry had been flattened by bombs in the small wadi while an armored vehicle, burnt out, lay on the edge of a 400-foot precipice.
>
> Through the orchards, mingled with the dark green foliage, a score of bright golden fires burnt out of control, incinerated tanks whose crews had already been burned alive. The orchards had born bitter fruit in Ain Dara that summer. In the center of the village street, a Syrian truck stood intact, its cargo of corpses and wounded heaped together, the blood of the living onto the bodies of their comrades. A soldier sat on the back, the top of his head broken open and some kind of white liquid mixing with the blood

that poured in a torrent down his face. He, too, was weeping, and his lips were moving slowly in what might have been a prayer.

Ain Dara had been a mountain village, a small section of descending road which curved back on itself, lined on both sides with pleasant shambling villas, many of them now burning. From their ruins came other soldiers, some with bandages around their heads or arms, but still holding their rifles and wearing their steel helmets. They had fought off the Israelis for almost two days and the proof of their victory could just be seen at the corner of the village road. Across the valley, amid the pine trees, columns of blue smoke rose from burning Israeli tanks. They had been ambushed, not only by the Syrian armor that had just been destroyed from the air, but by Syrian troops firing Sagger missiles out of Ain Dara and the surrounding forest. The invincible army had been brought to a halt.[3]

Aggravated by the delay at Ain Dara, Sharon ordered decisive action. The IDF would destroy the surface-to-air missile batteries that had caused so much damage in the 1973 war. The air force had put a tremendous effort into defeating these batteries. Using American-built F-15s and Israeli-built Kfir fighter planes, the plan worked to perfection, as nearly all the Syrian missile sites were destroyed in a complex secret operation. The IAF then trounced the Syrian air force, destroying about eighty enemy planes, with no losses of their own. With the Syrian ground troops denuded of cover, the IDF mauled the Syrians in the battles that followed. An IAF pilot described a successful mission:

> I was given a ground support mission to hit a target near the road that led east from Beirut. We came in from the east because we wanted the sun behind us, and since there was very little SAM activity at the time, there wasn't a problem. As we approached our target, we communicated with our forces on the ground and tried to get the exact location of their vehicles. The sky was constantly disturbed by black puffs at about 10,000 feet, but the forces underneath were living through a shelling attack. It was very hard to get an exact location from them. We circled around the approxi-

mate point, but could not identify any of our troops. At last, I spotted some heavy artillery with help from a guiding voice from an officer on the ground. All systems were go and we dove for a positive identification of the target. After verifying with some local groups that we were not going against our own troops, we went in. I dropped first and my wingman a few seconds after me. It was a hit. Another pair of Kfirs joined in on the channel, and I directed them to another battery a bit west of the one we had just hit. Since there were explosions still going on the ground, it was easy for them to come in after us and destroy their target. It did not take more than thirty seconds before we heard the ground forces cheer on the radio.[4]

The Soviets, worried about their client, began stockpiling weapons in preparation for an airlift to Syria if needed. The United States, mindful of avoiding another superpower confrontation like in 1973, imposed a ceasefire on Israel before they could eject the Syrians from Lebanon as Sharon had hoped.

Into Beirut

The ceasefire did not apply to Israeli forces engaged against the PLO, however, and by June 14, IDF forces had surrounded Beirut—despite Sharon's previous assertions to the cabinet that Beirut was not part of the operation's objectives. Yasir Arafat, the PLO leader, kept the PLO headquarters and fighters in the western part of the city. Israel's leaders faced another quandary: a ground assault into Beirut would cause massive casualties among the local populace, as well as for the IDF. But not attacking would be dangerous as well, as Begin told the cabinet:

> Gentlemen, if we continue to remain at the gates of Beirut as we are doing now, we may bring disaster on ourselves. . . . Do we want to harm the civilian population? But to argue that in case we may hit some civilians we shouldn't do anything—where would such an argument lead us? If we do not enter Beirut, the victory will be the PLO's. Arafat will claim that the PLO is alive, in position, and armed. . . . Gentlemen, we are at a turning point that may lead to

a national crisis. Our people will not tolerate weeks and months of an unnecessary mobilization of the army, with extended service, where we are being shot at and our boys are being hurt. We cannot withstand a static war without anything being done for victory.[5]

Begin and the cabinet settled on a policy of air, naval, and artillery strikes. The bombardment continued for seven weeks. In addition, the IDF cut the city's water and electricity. Slowly, west Beirut was demolished under the weight of the massive strikes. Fisk described the situation inside the besieged capital: "After a month under siege and under repeated bombardment and air attack, it had become a place of anxiety and filth. It smelled dirty. Even when the city was not under fire, clouds of smoke drifted through the streets from piles of burning garbage. The streets reeked of feces, for now that the Israelis had cut the water supply, the residents and refugees emptied their ordure in the gutters, just as the inhabitants of medieval cities had done."[6]

As Begin and Sharon hoped, the PLO took heavy losses. But so did the civilian population of Beirut—thousands were killed and wounded. The siege of Beirut came at a heavy price for the Jewish state. According to one historian, "The Lebanese war was the most televised war in history up to that time. The daily television transmission of Israeli artillery bombarding Beirut, the columns of smoke, dust and fire rising in the air, and the close-up pictures of the destruction, including serious damage to a hospital, caused immense harm to Israel's international image and much anguished discussion within Israel itself."[7] Arafat would regularly appear in front of the cameras with civilians injured during the attacks. The West, once solidly behind the Jewish state, began to shift toward the PLO. In Tel Aviv tens of thousands of Israelis protested the war, the first such protests in the Jewish state's history.

Determined to crush the PLO at all costs, Sharon stepped up the attacks in early August. Israeli aircraft pummeled west Beirut continuously. Robert Fisk described the ensuing carnage:

At the height of the shelling, I ran from house to house like a frightened cat, scampering between doorways, all the way from the AP bureau to the American University hospital. There was blood everywhere. In the emergency wards, I found at least 100 men, women, and children lying in their own blood on the floor or moaning on trolleys in the corridors. There was vomit and blood on the walls. An old half-naked woman was lying on a stretcher, whimpering and crying with her breasts lolling off the stretcher, in other people's blood on the floor.

I ran across the mortuary. Limbs and arms—dozens of them— had been stacked against the wall. There were several dead babies laying in plastic bags on the floor, neatly packaged up, the cellophane stapled above the tiny heads, as if they were being sent back to a manufacturer for repairs. Human entrails lay across the pathway outside. Someone had been trying to piece bodies together. They had found a leg, a torso, but three arms lay next to the torso. The place was slippery, and it reeked of people's stomachs.[8]

As Israeli air strikes reached their crescendo, the United States finally brokered a deal. The PLO would be evacuated to distant Tunisia. Prime Minister Begin was pleased. At a speech on August 8, he explained why he had made the decision to go to war: "We could have gone on seeing our civilians injured in Metulla or Kiryat Shmona or Nahariya. We could have gone on counting those killed by explosive charges left in a Jerusalem supermarket, or a Petah Tikva bus stop. All the orders to carry out these acts of murder and sabotage came from Beirut. Should we have reconciled ourselves to the ceaseless killing of civilians, even the agreement ending hostilities reached last summer, which the terrorists interpreted as an agreement permitting them to strike at us from every side, besides Southern Lebanon?" Begin then summed up what the war had accomplished: "During the past nine weeks, we have, in effect, destroyed the combat potential of 20,000 terrorists. We hold 9,000 in prison camp. Between 2,000 and 3,000 were killed and between 7,000 and 9,000 have been captured and cut off in Beirut. They have decided to leave there only because they have no possibility of remaining there. The problem will be solved."[9]

Israel had driven the PLO out of its base in Lebanon and secured safety from the artillery attacks that had crippled the lives of its citizens in the northern part of the country. But the PLO was not dead. Most of all, the Palestinian issue remained unresolved: the Palestinians still had no state, Israel still ruled over hostile populations in Gaza and the West Bank, and huge numbers of their people remained in refugee camps. Israel may have won the battle in Lebanon, but it only delayed another day of reckoning with the Palestinians. The only question was when and where it would come.

But before the next showdown between Israel and the Palestinians occurred, a horrific event that still stains the collective memory of the Palestinians and the Israeli-Arab conflict took place. Although the PLO had evacuated Beirut, Sharon worried about PLO fighters hiding among the civilians in the Sabra and Shatilla refugee camps in the western portion of the city. The IDF agreed to secure the city while the Christian militia, known as the Phalange, would enter the camps and root out the remaining PLO fighters. Sharon later explained that by letting the Phalange go into the camps, the IDF would avoid taking casualties, and the Arabic-speaking Lebanese soldiers, who were familiar with the PLO's fighting methods, would be better equipped for the situation. Israeli commanders ordered the Phalange not to harm any civilians. Phalange leaders, however, quickly countermanded these orders, telling their men to shoot young Palestinians in order to precipitate a mass flight from the camp.

As the Phalange moved into the refugee camps, the IDF provided searchlights to illuminate the camps at night. The Phalangists quickly moved into the back alleys and out of sight of the surrounding IDF officers. As they did, they began to massacre the refugees. An Israeli journalist described what he saw after the Phalangists had been in the camps for two nights:

> The Phalangists were driving a long line of women, children, and elderly people ahead of them at a run. Some of these people were covered with blood, others were wailing and shouting and some had their faces streaked with dirt. [The refugees] shouted at us

that they had been separated from their menfolk, whom the Phalangists had marched off elsewhere. The members of the Lebanese Forces tried to prevent us from filming by shooing us away from the edge of the camp. While we were arguing with them, a senior IDF officer brought the procession to a halt. Through a loudspeaker mounted on one of the buildings, the women and children were told to return to their homes. The Christian militiamen were ordered to leave the area, and thus the massacre was halted.[10]

As the Phalange left, journalists entered the camps, only to behold a terrible spectacle: hundreds of bodies littered the streets, and corpses were piled on top of each other, their blood pouring out on the ground. One of the first reporters to arrive on the scene wrote:

They were everywhere—in the road, in laneways, in back yards and broken rooms, beneath crumpled masonry and across the top of garbage tips. The murderers—the Christian militiamen whom Israel had let into the camps to "flush out the terrorists"— had only just left. In some cases, the blood was still wet on the ground. When we had seen a hundred bodies, we stopped counting. Down every alleyway, there were corpses—women, young men, babies and grandparents—lying together in lazy and terrible profusion where they had been knifed or machine-gunned to death. Each corridor through the rubble produced more bodies. The patients at a Palestinian hospital had disappeared after gunmen ordered the doctors to leave. Everywhere we found signs of hastily dug graves. Perhaps 1,000 people were butchered; probably half that number again. . . .

Inside the ruins of the Shatilla hovels, families had retreated to their bedrooms, when the militiamen came through the front door and there they lay, slumped over the beds, pushed beneath chairs, hurled over cooking pots. Many of the women here had been raped, their clothes lying across the floor, their naked bodies thrown on top of their husbands or brothers, all now dark with death.

There was another laneway deeper inside the camp, where

another bulldozer had left its tracks in the mud. We followed these tracks until we came to 100 square yards of newly ploughed earth. Flies carpeted the ground and there again was the familiar, fine, sweet, terrible smell. We looked at this place, all of us suspecting what was indeed the terrible truth, that this was a hastily dug mass grave.[11]

As the photographs were relayed in Israel and around the world, the Israeli public exploded. The citizen-soldiers of the Jewish state were well aware of the realities of war, but the deliberate mass slaughter of civilians was well beyond the realm of Israeli sensibilities. The war itself had been longer and bloodier than they were expecting. The bombing of Beirut with its many civilian casualties had been difficult to accept, but at least it had served a military purpose. The massacre at Sabra and Shatilla, however, served no military purpose. It had stained the honor of the previously unimpeachable Israel Defense Forces, the pride of the Jewish state.[12]

Shortly afterward, a massive crowd numbering in the hundreds of thousands gathered in Tel Aviv and demanded an investigation. Prime Minister Begin resisted at first, but the public sentiment was overwhelming. Begin bowed to public pressure and approved an independent commission, led by Chief Justice Yitzchak Kahan. The Kahan Commission found that there had been no Israeli conspiracy to commit a massacre, but that the highest echelons of the policymakers should have known that the Phalange would commit such actions, and that the high command had been derelict in their duties. Most of all, the commission singled out Minister of Defense Sharon, charging him with having failed to take into account the possibility that the Phalange would seek to take revenge on the people of the camps and not ordering measures to ensure that such an event would occur. Only a month before the massacre, Israel's chief of intelligence warned, "There will still be terrorists in Beirut, and the Phalange will find a way to get them and settle old scores. One day, the murders will start, and they will just go on and on without end. Every paper in the world will be there to cover the extermination. They'll photograph anyone who is so much as scratched! How can we operate without being tainted? They'll lay everything at our doorstep!"[13] This warning was prescient. Palestinians continue to blame Israel—and Sharon, in particular—for the massacres at Sabra and Shatilla to this day. As for the minister of defense, Sharon resigned his post but remained in the cabinet. He had expelled the PLO from Lebanon, but the cost had been higher than he, or anyone else, had expected.

"A Pressure-Cooker Ready to Explode": The Intifada

Begin and Sharon had hoped the expulsion of the PLO from Lebanon would lead to a more pliable Palestinian leadership in the occupied territories, one that would acquiesce to Israeli rule. It became clear after the expulsion that no such leadership was emerging. Quite to the contrary, the Palestinians became increasingly disgruntled with their situation. Aside from the humiliation of being ruled by the IDF, Palestinians chafed at the increasing Jewish population in the West Bank and Gaza. Since the 1967 war, Israel had established civilian towns and outposts in the territories, known as "settlements." These settlements had grown greatly since the Likud takeover in 1977. All these factors combined to make a highly combustible situation. By 1987 the tension was palpable. A noted Palestinian scholar wrote, "Gaza resembles a pressure-cooker ready to explode. In this 'forgotten corner of Palestine,' one witnesses overcrowding, poverty, hatred, violence, oppression, poor sanitation, anger, frustration, drugs, and crime. The Palestinian population is daily becoming more resentful and rebellious."[14] This state of affairs was not lost on Israelis. A journalist described the situation in Jerusalem: "You can feel the tension. Worshippers—Jews and Muslims alike—scurry rather than walk. Tourists cluster together and are protected by armed soldiers. Shopkeepers keep one hand on their shutters in anticipation of the next riot. In Gaza, you drive a car with Israeli plates at peril. . . . The atmosphere is reflected throughout Judea and Samaria and even some parts of Galilee. . . . Suspicion has become endemic in our lives. . . . Fear, suspicion, and growing hatred have replaced any hope of dialogue between Israelis and Palestinians."[15]

The tension finally erupted in December 1987. It began with riots in Gaza's refugee camps and quickly spread to the rest of the Gaza Strip, reaching a crescendo at Gaza City. For twelve straight days Palestinian protestors blocked large portions of Gaza City with stone barricades and burning tires. Large groups of youths surrounded the burning tires, shouting anti-Israel slogans. The smoke billowed for hours at a time. The youthful rebels threw stones at IDF patrols and congregated outside of mosques, daring the army to disperse them by force. In short order, the entire Gaza Strip and West Bank rose up against Israeli rule. Led by youthful demonstrators, the rioters waved Palestinian flags, sang slogans, threw stones at Israeli vehicles, and set up roadblocks to prevent Israeli civilians and the military from entering. The civil disobedience became known as the intifada (Arabic for "shaking off"). Underground pamphlets encouraged the demonstrators. One leaflet read:

> We will die standing, we will not submit. They will not pass, and the uprising will triumph. O masses of our heroic people; O people of stones and Molotov cocktails; you are recording in blood and light the history of your Arab nation. You are making light with your blood to brighten the long darkness of the Arabs. O children of the triumphant uprising, our uprising is continuing, baptized in chaste blood day after day, watering the beloved soil of the homeland, realizing important achievements and strengthened by the little triumphs which are accumulating one above the other to make great victories and establish the independent Palestinian state.[16]

An American observer described a typical intifada scene during her visit to the West Bank:

> As we turned west from the main highway onto a narrow road, our path was blocked by boulders. Only a bicycle could weave

between them. Youths from the next village had blocked the way so that army vehicles and settlers' cars could not pass. The army used to enter the village with a convoy of jeeps and busses. . . . Settlers drove through the village late at night, honking the car horns, shouting curses. . . . The villagers' stone barrier thus kept out—or at least slowed down—the intruder. Once their youthful outpost decided that we had friendly intentions, they helped us remove enough boulders so that our bus could pass. Then they rolled the rocks back into place. . . . Hand-painted Palestinian flags fluttered from the electricity wires, and graffiti were scrawled on the walls—"Down with the Occupation," and "Palestine Lives." Behind their makeshift barricades, the villagers viewed themselves as a liberated island.[17]

Another foreign correspondent captured the squalor and anger at a Gaza refugee camp:

A strong breeze blew off the Mediterranean, carrying the stench from Gaza's open sewers and rotting garbage into our nostrils as we drove through a labyrinth of tumbledown streets heading for Beach Refugee Camp. In one deserted alleyway hemmed in by low stone buildings and almost too narrow for our car to pass, a few lumps of concrete and twisted metal beams had been laid across the street as a makeshift roadblock. . . . Within minutes, we pulled up again in another rutted dirt street inside Beach Camp itself. Home to more than 50,000 people, half of them under age 15, all across the camp, these kids moved in wandering bands, scavenging, cursing, and falling into stone-throwing battles with the Israeli patrols. The place was a warren of flimsy huts with asbestos sheeting on the roofs. Here and there, rivulets of raw sewage ran through the camp, which overflowed when the rains came, flooding the place with waste. Rough open latrines lay outside shacks. From time to time these pits overflowed, the filthy water sloshing into the cramped rooms where people ate and slept.[18]

Israeli forces regularly clashed with the demonstrators. At first they used live ammunition, and then tear gas and rubber bullets—

nothing seemed to work. It was not the type of action the military was equipped to handle. The men of the IDF were trained to fight other armies in conventional battles. They had no experience or practice in dispersing demonstrators. The first time they used tear gas, it wafted back in their direction, affecting them more than the rioters. Nor did the soldiers know how to deal with mass demonstrations that involved young and old, men and women. Foot patrols proved inadequate. If the patrols faced down the demonstrators without using deadly force, they might have their weapons taken from them or be trampled. When the IDF switched to car patrols, the demonstrators laid nails and broken glass on the roads, rendering the motorized vehicles useless. The streets belonged to the demonstrators.

As with the Lebanon war, television cameras were everywhere, transmitting pictures of heavily armed Israeli troops shooting at stone-throwing youths. As Palestinian casualties mounted, Israel's image plummeted in the West. Conversely, the intifada was a massive public relations coup for the Palestinians. Meanwhile, an internal debate raged within Israel on how to deal with the uprising. The government of Yitzchak Shamir refused to negotiate with the PLO, which it viewed as a terrorist organization. Instead, the administration launched a massive crackdown on the demonstrators. By 1990, ten thousand heavily armed IDF soldiers patrolled the alleys and streets of the West Bank and Gaza, breaking into homes and stores where they suspected arms were being held, broke up demonstrations forcefully using clubs, arrests, and occasional shootings. Hastily-built Israeli prisons soon overflowed with an estimated 13,000 Palestinians arrested for civil disobedience.

One such prison was the Gaza Beach Detention Camp, housing 1,000 inmates, mostly teenage demonstrators. Penned into crammed cages, the inmates were routinely interrogated by the security services with harsh methods, including beatings and physical abuse. Israeli peace activist and journalist Ari Shavit, assigned to the camp as part of his reservist duties in 1991, described his experiences there: "Most of the reservists are shocked when they first arrive here. They find the sight of other people caged in pens inconceivable. When they hear the screaming for the first time, they are shaken."[19] But if the brutality of the crackdown in Gaza was bad, what Shavit noted most of all was that it was unnecessary: "in Gaza there are no excuses. Gaza is not even needed for our defense like some strategic heights in the West Bank; it is not even a historically charged terrain like some parts of Judea and Samaria. Gaza is clear and simple. It is the epitome of the absurdity of occupation." Shavit saw the occupation in Gaza as a violation of Zionist ethics: "if we are to have such a prison, we must betray ourselves. We must betray everything we were to be and everything we are to be. So the question now is not land for peace. The question is land for our decency. Land for our humanity. Land for our very soul."[20]

The intifada dragged on for years, leading to one of the most divisive and tortured periods in the Jewish state's turbulent history. The dilemma was grave; continued rule over the Palestinians eroded morale within the state and sapped Israel's credibility abroad, but withdrawal from the territories could also lead to increased attacks by those who wanted to return all of Israel to the Palestinians. There were other important issues as well: ruling over disenfranchised Arabs countered the democratic nature of the state, but extending citizenship to them would defeat the purpose of a Jewish state.

An increasing loud Israeli left launched scathing attacks on the right-wing Likud government and its allies, who would not consider withdrawal from the territories. A former Labor Knesset member wrote, "The 'Greater Israel' movement, whose aim is to incorporate the West Bank and Gaza into the nation's borders, had led Zionism and Israel astray, diverting them from their proper path and deflecting them from the achievement of their fundamental goals. We must now ask ourselves some painful questions. Is Israel still a Jewish state? Is Israel still a democratic state? Are Israel's economy and society still productive? Is Israel a state—or society—of tolerance? And is Israel approaching peace?"[21] Similarly, novelist Yitzhar Smilansky wrote in Israel's largest newspaper, "I am not blind to the fact that there are two sides to this painful situation, that it is not a question of evil oppressors persecuting the righteous oppressed. But neither am I blind to the fact that there is a way out of this quagmire . . . that in the end there will be no choice but to talk, and to negotiate a solution that will bring peace. So why not do it now instead of later—after another death and another and another?"[22] Indeed, a large and vocal peace movement grew during these years, calling for an immediate end to the occupation.

The uprising changed daily for ordinary Israeli citizens as well. The very same Arab neighborhoods and bazaars that Israelis had so enthusiastically flocked to after the 1967 war became places of danger, where a wayward Jew could expect a stone thrown at their car or even be stabbed to death. Young army conscripts feared that they would be sent into the West Bank to quash youth demonstrations, an assignment few cherished. American Jews, once so proud of their Israeli brethren, spoke in harsher terms than ever about the Jewish state. Israel's relations with the United States became strained, a grave development for the tiny state in need of stronger allies. For the first time, Israel's long-term future seemed bleak. But no solution emerged.

The debate within the country continued for years, with no discernible change. The deadlock was finally broken in June 1992, when Yitzchak Rabin's Labor Party soundly defeated Yitzchak Shamir's Likud Party. Rabin had campaigned on a platform of negotiations with the Palestinians. The stage was set for a new era in the Middle East.

-17-

Enough of Blood and Tears!

The Oslo Peace Process, 1992–2001

A Time of High Hopes

On July 13, 1992, newly elected prime minister Yitzchak Rabin outlined the new Israeli policy toward the Palestinians in his inaugural speech to the Knesset: "As a first step toward a permanent solution, we shall discuss the institution of autonomy in Judea, Samaria, and the Gaza district. We do not intend to lose precious time. The Government's first directive to the negotiating teams will be to step up the talks and hold ongoing discussion between the two sides."[1]

This was a major departure from previous Israeli policy. Rabin then appealed directly to the Palestinians:

> I wish to say from this rostrum: we have been fated to live together on the same patch of land, in the same country. We lead our lives with you, beside you and against you.
>
> You have failed in the war against us. One hundred years of your bloodshed and terror against us have brought you only suffering, humiliation, bereavement, and pain. You have lost thousands of your sons and daughters, and you are losing ground all the time. For forty-four years, you have been living under a delusion. Your leaders have led you all through lies and deceit. They

have missed every opportunity, rejected all the proposals for a settlement, and have taken you from one tragedy to another.

And you, Palestinians who live in the territories, who live in the wretched poverty of Gaza and Khan Yunis, in the refugee camps of Hebron and Nablus; you who have never known a single day of freedom and joy in your lives—listen to us, if only this once. We offer you the fairest and most viable proposal from our standpoint today—autonomy-self-government—with all its advantages and limitations. You will not get everything you want. Perhaps neither will we.

So once and for all, take your destiny in your hands. Don't lose this opportunity that may never return. Take our proposal seriously—to avoid further suffering and grief; to end the shedding of tears and blood. Enough of tears and blood![2]

Rabin quickly authorized talks with the Palestinians. Foreign Minister Shimon Peres conducted high-level negotiations with PLO representatives in Oslo, Norway. During the talks, Peres and the Palestinians forged a Declaration of Principles designed to turn over responsibility for government in Gaza and the West Bank to the PLO. The Declaration of Principles did not deal with every issue, however. The tricky questions of Jerusalem, borders, and refugees would be dealt with at a later date. By the summer of 1993 the two sides were ready to sign the Declaration of Principles. Israeli negotiators demanded that before any signing take place, the PLO renounce violence and terror and recognize the State of Israel. When Arafat agreed to this demand in a letter, Rabin responded by recognizing the PLO as the representative of the Palestinian people for the first time. The breakthrough had finally occurred. The next step was the formal signing of the Declaration of Principles, the first-ever agreement between the Israelis and Palestinians.

The sun shone brightly on the south lawn of the White House on the morning of September 13, 1993. September is normally the most pleasant time of year in the nation's capital, the heat and humidity of the summer months having given way to mild temperatures and cool breezes, but that day was particularly gorgeous. It was the perfect setting for the momentous event that was to take place. As foreign dignitaries and former presidents gathered, Israel and the PLO, for so long mortal enemies, prepared to sign the Declaration of Principles that would formally end the state of war between them and enter a peace process designed to turn over authority for the rule of the West Bank and Gaza to the PLO. As television cameras from all over the world rolled, PLO leader Yasir Arafat and Israeli prime minister Yitzchak Rabin signed all the relevant papers while Foreign Minister Shimon Peres, the main architect of the accords, looked on. Once the documents were signed, President Bill Clinton wrapped his long arms around the two men and brought them together. Arafat, beaming with pleasure, eagerly grasped Rabin's hand and shook it vigorously several times. For years an international pariah, Arafat reveled in his newfound respectability.

Rabin, however, was clearly uneasy with the gesture. He was well aware that Arafat had personally ordered the killings of numerous Israelis. He did not want to shake hands with the murderer of his people. But he also knew that by doing so he would show the world that Israel wanted peace and was willing to take major risks to achieve it, including shaking hands with the seemingly bitterest and most implacable of foes. Breathing in deeply, he gingerly accepted Arafat's hand. Arafat vigorously shook the old warrior's hand.

People the world over saw the handshake—a sight most thought not possible. Much had changed in recent years: the Soviet Union had fallen, apartheid was being dismantled in South Africa, and now at last, it seemed Arabs and Jews were ending their war. The drama of the moment was heightened by Rabin's unforgettable words:

> Let me say to you, the Palestinians, we are destined to live together on the same soil in the same land. We, the soldiers who have returned from battle stained with blood, we who have seen our relatives and friends killed before our eyes, we who have attended

their funerals and cannot look into the eyes of their parents and orphans, we who have come from a land where parents bury their children, we who have fought against you, the Palestinians—we say to you in a loud and clear voice: Enough of blood and tears. Enough! We harbor no hatred toward you. We have no desire for revenge. We, like you, are people who want to build a home, plant a tree, love, live side by side with you—in dignity, in empathy, as human beings, as free men. We are today giving peace a chance and saying to you: Enough. Let's pray that a day will come when we all will say farewell to arms.[3]

It was a moment of high expectations, yet it was also clear that the road ahead would be difficult. The peace process had opponents among Palestinians and Israelis. Many Palestinians viewed any accommodation with Israel as a capitulation and would accept only the destruction of the Jewish state and its replacement with a Palestinian one. Others claimed Israel would never agree to terms most Palestinians expected, such as the return of refugees, a complete withdrawal to the pre-1967 borders, and a Palestinian capital in Jerusalem. In Israel, critics charged that the peace process would give Arafat the legitimacy to build an armed terror network inside the territories that would be dedicated to the destruction of the Jewish state. Rabin addressed these criticisms in a speech presenting the accords to the Knesset for their approval:

> We cannot choose our neighbors and our enemies, including the cruelest of them. We must deal with what we have: the PLO, which has fought against us and against whom we fought. . . . We could have rejected the proposals of the PLO with disgust, in which case we would have unwittingly been among those responsible for the continuation of the vicious circle in which we have been forced to live so far: war, terrorism, and violence.
>
> We chose to adopt another way, one which offers chance and hope. We decided to recognize the PLO as the representative of the Palestinian people. . . . We took this step only after the PLO undertook, in its letters to the prime minister, the following: recognition of Israel's right to live in peace and security, and a com-

mitment to settle any future controversy by peaceful means and through negotiations.[4]

By a close vote, the Knesset approved the accords. The peace process continued. The Declaration of Principles was an agreement on the framework of an autonomy plan; no tangible change occurred on the ground. But in March 1994, Israel and the PLO signed the "Cairo Accords," under which Israeli troops would withdraw from the entire Gaza Strip and the West Bank town of Jericho. Once again, there was strong opposition within Israel. Rabin spoke to the Knesset: "I want to tell the truth. For twenty-seven years, we have controlled another people that do not want our rule. . . . It cannot be denied: the continued rule of a foreign people who does not want us has a price. There is first of all, a painful price: the price of constant confrontation between us and them. For six and a half years, we have witnessed a popular Palestinian uprising against our rule—the intifada."[5] Israelis were tired of the intifada. The Cairo Accords passed.

In May 1994 Israeli troops pulled out of Gaza for the first time since 1967. Joyous throngs raised the Palestinian flag and cheered their newfound autonomy. But for many Palestinians the highlight was the return of their long-exiled leader Yasir Arafat to Gaza, where he made his new headquarters. On the long-anticipated day, Arafat was escorted to the Gaza border by Egyptian president Hosni Mubarak. At the Rafa border crossing, Arafat entered Palestine for the first time in twenty-seven years. Upon arrival, he flashed a victory sign to the cheering throng, before dropping to his knees and kissing the ground and offering a prayer. A slew of Palestinian police officers surrounded him and raised him up, eliciting more cheers from the crowd. The Palestinian leader then entered a motorcade and sped toward Gaza City. The largest city in Gaza was lined with Palestinian flags, welcome banners, and thousands of cheering people. The motorcade pulled up in front of the legislative council building, while people sang and danced. When Arafat exited the motorcade, a wild roar ran through the crowd. Arafat beamed with delight and waved to his people. Celebration shots rang through the area. Israelis looked on with skepticism. Many charged that by allowing Arafat to return, Israel was allowing the terrorist mastermind to build a new base closer to his target, the Jewish state. Even those who supported the peace process doubted that the former terrorist had really changed. But for the time being, Israel's old enemy was its partner in peace, and many hoped it was the beginning of the end of decades of violence.

Momentous changes continued to ripple through the region. After brief negotiations, Israel and Jordan signed a peace treaty in October 1994. Coming on the heels of the Oslo Accords, it was another sign of a potential new Middle East and another victory for Rabin and his push to end the Arab-Israeli conflict. At a bleak desert outpost between the two countries in the Arava desert, the leaders of Israel and Jordan staged an impressive ceremony attended by more than forty-five hundred dignitaries and presided over by Bill Clinton. The atmosphere differed drastically from the signing ceremony at the White House the year before. This time Rabin was clearly at ease, signing the documents with no reservations or doubts about the correctness of his course of action. His handshake with King Hussein was warm and enthusiastic. All the speakers envisioned a bright future. Clinton declared the peace would last generations, benefiting both people and growing to new heights. King Hussein called the Arava a "valley of peace," while Rabin spoke of replacing the land mines along the border with fields of grain.[6] There were grandiose plans for joint Israeli-Jordanian cooperation. Shimon Peres even proposed building a canal from the Red Sea to the Dead Sea. Anything, it seemed, would be possible in the new Middle East that was taking shape.

With peace treaties signed with their neighbors and negotiations ongoing with the Palestinians, many Israeli began to feel that the siege might finally be coming to an end. Fifty nations had recognized Israel since the Oslo Accords, including several Muslim ones. Foreign investment tripled in four years, tourism increased, and the economy grew by a staggering 20 percent. A typical citizen could now afford a car for use on the new highway system, book a vacation abroad, and shop in the many malls that were sprouting up across the country. Israel had never experienced such prosperity. Even defense spending decreased. Adding to the growing sense of security was a massive influx of immigrants from the former Soviet Union. Now free to choose their homes, hundreds of thousands of Jews fled Eastern Europe, mainly to Israel. By the end of the decade, nearly one million had arrived in the Promised Land. Like all immigrants, they experienced hardships, but their road to integration in Israeli society was much easier than their North African or Middle Eastern predecessors. Their expertise in technical fields stimulated the economy, and their sheer numbers made it less likely that an enemy coalition would wipe away the Jewish state. It was a time of growing optimism and expectation in Israel. The peace process had already brought tangible gains to the people. But the negotiations were far from over.

Throughout 1995 talks centered on extending Palestinian autonomy to the West Bank. In the midst of the negotiations, the Islamic rejectionist group Hamas exploded a bomb on a Jerusalem bus. The *New York Times* reported on the attack, as well as on the charged political environment surrounding it:

> The explosion tore through the back of the bus at about 7:45 a.m. in the Ramat Eshkol neighborhood of northern Jerusalem, ripping apart its rear section and shattering the windows of a second bus that the first was overtaking. . . .
>
> One witness to the blast, Rahel Shamir, was just opening the shutters of her ground-floor bedroom on the Levi Eshkol Boulevard when a fierce explosion sent a fireball high into the air. "The fire moved to the next bus, and I saw dead people—one without a head, some on the ground," she said between bouts of emotion. "Two girls came toward me totally naked, covered with blood, with no hair. I washed their faces. One asked me, "Am I going to die?"
>
> . . . Helicopters hovered overhead and the smell of spilled diesel fuel filled the air as investigators poured over the wreckage, followed by ultra-orthodox Jews whose function it is in such disasters to gather every bit of human flesh and blood.

But no sooner were the dead and wounded taken away than several hundred protestors became increasingly loud and sometimes violent. Their target was the ongoing negotiations over self-rule in the occupied Arab territories, which have drawn increasingly desperate resistance from Israeli settlers and conservatives. . . . The most militant demonstrators, members of the Jewish Defense League, screamed "Death to Rabin" and "Death to Arabs" and tangled several, times with the police.[7]

Despite the opposition, Israel and the PLO agreed that Israeli troops would withdraw from the largest Palestinian cities in the West Bank. After a rancorous debate, the Knesset approved the Oslo II Accords by a razor-thin margin of sixty-one to fifty-nine. Israeli troops began withdrawing from West Bank towns shortly afterward and were replaced by the Palestinian Authority. Turning over the West Bank, however, polarized Israeli society. Many viewed the land as an inviolable part of Eretz Israel. Others charged that Arafat was not restraining the terror attacks that were becoming a routine part of Israeli life. Critics pointed out that terror had increased since the Oslo process began.

To counter these charges, those in favor of the process held a massive rally in Tel Aviv on November 4, 1995. Perhaps one hundred thousand people joined in singing "The Song of Peace," led by none other than Yitzchak Rabin and Shimon Peres. Rabin addressed the crowd: "This rally must send a message to the Israeli public, to the Jewish community throughout the world, to many, many in the Arab world and in the entire world, that the people of Israel want peace, support peace, and for that, I thank you very much."[8]

It would be his last public speech. A few minutes later, Rabin was shot to death by an ultra-Orthodox religious student. A wave of horror and disgust spread across the Jewish state. It had never seemed possible that one of their own could do such a thing. Moreover, without the hard-nosed general, the peace process seemed imperiled. This fact was not lost on the eighty-five heads of state who attended Rabin's funeral on Mount Herzl in West Jerusalem.

In a solemn ceremony, the fallen soldier was laid to rest alongside Israel's other founders and prime ministers. The speakers included two Arab heads of state, Egypt's Hosni Mubarak, who called on all sides to redouble their efforts toward peace, and Jordan's King Hussein, who called Rabin "a soldier of peace." But it was U.S. president Bill Clinton's two simple words delivered in Hebrew, "Shalom haver" (Good-bye friend), that captured the Israeli public's imagination. The American president pleaded with Israelis to stay on the righteous course, even in the face of the loss of their beloved leader.

The fears of the speakers at Rabin's funeral were soon realized. The popularity of his successor, Shimon Peres, was crippled by a wave of Hamas bombing attacks. As a result, the right-wing government of Benjamin Netanyahu won the elections of 1996. As promised, Netanyahu slowed down the peace process, demanding concrete efforts from Arafat in fighting terror and slackening the pace of IDF withdrawals from the West Bank. In January 1997, after months of drawn-out negotiations, Netanyahu agreed to an IDF withdrawal from 80 percent of the West Bank town of Hebron. The peace process kept going.

So did the violence. On July 30, 1997, two simultaneous suicide bombs killed sixteen and wounded over one hundred at Jerusalem's main fruit and vegetable market. A twenty-two-year-old American student taking summer classes at Hebrew University's Mount Scopus campus recalled:

> When the news came in of the attacks, several of the overseas students rushed to call home and inform their family they were not harmed. Our Israeli teachers were much more composed. They shrugged off the news, saying in effect, "Life must go on." It was their way of dealing with terror. They would not let it cripple them. A few days later, I saw this code in action. I was riding the bus through central Jerusalem when we passed the market that had been the site of the attack. I remembered the pictures in the newspapers of the mayhem, destruction, and blood. Yet they had already rebuilt the destroyed stalls, the vendors were

selling their goods, and the customers had returned. "This is how it needs to be," a young Israeli woman explained to me. When I got off at Jerusalem's central bus station a few minutes later, another bus pulled up and its passengers disembarked. With the two buses emptied, the station platform was densely packed. I suddenly realized that it would be the perfect opportunity for a suicide bomber to attack. If there were two suicide attacks like at the fruit market, the damage would be enormous. I panicked as I realized that my life might be in jeopardy. When I regained my composure, it occurred to me that this was the fear that Israelis lived with every day. It was a lesson I never forgot. I never experienced fear like that in America, even after the September 11 attacks.[9]

Against this backdrop of violence, the peace process crawled forward. In October 1998 Netanyahu agreed to the Wye River Accords, which mandated further withdrawals from the West Bank. The following year, Netanyahu lost the premiership to Ehud Barak, who came into office convinced that he could conclude a lasting peace with the Palestinians. The stage was stage for the climax of the Oslo peace process.

Things Fall Apart

In the summer of 2000 outgoing U.S. president Bill Clinton, eager to burnish his legacy with a major foreign policy triumph, gathered the two sides together for intensive talks aimed at a final settlement. The site he chose was Camp David, hoping that the location would help recapture some of the spirit of the previous Arab-Israel peacemaking breakthrough. After fourteen days, the two sides were not able to complete a final deal. Clinton and Barak were sorely disappointed, but negotiations continued afterward. U.S. negotiators were impressed that Barak seemed willing to go further than any previous Israeli leader, but it remained unclear if the terms Barak offered would be acceptable to his cabinet and the Knesset, in particular his apparent willingness to accept Palestinian sovereignty over the Temple Mount. Barak responded that it was simply a negotiating point and that he had not accepted anything yet. The peace process spurted on.

However, on September 28, new Likud leader Ariel Sharon visited the Temple Mount, sacred to Muslims as the Haram al-Sharif, site of the Al-Aqsa Mosque. Sharon's visit to the site was seen as a provocation by the Arabs. Sharon was a hated figure among the Arabs, considered as the architect of the Sabra and Shatilla massacres. Arab opposition to his visit mounted well ahead of time. On the day of the visit, Israeli security forces were on high alert. Over a thousand policemen were deployed around the Temple Mount, including snipers positioned at key points, as well as riot officers armed with clubs, helmets, and plastic shields. Helicopters circled above as Sharon entered the compound. The Likud leader spoke briefly, declaring that the Temple Mount would remain under Israeli control forever. As he walked around the mount, he was ringed in tightly by an entourage of security personnel, protecting him from danger. Despite the precautions, Arab anger boiled over, and shouts of "Murderer!" "We remember Sabra and Shatilla!" "With blood and fire we'll free Al-Aqsa!" rang out all over the compound. As Sharon left, he could not resist repeating Motta Gur's famous words from 1967: "The Temple Mount is still in our hands!" A full-scale riot broke out, and Arab youth shouting "God is great!" hurled stones, chairs, and anything else they could get their hands on at the riot police.[10] The police fought back, firing rubber bullets at the crowd, injuring four. The riots soon spread out to East Jerusalem, where angry youth hurled stones at Israeli police and buses.

Riots erupted all over the West Bank and Gaza as Palestinians clashed with Israelis. This time, however, the Palestinians had guns. At one particularly fierce firefight, a French TV crew captured a twelve-year-old Palestinian boy, Muhammad Dura, and his father caught between the two sides. The boy's terror and his father's attempts to protect him could clearly be seen. The boy was killed by the crossfire, shot four times. The video and the boy's death became symbolic to the Palestinians of the Israelis' callousness and brutality, and the scene was played repeatedly on Palestinian television.

Similarly, an incident in the West Bank came to represent to the Israelis the Arabs' barbarism. Three army reservists took a wrong turn and ended up in Ramallah. When several Palestinians began chasing the car, the soldiers ran into a Palestinian police station. The policemen tried to protect them, but a huge mob quickly gathered outside the building and called for their deaths. After a brief standoff, the mob, consisting of well over one thousand people, broke into the station and overpowered the policemen. In full view of television cameras, the mob ran through the station and beat the reservists to death. One man ran to a window, proudly displayed his bloodstained hands, and flashed a victory sign, to the cheers of the massive crowd. The mob proceeded to attach one of the bodies to a rope and lowered it down to the courtyard, where the mob stomped and beat the corpse. Around the same time, the wife of one of the reservists called her husband on his cell phone. "I have just killed your husband," an unfamiliar voice told her.[11] The bodies of the mutilated soldiers were delivered to the Israeli army later that day.

The second intifada had begun, and it was even bloodier than the first. Nonetheless, negotiations for a final settlement continued, driven by Bill Clinton's personal involvement in the process. The final proposal made in December 2000, known as the Clinton Plan, offered the Palestinians a state in Gaza and 95 percent of the West Bank. The Palestinians would control East Jerusalem and the Haram al-Sharif, while the Israelis would rule West Jerusalem and the Western Wall. Prime Minister Ehud Barak's government accepted the proposal. It was now the Palestinians' turn. If they accepted, the Jewish state might finally join the ranks of other nations, whose citizens go about their daily affairs in peace and safety. Although Israel's survival was ensured regardless of the outcome, its people yearned for a normal existence. Barak felt confident the Palestinians would accept.

But it was not to be. Arafat expressed reservations about the status of Jerusalem's holy sites, refusing to accept no less than the entire Western Wall and the Dome of the Rock, a demand the Israelis could not accept. Arafat also demanded the right of return for all Palestinians to their former homes, including those in Israel. In their response to the Clinton Plan, the Palestinian negotiators concluded, "We cannot accept a proposal that secures neither the establishment of a viable Palestinian state nor the right of the Palestinian refugees to return to their homes."[12]

The peace process was dead. With it died any chance for a truly normal life in Israel. Masada might not have been in danger of falling, but true security remained as elusive as ever. The next decade would feature new methods of gaining security.

-18-

The Third Way

Second Intifada and Beyond, 2001–2014

"The Bulldozer" Takes Command

On February 6, 2001, Israelis went to the polls to elect a prime minister. Before them were two starkly contrasting choices: incumbent Ehud Barak favored continued negotiations with the Palestinian Authority, while challenger Ariel Sharon, known as "the Bulldozer," promised security. In a sweeping mandate, Israelis chose Sharon.

It was not clear how Sharon would achieve his stated goal. From 1967 to 1993 Israel had sought to control the Palestinian areas. That policy had failed. From 1993 to 2001 Israel had tried to negotiate a settlement with the Palestinians. That policy, too, had failed. A third way had to be found. Sharon's policies would eventually come to be known as "unilateral separation," or "disengagement." It was not a preplanned policy, but the result of events and the government's responses to them.

The first priority was dealing with the suicide attacks that were crippling life in Israel. In response to these attacks, Sharon adopted a policy of targeted killings of Hamas leaders. Yet there was no letup in the bombings. A journalist recorded the aftermath of one such attack that killed twelve people at Jerusalem's Moment Café, a popular meeting place for members of the Peace Now movement:

Amidst the bedlam the police were already taping off an area around the still-smoking black shell of the café. I managed to slip across the cordon into the immediate area of the explosion. It was a scene that stays etched in my memory. Gelled blood and torn clothing lay everywhere across the pavement. I picked my way past a handbag, a mobile phone, pieces of a barstool, and a woman's high-heeled shoe still containing her severed foot. On stretchers and along the side of the road outside the café, dozens of people lay shredded by flying glass and timber, doctors working quickly to staunch the bleeding and relieve the pain. Some of those caught up in the blast for who it was too late had already been zipped up in black body bags. After examining each patient the paramedics would discard their surgical gloves, which lay strewn across the street. Trampled underfoot by the rescue workers or run over by the wheels of passing ambulances, they would fill with air before making a peculiar popping sound. Overhead a helicopter hovered, its floodlight beam and that of the blue beacons on the convoy of ambulances reflected eerily in the pools of blood along the street.[1]

The next day, an even deadlier suicide attack killed twenty-six people who had gathered to celebrate the first night of Passover at a hotel in the quiet seaside town of Netanya. Sharon determined that it was time for decisive action. Operation Defensive Shield was the largest IDF operation since the Lebanon war. The government called it a large-scale counterterrorism operation. IDF units rolled into all major West Bank towns, encountering heavy resistance as they went, particularly at Jenin. Palestinians referred to Jenin as "the capital of suicide attackers." At least twenty-eight attacks had been staged from Jenin since the second intifada erupted nearly two years earlier. The Palestinian fighters had prepared for an IDF incursion, laying hundreds of explosives in the streets, hoping they would be triggered by Israeli soldiers or vehicles. To deal with the bombs, the IDF sent massive bulldozers ahead of the main body to clear the explosives. The engineering units detonated hundreds of these devices. The IDF moved in slowly, hampered by the tight alleyways and houses within the city and refugee camp. Snipers hid among the urban edifices, shooting at the advancing soldiers. At the center of the city, the Palestinians defenses were the strongest. Fighters shot from rooftops and alleyways. The IDF called in helicopters to attack the roof positions, using overwhelming firepower. The roofs were cleared, but the fighters remained entrenched in the buildings. For this job the IDF brought in a special weapon: a huge armored bulldozer twenty feet high and weighing twenty tons, the D-9 caterpillar. At first they were used to clear the explosives. Now they were being used to break open houses containing fighters. The huge shovel was used to break off entire walls of houses. Perhaps two hundred buildings were leveled in this manner. Most civilians had fled, but some remained. Therefore, before going into a house, IDF officers would warn the residents, bellowing into megaphones, "People in the house, get out. We don't want you to be hurt," or "People in the house, we are going to come in." The civilians who came out were ordered to stand up and lift their shirts to reveal whether they were wearing suicide belts packed with explosives. It had become a standard IDF procedure. But in at least one case, soldiers mistook a medical support belt for a suicide vest and killed an innocent man. The combination of the D-9 bulldozers and superior firepower eventually carried the fight for the IDF. The remaining fighters were rooted out and captured. The brutal battle over, the Israeli troops withdrew from the urban inferno.

Palestinian sources claimed hundreds of civilians had been deliberately killed in Jenin, but a subsequent UN investigation cleared Israel of such charges. In addition to the battles in the West Bank towns, the IDF surrounded and cut off Arafat's Ramallah compound for over a month. Operation Defensive Shield was a great success from the Israeli perspective. They had captured huge weapons and ammunition stores and killed, wounded, and captured hundreds of fighters.

And yet the suicide attacks continued. Israel responded with a policy of "targeted assassinations" aimed at the planners behind the suicide operations. Under this plan, Israel killed the founder of Hamas, Sheik Ahmed Yassin, and shortly afterwards, his successor. Although this policy was controversial abroad, it had wide support in Israel. Another policy intended to stop suicide bombers and other attackers was the establishment of roadblocks and checkpoints throughout the West Bank. And some suicide bombers and arms smugglers were indeed caught before they could do any harm. Palestinians chafed at the massive delays and the lack of freedom of movement the roadblocks created. The IDF insisted on its continuation, yet it caused hardships for the soldiers manning the checkpoints as well. An Israeli conscript explained the moral ambiguity of halting civilians during the course of their daily affairs:

> The true nature of the soldier's mission usually dawns upon him shortly after he arrives on the scene. He might be told, as I was in one of my first shifts, to close a checkpoint for some reason or other. A Palestinian child comes by and asks to pass on his way home from school. When the child discovers the checkpoint is closed and he cannot get home, he begins to cry. Recalling the freedom and responsibility to exercise his clear-headed judgment, the soldier decides to let the child through. A while later, ten crying children come along. They all heard about a new way to pass through the checkpoint even when it is officially closed.
>
> At this point, facing the crying children, the soldier realizes he made a mistake—not because these children are dangerous, but because he cannot afford to be fooled by ten-year-olds, or by anyone, for that matter. There cannot be an efficient way to pass through his checkpoint. Any such weakness may be used against him, against his mission. He cannot tell harmless ten-year-olds from ten-year-olds who were sent to trick him. Everyone should know that at his checkpoint it is up to him and him alone to decide what will be their fate.
>
> The soldier realizes he should not act on empathy since empathy can be manipulated. But can he suppress this natural sentiment? It takes time. The next time a similar situation occurs, he does not let the child pass. Instead, he smiles at him or tries to

make him laugh. These are also signs of weakness. His lenience toward children, if it becomes known, may be used against him. He realizes this when families start encouraging their children to soften him up so they will pass through more quickly. If the harmless Palestinians manipulate him, so can the harmful ones. He makes a further effort to suppress his empathy.

But if sentiments such as empathy are not proper guides for his clear-headed judgment, which are? Strictly following orders leads to failure, as well. He was ordered to use his clear-headed judgment to recognize cases to which the orders do not apply. How should he recognize such cases? Any rule for recognizing exceptions will have to be assigned a higher-order rule by which to recognize its own exceptions. This seems to lead to an infinite regress. The soldier gradually realizes that he cannot but fail his mission: the rules and orders he had to guide him are conditional on his judgment, which cannot be guided by any rule.[2]

Nonetheless, Israeli society remained much more united than during the first intifada. This time the Israeli public felt they were entirely in the right; they were under attack, and the attacks had to be halted. The government's policies of targeted assassination, reprisals, and armed incursions were all overwhelmingly popular with the public. Unlike the first intifada, there was no soul-searching within Israel, no anguished debates over the morality of the Jewish state's actions. Those calling for negotiations and restraint met with incredulity from a people under constant bombardment.

In its quest to secure the lives and safety of its citizens, Israel would adopt a new project: a massive defense wall separating Israel from the West Bank. The barrier drew heavy criticism abroad and made life for ordinary Palestinians even more difficult, but Israelis saw it as a necessary step for their personal safety. Across the length of the West Bank, a huge separation barrier began to rise, signaling at least a temporary end to attempts at peaceable coexistence. The wall was decried as a land grab by the Palestinians, who bitterly opposed its construction on land they considered theirs. An Israeli activist described demonstrations in one Palestinian village against the barrier:

One day in early 2004, at 9:00 in the morning, farmers in the village of Bil'in noticed a bulldozer. It was accompanied by a force of Border Police troops and came to demarcate the route of the separation barrier. The village's residents were ready for it. They did not know precisely when the work would begin but they had prepared in advance for the day when the heavy machinery would clamber onto their land. The farmers who saw the approaching bulldozer and military force immediately informed the members of the village's popular committee that was formed to wage the struggle, together with the village council, against the construction of the barrier. Within minutes, dozens of villagers had left their homes, workplaces and agricultural plots, and advanced toward the point where the bulldozer was located. . . .

The demonstrations became a fixed routine: They marched each week on Fridays—sometimes dozens, usually hundreds, and in some cases even thousands—from the village's mosque, along the narrow asphalt path winding among the olive trees, toward the checkpoint marking the route of the separation barrier that was under construction. When the demonstrators reached a certain point, the soldiers or border policemen (the units alternated every few months) began to fire stun grenades, tear gas canisters, and rubber-coated bullets, and they also usually charged at the demonstrators in order to distance them from the barrier that was being built.

Dozens of demonstrators, mainly Palestinian, but also Israelis and foreign activists, were injured during these demonstrations. But the demonstrations did not stop. The protest against the barrier whose construction was advancing on Bil'ins land became a ritual that was covered by the Israeli, Palestinian and foreign media, and within a few months the struggle in Bil'in became a symbol of the popular Palestinian fight against the separation barrier.[3]

The issue of the barrier eventually reached the Israeli High Court of Justice. The High Court ordered some changes in the route of the barrier, but not a halt to the wall itself. Over the next few years, suicide attacks into Israel declined precipitously—by as much as 84 percent in two years. From the Israeli government's perspective, the barrier had been a necessity.

It was a major step in the direction of unilateral separation. Prime Minister Sharon announced the next step, what he called a "Disengagement Plan," to a surprised audience in December 2003. The plan was to withdraw army units and settlers from the most heavily populated Palestinian areas. Sharon hoped that this redeployment would reduce the friction between the Israelis and Palestinians. Although he was vague in this speech, Sharon would later reveal that he planned no less than the withdrawal of all Jewish settlers and troops from Gaza. Roughly five thousand Jewish settlers resided in Gaza, requiring a regular contingent of IDF forces to guard them. Critics argued that the army's withdrawal would allow for an arms buildup in the strip. But the plan had overwhelming support among the public, who viewed Gaza as an unnecessary drain of resources. There were no major sites of Jewish importance there; it had never been a part of the Land of Israel. Moreover, Sharon obtained two major diplomatic concessions from the United States as part of the disengagement plan. In exchange for the withdrawal, the Bush Administration announced that the Palestinian refugees should be settled in areas outside of Israel's pre-1967 borders. In addition, Bush announced that the United States did not expect a full and complete return to the 1949 Armistice lines as part of any future peace deal. The plan passed the Knesset by a vote of sixty-seven to forty-four.

Prior to the withdrawal, Sharon issued a stern warning to the Palestinians: "Those who continue to fight us will meet the full force of the Israeli army and security forces," Sharon declared, putting the burden of proof on the Palestinians. "The world is waiting for the Palestinian response—a hand stretched out to peace or the fire of terror. To an outstretched hand we shall respond with an olive branch, but we shall fight fire with harshest fire ever."[4] In the summer of 2005, the withdrawal was carried out with little resistance from the Gaza settlers and amidst praise from the

United States and Europe. Unilateral separation had been achieved in Gaza. It had also been achieved in Lebanon with the withdrawal of the IDF from a security zone in 2000. Israel's borders and troop deployments had been altered. The main architect of the new security plan, however, would not see its results. In January 2006 Ariel Sharon, the most popular prime minister in the Jewish state's history and the last remaining statesman from the pioneer generation Israelis so revered, slipped into a coma and did not recover. Still, the question remained: would the new policies finally achieve the security Israel had yearned for so many years?

"No One Believes This Will Be the Last War"

The answer came in the summer of 2006, less than a year after the Gaza withdrawal. Hamas, now in control after expelling the Palestinian Authority, began launching rocket attacks over the border fence into Israel. The IDF responded with raids into the Gaza Strip. Hamas fighters then surprised an Israeli unit, appearing on the other side of the border after having dug a one-thousand-foot tunnel. Two Israeli soldiers were killed and one was captured. Events quickly escalated, with Israel launching air strikes and then a ground operation into the strip. While southern Israel was under attack, northern Israel came under an even larger threat. The Lebanese Shiite group Hezbollah began launching Iranian-supplied rockets into Israeli cities, nearly bringing life to a halt in the north. Residents either fled to the southern part of the country or huddled in bomb shelters. The Israeli government responded with a massive military campaign, the largest since the 1982 war. The air force led the way, but they alone could not cripple Hezbollah's inventory hidden in tunnels and dug-in positions. It would be necessary to send in ground troops, and that would mean casualties.

The heaviest fighting occurred in the southern Lebanese town of Bint Jbail, known to Hezbollah as "the capital of the resistance." As the Israeli soldiers approached the town, most residents fled. Only a few fighters were reported to have stayed behind. The infantrymen entered the town to dead silence. It was their third day in Lebanon, and all had been quiet. The lead company entered an open area surrounded by apartment buildings. They had unknowingly walked into a Hezbollah ambush. The hidden fighters sprang from the buildings, peppering the soldiers with bullets, grenades, and missiles. Nearly all fifteen members of the lead platoon were hit. As they tended to their wounded, a commander threw himself on a grenade, losing his life but saving two of his men. More soldiers arrived at the scene and began firing back. Back at headquarters, command debated over whether to send in helicopters, as they might be vulnerable to the missile attacks. After six hours of fighting, Israeli artillery fired smoke shells, providing the necessary cover for the helicopters to fly in. The helicopters brought in fresh troops and took away the injured. IDF sources reported eight soldiers and 30 Hezbollah fighters killed in the battle. Israeli forces pulled back, allowing Hezbollah to claim victory. Before moving into any more areas, the IAF was sent in again to carpet bomb, clearing the areas of fighters, but also increasing civilian casualties.

The carpet bombing, however, increased the risk of civilian casualties. Hundreds of thousands of Lebanese civilians fled north as the IAF pounded the countryside in search of Hezbollah rocket-launching sites. At the town of Kfar Qana, thirty Lebanese civilians were killed in the largest single incident of the war. The event was televised the world over and caused great harm to Israel's position. Over a thousand Lebanese civilians were killed during the course of the war, leading to heavy international criticism of Israel. Hezbollah continued to fire rockets into northern Israel, leading nearly a million Israelis to flee from their homes in the north to safety elsewhere in the country. After a month of fighting, international and U.S. pressure led Israel and Hezbollah to accept a cease-fire. Life slowly returned to normal in northern Israel and southern Lebanon. The war ended with Hezbollah still entrenched in southern Lebanon.

Although large-scale fighting between Israel and Hezbollah did not return, the Gaza border remained the site of frequent violence. Hamas continued to target southern Israeli towns with rockets, and Israel responded with actions ranging from drone strikes to full-scale ground incursions. The largest such incursion was Operation Cast Lead in the winter of 2008, lasting three weeks and involving air, naval, and ground attacks into Gaza to destroy launch sites and Hamas fighters. It was a difficult battle. Hamas operatives had turned Gaza into a deadly maze of tunnels, booby traps, and hidden bombs. They had hidden their weapons in mosques, schools, and civilian housing. Hamas fighters dressed in civilian clothing to blend in with the population. A typical Hamas tactic was to quickly emerge from a hidden tunnel, fire a rifle or anti-tank missile, and then disappear back into the tunnel. To combat these tactics, the IDF treated the operation as a war instead of a police action. As they approached the battle zones, they warned civilians to leave. If they took fire, they responded with heavy artillery and air strikes. Then they moved in behind tanks and armored bulldozers, leveling buildings as they went. The infantry rode inside armored vehicles, spending as little time in the open as possible. They would then break into the side walls rather than going in the front and risk detonating a hidden bomb. Bomb-sniffing dogs sought out hidden bombs, and sappers would then defuse them. Snipers and suicide bombers dressed as civilians continued to harass the advancing units. It was a vicious, brutal, urban battle, and several hundred civilians were killed, mostly during the course of the air strikes.[5]

Facing world condemnation, the IDF brought a group of foreign journalists to observe the fighting from outer positions along the Gaza Strip. One astute reporter wrote:

> To the west, the Mediterranean sparkled and winked. To the east, columns of black smoke rose and gunfire pounded. In between, Israeli Merkava tanks plowed through potato and strawberry fields on Thursday as paratroopers guarded their ground, a mix of ruins that once were handsome two-story homes and farm fields that had been turned into rocket-launching pads against Israel by Hamas.
>
> On a day of unusually harsh Israeli attacks inside the center of Gaza City to the south, the neighborhood of Atara, in northwest

Gaza, was a scene of devastation, filled with impromptu tank-track roads, rusting greenhouses, and blown-up houses that had been booby-trapped with mannequins, explosive devices and tunnels. The area was a major site for Hamas launchers over the past eight years. But for the past 10 days, it has been a ghost town inhabited only by Israeli soldiers, many of them from a paratroopers' unit, the 101, founded in 1953 as the first elite Israeli unit aimed at striking Palestinian guerrillas infiltrating from Gaza.

The fact that more than half a century later Israel remains at war with the children and grandchildren of those guerillas has served as a kind of overpowering historical backdrop to the 20-day-old military confrontation that Israel says is aimed at ending Hamas rocket fire onto Israeli towns. No one believes this will be the last war.[6]

It certainly was not the last war. Rocket fire continued from Gaza, and even the deployment of the "Iron Dome" anti-missile system was not enough to prevent all rockets from reaching major Israeli population centers. Israel responded with Operation Pillar of Defense in November 2012, the largest incursion since Operation Cast Lead in 2008. For eight days, Israeli forces pounded suspected rocket sites in Gaza. The IDF also assassinated the military leader of Hamas, Ahmad Jabari, who had survived four previous attempts on his life. A newspaper report described the attack, along with the expected defiant aftermath:

Ahmad Jabari probably didn't even hear the missile that killed him, launched from a drone in the skies over Gaza City as he drove in an ordinary saloon car through a quiet residential street. It was a remarkably successful operation even for Israel's security forces, who pride themselves on their skill at dispatching their enemies. Grainy black and white footage taken from a drone showed a minibus full of passengers drive past the target's car to a safe distance, seconds before the missile exploded. A piece of chassis is seen spinning into the air, as the vehicle, in flames, continues drunkenly for a few yards. Unlike targeted killings in the past, there was no collateral damage except for some minor injuries from flying glass. Israel has learnt the hard way that accidentally killing civilians carries a damaging political cost. . . .

Jabari's funeral, less than twenty-four hours after his death, was emotional and angry. Supporters called for revenge, demanded more rocket attacks, and shot into the air in defiance. But the usual masked gunmen stayed away fearing Israeli attack, and a sense of fear took hold among Hamas supporters: Israel had tracked down and killed one of its wiliest enemies in the heart of his stronghold.[7]

In the wake of Operation Pillar of Defense and the ongoing tension in Gaza and the West Bank, it was clear that Israel would never experience true peace until the Palestinian issue was resolved. To this end U.S. secretary of state John Kerry launched yet another peace initiative in 2013. Kerry shuttled back and forth between Israeli and Palestinian leaders but was unable to produce any major breakthroughs. By early 2014 the latest U.S. peace drive seemed to be at an end, the latest diplomatic causality in a long line of failed peace initiatives. Since the end of the Oslo process the United States had attempted various talks, including the "Road Map" to peace in 2002–3, the Annapolis meetings in 2007, Secretary of State Hillary Clinton's peace initiative in 2012, and finally the Kerry initiative. None were able to achieve any substantial progress. True peace with the Palestinians remains as elusive as ever. It may continue to be so in the foreseeable future, much to the chagrin of Israelis, but the continued conflict with the Palestinians does not threaten the existence of the Jewish state. Unrest in Egypt and Syria in recent years has caused some to worry about what a reversal of Egyptian policy toward Israel would mean for the Jewish state. But Egypt and Syria combined do not possess the military strength to annihilate Israel, nor is there any indication that they intend do so.

While the lack of peace with the Palestinians remains a source of concern, a new threat has arisen that many Israelis do considered a danger to their very existence. Since its takeover by religious clerics in 1979, the Islamic Republic of Iran has been hostile to the Jewish state. Iran openly backed Hamas and Hezbollah, supplying them with weapons used against Israel. When Iran announced it was commencing a nuclear program (ostensibly for peaceful purposes), it raised great suspicion in Israel. Israeli leaders repeatedly stated that a nuclear-armed Iran would represent an existential danger to the Jewish state. These fears were reinforced by Iranian president Mahmoud Ahmadinejad's many pronouncements that Israel should be wiped off the map. Several rounds of international sanctions failed to dissuade Iran from continuing its nuclear program. In September 2012 Israeli prime minister Benjamin Netanyahu appeared at the UN General Assembly and warned that Iran was nearing a nuclear capability, and this represented a "red line" for Israel. The day before, Ahmadinejad had also appeared at the General Assembly, stating that Israel had no root in the Middle East and would not last. In March 2013 U.S. president Barack Obama met with Netanyahu in Jerusalem. Obama emphasized that diplomacy might still work, but Netanyahu stressed that time was running out.

Looking forward, the same pattern that has existed since the Camp David Accords will likely continue into the near future: a state of Israel that cannot be defeated by the conventional armies of its neighbors, but one whose citizens' security cannot be guaranteed from terror attacks. For while the Palestinians cannot defeat Israel, neither can the Jewish state impose a military solution on the Palestinians. Until a political accommodation is reached, violence will continue to be the norm in the Holy Land. The other major source of Israeli concern is nuclear weapons in the hands of an enemy state. And while a nuclear-armed Iran will not be beneficial for the Jewish state, it is also highly unlikely that it would mean the end of Israel. Peace may not be right around the corner, but the threat of annihilation that hung over the Jewish state for so many years seems to have finally passed.

Conclusion

Why Masada Did Not Fall

We now turn to the question posed at the beginning of this book: how was it possible that a scattered, stateless, and powerless people was able to reconstitute itself and overcome repeated threats of annihilation at the hands of its more numerous neighbors? We have seen how inauspicious the beginning of the Zionist movement was, when a few unprepared pioneers arrived to settle in Palestine. Yet they built up their numbers and began to reclaim the land and create a new society. They were then granted the charter they had been seeking, giving them a legal basis for their state. As the Mandate developed, Arab hostility grew, culminating in riots and a full-scale revolt in 1936, a war with the Palestinian Arabs in 1948, and a war with the Arab states the same year. The Jewish state teetered on the brink of annihilation, but not only survived the war, it expanded its boundaries. Egyptian military might threatened the new state in 1956, but Israel decisively defeated the Egyptian army, destroyed the fedayeen bases in Gaza, and opened the Straits of Tiran. This led to ten years of growth, but in 1967 Israel was again threatened: a ring of hostile armies greatly outnumbered the Israeli forces. But the IDF destroyed them in a single week. The surprise attack in 1973 might well have succeeded had the IDF not recovered and repelled the invaders from its borders. With the Camp David Accords in

1979, Israel's survival was ensured. Masada did not fall, despite the terrific odds.

The single greatest factor in the Zionists' triumph over the Arabs was their more advanced development. The Jews, coming from Europe, were a modern, literate, scientific people, whose level of development reflected the society from which they came. Once in Palestine, they were able to re-create a modern society similar to those in Europe, complete with financial institutions, universities, industries, and—most conspicuously—a strong military. By contrast, Arab society in the second half of the twentieth century was at a lower level of socioeconomic development than that of contemporaneous Europe and the Jews of Palestine. In terms of key indices such as literacy rates, education, and gross domestic product per capita, the Jews had an enormous advantage. A 1931 British census reported Arab literacy in Palestine at 18 percent, compared to near universal literacy for Jews;[1] only 30 percent of Palestinian children attended primary school, while almost all of the Yishuv's children did. The differences in literacy and education were even greater with Israel's Arab neighbors; Egypt's literacy rates by 1960 were at a mere 25 percent.[2] In addition, the Arab states' economies remained overwhelmingly agricultural; in 1939, 53 percent of the Palestinian workforce and 62 percent of Egypt's were agricultural workers, compared to only 19 percent of the Jews in Palestine.[3] The result was a far higher Jewish per capita output. In 1950, the Jewish state's per capita gross domestic product was three times that of the Palestinians and Egyptians, and by the time of the Six-Day War in 1967 it had grown to six times as much.[4] These differences would have enormous effects on the region's history.

British Mandatory officials were aware of these differences. A British report from 1937 noted, "The Jews in the main represent a cross-section of western society at its highest point of efficiency. As a result there is a de facto inequality which at every point of contact between the two societies expresses itself in visible material forms." A 1944 British report observed, "The Jewish economy of Palestine is radically different from the Arab economy and is in fact not very dissimilar to that of the UK."[5]

The Arabs were also aware of these differences and strived to overcome them. As early as 1798, Napoleon's defeat of the Egyptian forces made Middle Eastern leaders all too aware of the dramatic advances that Europe had made. Europe had become the first society in history to experience an industrial revolution, unleashing an explosion in technology, manufacturing, and wealth the likes of which the world had never seen before. Spurred by the changes in Europe, Arab rulers set out to put their nations on the path to modernization. These policies of modernization were planned programs of change that sought to borrow from the West military and economic principles that would restore the Arab world to its previous greatness. But the programs proved much harder to implement than the Arab rulers envisioned; changing entire ways of thinking, living, and organizing a society were tremendous challenges. The nineteenth century saw only minor progress in the Arabs states, as modernization gained even greater momentum in Europe. By the time the first Zionists arrived in Palestine in the 1880s, the gap between them and the local Arabs was very large indeed. Another century did little to close the chasm. In 1974 Egyptian leader Anwar Sadat explained the dilemma: "The real challenge confronting peoples with deep-rooted origins who are facing the problem of civilizational progress is precisely how to renovate their civilization. They should not reject the past in the name of the present and should not renounce the modern in the name of the past. . . . Modernism is knowing the right order of priorities. . . . We should compose the suitable environment and necessary stage of development which will make us capable of invention and creativeness and consequently of true contribution to human civilization."[6] But Sadat, like his predecessors, proved unable to implement significant reforms.

The developmental disparities are noticeable at all the major points in the history of the Arab-Israeli conflict. They were the very reason Churchill set up the Mandate in the first place; he believed the Jews could advance the interests of the British Empire by developing the land quicker than the Arabs. The disparate levels of development enabled the Jews to shatter the Palestinian

Arabs' society in 1948 before holding back the invading Arab states. Much has been written about which side was responsible for the flight of the Arab refugees during the war, but the Arabs' flight was due more to the collision between a lesser-developed society and a modern one than any particular policy. The Arabs could not match the Jews' cohesion, and once hostilities began, the fabric of their society quickly unraveled, leaving them without a state as the new nation of Israel was born. Once they had their own state, the Jews could bring in and assimilate immigrants much faster than any Arab country could, despite the myriad of social problems it caused. They were then able to build a modern army, capable of performing complex maneuvers and assimilating cutting-edge weaponry into their arsenal. The IDF was thus able to outperform its foes decisively in 1956 and 1967, when its existence was threatened by its Arab neighbors. The army was also able to rebound from the disastrous surprise of the first days of the 1973 war and repel the invasions, despite being greatly outnumbered on both fronts.

In contrast, the Arab armies' performances left much to be desired. Military analyst Kenneth Pollack points to four factors that hobbled the Arab war efforts. First and foremost was the performance of the lower-level officers: "Arab tactical commanders regularly failed to demonstrate initiative, flexibility, creativity, independence of thought, an understanding of combined-arms integration, or an appreciation for the benefits of maneuver in battle. These failings resulted in a dearth of aggressiveness, responsiveness, speed, movement, intelligence gathering, and adaptability in Arab tactical formations that proved crippling in every war they fought." Second, Arab armies handled information improperly. This included falsifying reports, hoarding and withholding key pieces of information, and inadequate intelligence gathering and analysis. The result was that the Arabs went into battle without a proper understanding of their enemy. Once the battle started, the generals could not get an accurate picture of the reality of the situation. Third, Arab soldiers displayed poor technical skills and weapons-handling ability: "They required long periods of time to learn how to use the new weapons and other equipment. . . . Arab armies and air forces were unable to take full advantage of the technology at their disposal. They rarely were able to employ the more advanced capabilities of their weapons."[7] For example, the ratio of Arab to Israeli airplane losses in dogfights averaged 25:1. Arab tankers suffered disproportionately as well. Fourth, Arab armies suffered from poor maintenance. Arab states often went to war with large numbers of nonoperational tanks and planes. Once the battles started, their soldiers tended to abandon damaged vehicles rather than repair them.

These patterns were apparent in all the wars and battles between the Arabs and Israelis. In the 1948 war, the large Egyptian army proved limited in its offensive capabilities, slowed by the fierce defense at Yad Mordechai and then stopped by a combined air and ground attack. The Syrian army proved similarly unable to take advantage of its larger numbers. In the 1956 war, Israeli forces used combined arms tactics to break the strong Egyptian defensive positions in the northern Sinai, simultaneously weakening the larger Egyptian army while capturing much-needed supplies. Ariel Sharon's paratroopers, surrounded and outnumbered in the Mitla Pass, managed to extricate themselves by skirting around the enemy positions and attacking from the side and rear. The last action of the war, the "Long Trek" to the Straits of Tiran, was a complicated operation that surprised and overwhelmed the Egyptian defenders. In the Six-Day War the IDF managed to break its enemy, despite being greatly outnumbered. The preemptive air attack that opened the war was a result of the Arabs' poor intelligence and warning capabilities. The ground action was even more lopsided than it had been in the 1956 war, because by 1967 the IDF had improved its combined arms capabilities. The classic example is the attack on Abu Agheila. In that battle, Ariel Sharon employed tanks, helicopters, infantry, and artillery in a coordinated fashion. His forces maneuvered around the defenders' positions, then attacked from the side and rear at a single point before moving forward and rolling up the defenders' lines. At no point in the battle did the Egyptians try to bring their tanks forward or turn to face the attackers approaching from the sides or rear. Israeli forces experienced similar success throughout the Sinai, attacking in coordinate waves against defenders who were unable to maneuver to meet them. The IDF defeated the Jordanian and Syrian armies in similar manners during that war. The Arabs' best chance to defeat Israel came in 1973, when they achieved surprise on two fronts. But their armies proved incapable of exploiting the surprise.

The reason for the Arabs' inability to fight effectively stemmed in part from their lower levels of socioeconomic development. Modern warfare demands well-educated officers who are able to think and act independently, pilots who are familiar and comfortable with advanced technology, intelligence officers who can accurately report on enemy positions, mechanics who are used to working with modern vehicles, and soldiers who can handle new weaponry. Arab societies lacked the necessary human material to field an effective modern army. The result was repeated and stunning Israeli victories, victories that seemed improbable given the numerical disparities, but when examined in the context above become much less inexplicable.

The second great factor in the Zionists' favor was outside intervention, as the Europeans and later the Americans aided the Jews for reasons of state interest. The first such outside intervention was the Balfour Declaration in 1917, issued not out of love for the Jews but out of a hard-headed British calculation that a commitment to a Jewish national home would further their war aims. Similarly, the British decided to build up the Jewish home as a means to develop the empire. Under British protection, the Jewish national home grew, such that by the time the British refuted a Jewish state in the late 1930s, the seeds had been firmly planted. The British crushed the anti-Zionist Arab revolt of 1936 to 1939, which may well have driven the Jews out had the British quit the Mandate. The British presence was also decisive in 1948, allowing the Jews to first battle the Palestinians before the Arab states invaded. Had the British departed earlier, the Arabs might have joined forces and defeated the fledgling state. In 1956, when the weak state faced the threat of an Egyptian army much larger than theirs in the wake of the Soviet arms deal, France and Britain agreed to arm and fight with Israel, as their interests dictated opposing Nasser. Without French arms, Israel would not have been able to defeat the Egyptian army, clean out the fedayeen bases in Gaza, and open the Straits of Tiran. France continued to provide arms for the next decade, allowing Israel to defeat the hostile encirclement that formed in 1967. When the French stopped their arms shipments, Israel was able to find another patron in the United States, whose Cold War interests dictated countering the Soviet Union's Arab clients, Egypt and Syria, who were Israel's enemies. American arms were important in the 1973 war.

The Arabs had outside help as well, most notably from the Soviet Union, but lacking a modern society, they proved incapable of using their arms as well as the Israelis did. The more developed Jewish society offered outside powers opportunities to expand their influence in ways that the Arabs could not. As the Great Powers supplied Israel with arms, the Jewish state incorporated them into their arsenal, building a modern army the Arabs could not match.

The role of Germany was critical in creating and sustaining the State of Israel, although unlike the other Great Power interventions, German policy was not dictated by national interest but by racial policy. Germany played a major role in the Jewish state's development three times. The first and most important instance was in the 1930s, when the Nazi persecution led to the flight of two hundred thousand Jews to Palestine, nearly doubling the Jewish population—and the economy—there. Without these people and the money, it is highly unlikely Israel would have survived the War of Independence. The second time was the arrival of roughly two hundred thousand displaced European Jews after the establishment of the State of Israel in 1948, a much-needed influx of people and skills to the tiny, besieged state. The third time was in the 1950s, when West Germany paid reparations, which developed the state's economy much quicker than would have been possible otherwise. It is often asserted that the Holocaust led to the creation of the Jewish state, as the UN voted for statehood partially on the basis of the genocide as proof of the need for a Jewish safe haven. But a de facto Jewish state already existed in Palestine in 1947. A war between the two sides would have occurred regardless of the outcome of the UN vote. Nazi Germany's influence on the development of Israel was much more important in the three other episodes described here.

The Jews also received help from their Diaspora brethren. The money donated by American Jews in early 1948 allowed the Haganah to purchase the desperately needed arms that proved decisive in the crucial battles later that year. The foreign Jews who came to fight for the state in 1948, including U.S. Army colonel David Daniel "Mickey" Marcus, were a major addition to the nascent state's small army. Diaspora contributions were key in settling the immigrants in the 1950s and in building the Jewish state's economy over the years. Without the active help of their overseas cousins, the history of the Jewish state may well have been different.

There were other important factors as well. The rise of anti-Semitism—first in Russia at the turn of the twentieth century, then in Germany in 1930s, and finally in the Arab world after the creation of the State of Israel—provided a steady stream of immigrants to the Jewish state. Anti-Semitism was the reason for the creation of the state in the first place, and as events transpired, anti-Jewish sentiment actively encouraged its development.

Sound leadership was also crucial. The charismatic aura that Theodor Herzl lent the Zionist movement was critical in moving it from a fringe group with few followers to a large, well-funded organization. Chaim Weizmann's efforts to secure the Balfour Declaration ensured the legal charter that had eluded Herzl. David Ben-Gurion's foresight in sending agents to Europe to secure arms for the war that broke out after the UN Resolution in 1947 proved key to winning the war, as did Golda Meir's fund-raising in America. Menachem Begin's reluctant acceptance of the Camp David Accords secured the state's long-term survival. The talented military leaders, from Yigal Allon to Moshe Dayan, Yitzchak Rabin to Yigael Yadin, Ariel Sharon to Ezer Weizman, made risky decisions that worked out in the long term.

And finally, beyond the well-known names of Israeli history, there were the people themselves. Dedicated to their very core to securing a safe haven for the Jews, they accomplished monumental feats, reclaiming the land, creating a new language, building towns and cities, and fighting to defend themselves. Through their efforts, and despite vast odds, Masada did not fall again.

Notes

Introduction

1. Josephus, *Destruction of the Jews*, 226–27.
2. Josephus, *Works of Flavius Josephus*, 874–75.
3. Josephus, *Works of Flavius Josephus*, 875.

1. A Pillar of Fire on the Road to Zion

1. Radzinsky, *Alexander II*, 415.
2. Howe, *World of Our Fathers*, 10.
3. Kurzman, *Ben-Gurion*, 44.
4. Kurzman, *Ben-Gurion*, 45.
5. Howe, *World of Our Fathers*, 13.
6. Howe, *World of Our Fathers*, 9.
7. Howe, *World of Our Fathers*, 9.
8. Stein, *Hope Fulfilled*, 7.
9. Howe, *World of Our Fathers*, 7.
10. Morris, *Righteous Victims*, 15–16.
11. Mendes-Flohr and Reinharz, *Jew in the Modern World*, 408.
12. Sachar, *History of Israel*, 12.
13. Howe, *World of Our Fathers*, 14.
14. Howe, *World of Our Fathers*, 25.
15. Howe, *World of Our Fathers*, 27
16. Eban, *My Country*, 26.
17. O'Brien, *The Siege*, 47–48.
18. Laqueur and Rubin, *Israel-Arab Reader*, 3–4.
19. Sachar, *History of Israel*, 33.
20. Stein, *Hope Fulfilled*, 27.

2. An Eye toward Zion

1. Bein, *Theodore Herzl*, 113–14.
2. Bein, *Theodore Herzl*, 115–16.
3. Bein, *Theodore Herzl*, 114.
4. Laqueur and Rubin, *Israel-Arab Reader*, 5–7.
5. Bein, *Theodore Herzl*, 170.
6. Bein, *Theodore Herzl*, 183.
7. Bein, *Theodore Herzl*, 183–84.
8. O'Brien, *The Siege*, 73.
9. Bein, *Theodore Herzl*, 231–32.
10. Bein, *Theodore Herzl*, 232, 235.
11. O'Brien, *The Siege*, 76.
12. Laqueur and Rubin, *Israel-Arab Reader*, 9.
13. O'Brien, *The Siege*, 80
14. Sachar, *History of Israel*, 51.
15. Bein, *Theodore Herzl*, 504–5.
16. Rubin, *Scattered among the Nations*, 197.
17. Eban, *My Country*, 284.
18. Kurzman, *Ben-Gurion*, 80.
19. Gilbert, *Israel*, 51.
20. Sachar, *History of Israel*, 82.
21. Laqueur, *History of Zionism*, 204.
22. Dwork and Van Pelt, *Flight from the Reich*, 30.

3. It Is Good to Die for Our Country

1. O'Brien, *The Siege*, 112.
2. O'Brien, *The Siege*, 112.
3. Khalidi, "The Arab Perspective," in Louis and Stookey, *End of the Palestine Mandate*, 104.
4. Ari Shavit. *My Promised Land*. New York: Random House, 2013, 33.
5. Shavit, *My Promised Land*, 43.
6. Sachar, *History of Israel*, 143.
7. Morris, *Righteous Victims*, 95.
8. Fromkin, *Peace to End All Peace*, 520.
9. Fromkin, *Peace to End All Peace*, 519.
10. Fromkin, *Peace to End All Peace*, 523.
11. Laqueur and Rubin, *Israel-Arab Reader*, 26.
12. Gilbert, *Israel*, 53.
13. Silberman, *Prophet from Amongst You*, 26.
14. Gilbert, *Israel*, 74–75.
15. Morris, *Righteous Victims*, 108.
16. O'Brien, *The Siege*, 175.
17. Segev, *One Palestine Complete*, 322–23.

4. The Great Catastrophe

1. Kurzman, *Ben-Gurion*, 189.
2. Black, *Transfer Agreement*, 313.
3. Black, *Transfer Agreement*, 336.
4. Black, *Transfer Agreement*, 300.
5. Black, *Transfer Agreement*, 338.
6. Black, *Transfer Agreement*, 337.
7. O'Brien, *The Siege*, 203–04.
8. O'Brien, *The Siege*, 204.
9. Meir, *My Life*, 148.
10. Gilbert, *Israel*, 83–84.
11. Gilbert, *Israel*, 81.
12. O'Brien, *The Siege*, 226.
13. Deem, *Kristallnacht*, 99.
14. Deem, *Kristallnacht*, 26.
15. Deem, *Kristallnacht*, 13.
16. Deem, *Kristallnacht*, 42–44.
17. Deem, *Kristallnacht*, 77.
18. Gilbert, *The Holocaust*, 71–72.
19. Deem, *Kristallnacht*, 90.
20. Kurzman, *Ben-Gurion*, 222–24.
21. Eban, *My Country*, 37.
22. Meir, *My Life*, 165.

5. An Indifferent World

1. Gilbert, *Israel*, 106.
2. Stein, *Hope Fulfilled*, 228.
3. Mendes-Flohr and Reinharz, *Jew in the Modern World*, 684.
4. Eban, *My Country*, 40.
5. Gilbert, *Holocaust*, 231–32.
6. Dwork and Van Pelt, *Flight from the Reich*, 302.
7. Dwork and Van Pelt, *Flight from the Reich*, 312.
8. Kurzman, *Ben-Gurion*, 263.
9. Karpin, *Bomb in the Basement*, 7.
10. Karpin, *Bomb in the Basement*, 28.
11. Gilbert, *Israel*, 128.
12. Laqueur and Rubin, *Israel-Arab Reader*, 57.
13. Meir, *My Life*, 189.

6. Nothing Can Keep Us from Our Jewish Homeland

1. Sachar, *History of Israel*, 270.
2. Gruber, *Exodus 1947*, 103–8.
3. Meir, *My Life*, 203.

4. Rose, *Senseless Squalid War*, 157–58.
5. Gruber, *Exodus 1947*, 51–65.
6. Gruber, *Exodus 1947*, 164–69.
7. Gruber, *Exodus 1947*, 181.
8. Gruber, *Exodus 1947*, 183.
9. Rose, *Senseless Squalid War*, 132.
10. Rose, *Senseless Squalid War*, 114.
11. Gervasi, *Life and Times of Menachem Begin*, 157.
12. Rose, *Senseless Squalid War*, 164–65.
13. Rose, *Senseless Squalid War*, 165.
14. Sachar, *History of Israel*, 259.
15. Gilbert, *Israel*, 146.
16. Laqueur and Rubin, *Israel-Arab Reader*, 57–59.
17. Eban, *My Country*, 45.
18. Dayan, *Story of My Life*.

7. The Darkest Moment of Our Struggle

1. Collins and Lapierre, *O Jerusalem!*, 87.
2. Eshel, *Chariots of the Desert*, 5–8.
3. Rose, *Senseless Squalid War*, 187–88
4. Gilbert, *Israel*, 166–67.
5. Meir, *My Life*, 213–14.
6. Karsh, *Palestine War 1948*, 81.
7. Collins and Lapierre, *O Jerusalem*, 265.
8. Collins and Lapierre, *O Jerusalem*, 278–79.
9. Begin, *The Revolt*, 163–64.
10. Karsh, *Palestine War 1948*, 81.
11. Morris, *Birth of the Palestinian Refugee Problem*, 82.
12. Begin, *The Revolt*, 354–64.
13. Begin, *The Revolt*, 354–64.
14. Sachar, *History of Israel*, 334.
15. Gilbert, *Israel*, 177–78
16. Gilbert, *Israel*, 174.
17. Morris, *Birth of the Palestinian Refugee Problem*, 110–11.
18. Morris, *Birth of the Palestinian Refugee Problem*, 199.
19. Segev, *One Palestine Complete*, 508.
20. Morris, *Birth of the Palestinian Refugee Problem*, 231.

8. We Shall Triumph!

1. Gilbert, *Israel*, 181.
2. Gilbert, *Israel*, 182.
3. Collins and Lappierre, *O Jerusalem*, 356.
4. Gilbert, *Israel*, 187.

5. Gilbert, *Israel*, 182–83.

6. Lapierre and Collins, *O Jerusalem*, 362.

7. Lapierre and Collins, *O Jerusalem*, 382

8. Sachar, *A History of Israel*, 315.

9. Sachar, *History of Israel*, 315.

10. Silberman, *Prophet from Amongst You*, 118–19.

11. Collins and Lapierre, *O Jerusalem*, 465–66.

12. Hefez and Bloom, *Ariel Sharon*, 6–7.

13. Hefez and Bloom, *Ariel Sharon*, 8–12.

14. Hefez and Bloom, *Ariel Sharon*, 12. See also Sharon, *Warrior*, 54–61.

15. Weizman, *Battle for Peace*, 6.

16. Morris, *1948*, 240.

17. Gilbert, *Israel*, 212.

18. Kurzman, *Ben-Gurion*, 295–96.

19. Gilbert, *Israel*, 213.

20. Gilbert, *Israel*, 218.

21. Shavit, *My Promised Land*, 125. See also Tolan, *Lemon Tree*, 65–69.

22. Sachar, *History of Israel*, 335.

23. Sachar, *History of Israel*, 436.

24. Gilbert, *Israel*, 241.

9. A Heavy Burden

1. Segev, *1949*, 110.

2. Segev, *1949*, 162–63.

3. Segev, *1949*, 169.

4. Segev, *1949*, 123.

5. Meir, *My Life*, 264–65.

6. Gilbert, *Israel*, 280–84.

7. Gilbert, *Israel*, 284.

8. Sharon, *Warrior*, 88.

9. Sharon, *Warrior*, 89.

10. Sharon, *Warrior*, 91.

11. Kissinger, *Diplomacy*, 530.

12. Sharon, *Warrior*, 147–49.

13. Sharon, *Warrior*, 147–49.

14. Meir, *My Life*, 302.

15. Eban, *My Country*, 139.

16. Kissinger, *Diplomacy*, 543.

17. Meir, *My Life*, 302.

18. Sachar, *History of Israel*, 508.

10. Masada Shall Not Fall Again!

1. Kurzman, *Ben-Gurion*, 396.

2. Sachar, *History of Israel*, 552.

3. Gilbert, *Israel*, 336.

4. Kurzman, *Ben-Gurion*, 425.

5. Mendes-Flohr and Reinharz, *Jew in the Modern World*, 697.

6. Mendes-Flohr and Reinharz, *Jew in the Modern World*, 690.

7. Sachar, *History of Israel*, 557–59.

8. Karpin, *Bomb in the Basement*, 162.

9. Cohen, *Israel and the Bomb*, 13.

10. See Cohen, *Israel and the Bomb*, and Karpin, *Bomb in the Basement*.

11. Silberman, *Prophet from Amongst You*, 261.

12. Gilbert, *Israel*, 341.

13. Silberman, *Prophet from Amongst You*, 289–90.

14. Silberman, *Prophet from Amongst You*, 275.

15. Silberman, *Prophet from Amongst You*, 291.

16. Laqueur and Rubin, *Israel-Arab Reader*, 90.

17. Laqueur and Rubin, *Israel-Arab Reader*, 90.

18. Laqueur and Rubin, *Israel-Arab Reader*, 91.

19. Eban, *My Country*, 162.

20. Shlaim, *Iron Wall*, 229–30.

21. Sharon, *Warrior*, 165.

11. To Live or Perish

1. Ginor and Remez, *Foxbats over Dimona*, 2007.

2. Meir, *My Life*, 358.

3. Laqueur and Rubin, *Israel-Arab Reader*, 97.

4. Eban, *My Country*, 208.

5. Kurzman, *Soldier of Peace*, 211–12.

6. Laqueur and Rubin, *Israel-Arab Reader*, 99.

7. Laqueur and Rubin, *Israel-Arab Reader*, 101–02.

8. Meir, *My Life*, 359.

9. Nakleh, "June 1967 and October 1973 Arab-Israeli Wars."

10. Laqueur and Rubin, *Israel-Arab Reader*, 103.

11. Gilbert, *Israel*, 377.

12. Laqueur and Rubin, *Israel-Arab Reader*, 107.

13. Sharon, *Warrior*, 181.

14. Oren, *Six Days of War*, 157.

15. Eban, *My Country*, 219.

12. Israel's Golden Summer

1. Oren, *Six Days of War*, 170.

2. Cohen, *Israel's Best Defense*, 200.

3. Oren, *Six Days of War*, 171.

4. Oren, *Six Days of War*, 172.

5. Dayan, *Story of My Life*.

6. Cohen, *Israel's Best Defense*, 232.

7. Oren, *Six Days of War*, 188.

8. Oren, *Six Days of War*, 227.

9. Oren *Six Days of War*, 243.

10. Oren, *Six Days of War*, 245.

11. Eban, *My Country*, 225.

12. Rabin, *Rabin Memoirs*, 112–13.

13. Rabin, *Rabin Memoirs*, 113.

14. Bar-On, *Moshe Dayan*.

15. Associated Press, *Lightning Out of Israel*, 111–12, 135–37.

16. Oren, "The uss *Liberty*."

17. cia Directorate of Intelligence, "Israeli Attack on the uss *Liberty*."

18. cia Directorate of Intelligence, "Israeli Statement on the Attack on the uss *Liberty*."

19. Oren, "The uss *Liberty*."

20. Rabin, *Rabin Memoirs*, 110.

21. Oren. "The uss *Liberty*." For additional information on the *Liberty* incident, see Cristol, *Liberty Incident Revealed*.

22. Oren, *Six Days of War*, 275.

23. Oren, *Six Days of War*, 277.

24. Oren, *Six Days of War*, 279.

25. Oren, *Six Days of War*, 281.

26. Sachar, *History of Israel*, 667.

27. Eban, *My Country*, 243.

28. Eban, *My Country*, 247.

29. Shehadeh, *Strangers in the House*, 48.

30. Sachar, *History of Israel*, 676.

31. Weizman, *Battle for Peace*, 18.

13. We May Be in Trouble

1. U.S. Embassy Israel, Cable 7766 to Department of State, 6 October 9988, "goi Concern about Possible Syrian and Egyptian Attack Today."

2. Message from Secretary Kissinger, New York, to White House Situation Room, for delivery to President Nixon at 9:00 a.m., 6 October 1973.

3. Rabinovich, *Yom Kippur War*, 16.

4. Bar-Joseph, *Watchman Fell Asleep*, 11.

5. Bar-Joseph, *Watchman Fell Asleep*, 12.

6. Bar-Joseph, *Watchman Fell Asleep*, 90.

7. Rabinovich, *Yom Kippur War*, 51.

8. Bar-Joseph, *Watchman Fell Asleep*, 97.

9. Rabinovich, *Yom Kippur War*, 58.

10. Blum, *Eve of Destruction*, 120.

11. Rabinovich, *Yom Kippur War*, 60.

12. Bar-Joseph, *Watchman Fell Asleep*, 245.

13. Bar-Joseph, "Special Means of Collection."

14. Rabinovich, *Yom Kippur War*, 71.

15. Bar-Joseph, *Watchman Fell Asleep*, 143.

16. Rabinovich, *Yom Kippur War*, 73.

17. Bar-Joseph, *Watchman Fell Asleep*, 172.

18. Bar-Joseph, *Watchman Fell Asleep*, 196.

19. Kissinger, *Years of Upheaval*, 461.

20. Sadat, *In Search of Identity*, 241.

21. Central Intelligence Bulletin, 29 September 1973.

22. Sadat, *In Search of Identity*, 241.

23. Kissinger, *Years of Upheaval*, 464.

24. Brugioni, "Overhead Imagery during the Yom Kippur War," 5.

25. Central Intelligence Bulletin, 5 October 1973.

26. Kissinger, *Years of Upheaval*, 465.

27. Kissinger, *Years of Upheaval*, 466.

28. Central Intelligence Bulletin, 6 October 1973.

29. Colby, *Honorable Men*, 366.

30. Harold Ford, *Estimative Intelligence* (Lanham ME: University Press of America, 1993), 245.

31. Kissinger, *Years of Upheaval*, 458.

32. Memorandum from William B. Quandt to Brent Scowcroft, "Arab-Israeli Tensions," 6 October 1973.

14. Destruction of the Third Temple

1. Rabinovich, *Yom Kippur War*, 101–3.

2. Blum, *Eve of Destruction*, 186.

3. Blum, *Eve of Destruction*, 190.

4. Bar-Joseph, *Watchman Fell Asleep*, 222–23.

5. Herzog, *The War of Atonement*, 106.

6. Kahalani, *The Heights of Courage*, 64.

7. Rabinovich, *Yom Kippur War*, 232.

8. Sharon, *Warrior*, 303.

9. See Blum, *Eve of Destruction*, 309, 227–29; Rabinovich, *Yom Kippur War*, 269.

10. Eshel, *Chariots of the Desert*, 121.

11. Sharon, *Warrior*, 316.

12. Sharon, *Warrior*, 322–23.

13. Message from Brezhnev to Nixon, 24 October 1973, received at State Department, 10:00 p.m.

14. Nixon to Brezhnev, 25 October 1973, delivered to Soviet Embassy, 5:40 a.m.

15. Dobrynin to Kissinger, enclosing letter from Brezhnev to Nixon, 25 October 1973, received 15:40 hours.
16. Gilbert, *Israel*, 466.
17. Gilbert, *Israel*, 467.
18. Gilbert, *Israel*, 467.
19. Morris, *Righteous Victims*, 440.

15. Nation Shall Not Lift Up Sword Against Nation

1. Laqueur and Rubin, *Israel-Arab Reader*, 206–7.
2. O'Brien, *The Siege*, 462.
3. O'Brien, *The Siege*, 560.
4. Sadat, *Those I Have Known*, 104–6.
5. Weizman, *Battle for Peace*, 22.
6. O'Brien, *The Siege*, 274.
7. Morris, *Righteous Victims*, 450.
8. Morris, *Righteous Victims*, 452.
9. Laqueur and Rubin, *Israel-Arab Reader*, 209–12.
10. Weizman, *Battle for Peace*, 34.
11. O'Brien, *The Siege*, 578.
12. Weizman, *Battle for Peace*, 56–59.
13. Weizman, *Battle for Peace*, 68.
14. Weizman, *Battle for Peace*, 88–90.
15. Morris, *Righteous Victims*, 466.
16. Weizman, *Battle for Peace*, 371.
17. Morris, *Righteous Victims*, 468.
18. Reich, *Brief History of Israel*, 132.
19. O'Brien, *The Siege*, 610.
20. O'Brien, *The Siege*, 611.

16. Most Televised War in History

1. Sharon, *Warrior*, 432.
2. Sharon, *Warrior*, 461–62.
3. Fisk, *Pity the Nation*, 229–230.
4. Nordeen, *Fighters over Israel*, 177.
5. Sharon, *Warrior*, 486.
6. Fisk, *Pity the Nation*, 293.
7. Gilbert, *Israel*, 508.
8. Fisk, *Pity the Nation*, 315.
9. Laqueur and Rubin, *Israel-Arab Reader*, 255–56.
10. Schiff and Yaari, *Israel's Lebanon War*, 275.
11. Fisk, *Pity the Nation*, 359–60, 364–65.
12. Schiff and Yaari, *Israel's Lebanon War*, 280.
13. Schiff and Yaari, *Israel's Lebanon War*, 250.

14. Tessler, *History of the Israeli-Palestinian Conflict*, 683.

15. Tessler, *History of the Israeli-Palestinian Conflict*, 684.

16. Laqueur and Rubin, *Israel-Arab Reader*, 326.

17. Tessler, *History of the Israeli-Palestinian Conflict*, 686.

18. Pratt, *Intifada*, 45, 49.

19. Ari Shavit. *My Promised Land.* New York: Random House, 2013, 233.

20. Ari Shavit. *My Promised Land.* New York: Random House, 2013, 235.

21. Gilbert, *Israel*, 530.

22. Sachar, *History of Israel*, 966.

17. Enough of Blood and Tears!

1. Laqueur and Rubin, *Israel-Arab Reader*, 404.

2. Gilbert, *Israel*, 553.

3. Laqueur and Rubin, *Israel Arab Reader*, 426

4. Laqueur and Rubin, *Israel-Arab Reader*, 437.

5. Laqueur and Rubin, *Israel Arab Reader*, 461.

6. Clyde Haberman, "The Jordan-Israel Accord: The Overview; Israel and Jordan Sign a Peace Accord," *New York Times*, October 27, 1994.

7. Serge Schemann, "Bus Bombing Kills Five in Jerusalem; 100 Are Wounded," *New York Times*, August 22, 1995.

8. Laqueur and Rubin, *Israel-Arab Reader*, 522.

9. Author's personal recollection of Mahane Yehuda bombing and aftermath on July 31, 1997, during Summer School at Hebrew University in Jerusalem.

10. Joel Greenberg, "Sharon Touches a Nerve and Jerusalem Explodes," *New York Times*, September 29, 2000; Hefez and Bloom, *Ariel Sharon*, 335.

11. Alan Philps, "A Day of Rage, Revenge and Bloodshed," *Telegraph*, October 13, 2000.

12. Laqueur and Rubin, *Israel-Arab Reader*, 473.

18. The Third Way

1. Pratt, *Intifada*, 132.

2. Oded Na'aman, "The Checkpoint," *Boston Review*, July/August 2012.

3. Shaul Arieli, "It's Not a Barrier, It's a Neighborhood: The Battle of the Village Bil'in."

4. Laqueur and Rubin, *Israel-Arab Reader*, 594.

5. Steven Erlanger, "A Gaza War Full of Traps and Terror," *New York Times*, January 10, 2009.

6. Ethan Bronner, "Israel Lets Reporters See Devastated Gaza Site and Image of a Confident Military," *New York Times*, January 18, 2009.

7. Nick Meo, "How Israel Killed Ahmed Jabari, Its Toughest Enemy in Gaza," *Telegraph*, November 17, 2012.

Conclusion

1. Tessler, *History of the Israeli-Palestinian Conflict*, 214.
2. "A Slow Learning Curve," *Economist*, July 15, 2010.
3. Tessler, *History of the Israeli-Palestinian Conflict*, 218.
4. Angus Maddison, "Historical Statistics of the World Economy: 1–2008 A D."
5. Walid Khalidi, "The Arab Perspective," in Louis and Stookey, *End of the Palestine Mandate*, 106.
6. Von Laue, *World Revolution of Westernization*, 263.
7. Pollack, *Arabs at War*, 557–74.

Bibliography

Government Documents

Central Intelligence Bulletin, 23 May 1967. *Fifty Years of Informing Policy.* United States Central Intelligence Agency. Washington DC: Center for the Study of Intelligence, 2002.

Central Intelligence Bulletin, 29 September 1973. *Fifty Years of Informing Policy.* United States Central Intelligence Agency. Washington DC: Center for the Study of Intelligence, 2002.

Central Intelligence Bulletin, 5 October 1973. *Fifty Years of Informing Policy.* United States Central Intelligence Agency. Washington DC: Center for the Study of Intelligence, 2002.

Central Intelligence Bulletin, 6 October 1973. *Fifty Years of Informing Policy.* United States Central Intelligence Agency. Washington DC: Center for the Study of Intelligence, 2002.

CIA Directorate of Intelligence. "The Israeli Attack on the USS *Liberty*." June 13 1967. Approved for release June 2006.

CIA Directorate of Intelligence. "The Israeli Statement on the Attack on the USS *Liberty*." June 21, 1967. Approved for release June 2006.

Nakleh, Emile. "The June 1967 and October 1973 Arab-Israeli Wars." In *Fifty Years of Informing Policy.* United States Central Intelligence Agency. Washington DC: Center for the Study of Intelligence, 2002.

U.S. Embassy Israel, Cable 7766 to Department of State, 6 October 9988, "GOI Concern about Possible Syrian and Egyptian Attack Today." National Security Archive. These materials are reproduced from www.nsarchive.org with the permission of the National Security Archive.

Message from Secretary Kissinger, New York, to White House Situation Room, for delivery to President Nixon at 9:00 a.m., 6 October 1973. National

Security Archive. These materials are reproduced from www.nsarchive.
org with the permission of the National Security Archive.

Memorandum from William B. Quandt to Brent Scowcroft, "Arab-Israeli Tensions," 6 October 1973. National Security Archive. These materials are reproduced from www.nsarchive.org with the permission of the National Security Archive.

Message from Brezhnev to Nixon, 24 October 1973, received at State Department, 10:00 p.m. National Security Archive. These materials are reproduced from www.nsarchive.org with the permission of the National Security Archive.

Nixon to Brezhnev, 25 October 1973, delivered to Soviet Embassy, 5:40 a.m. National Security Archive. These materials are reproduced from www.nsarchive.org with the permission of the National Security Archive.

Dobrynin to Kissinger, enclosing letter from Brezhnev to Nixon, 25 October 1973, received 15:40 hours. National Security Archive. These materials are reproduced from www.nsarchive.org with the permission of the National Security Archive.

Published Works

Associated Press. *Lightning Out of Israel*. New York: Western Printing and Lithographing Company, 1967.

Badri, Hassan, Taha Magdoub, and Mohammed Dia en Din Zody. *The Ramadan War*. New York: Hippocrene, 1978.

Bar-Joseph, Uri. *The Watchman Fell Asleep*. Albany: State University of New York Press, 2005.

———. "The 'Special Means of Collection': The Missing Link in the Surprise of the Yom Kippur War." *Middle East Journal* 67, no. 4 (Autumn 2013).

Bar-On, Mordechai. *Moshe Dayan: Israel's Controversial Hero*. New Haven CT: Yale University Press, 2012.

Begin, Menachem. *The Revolt*. New York: Nash Publishing, 1977.

Bein, Alex. *Theodore Herzl*. Philadelphia: Jewish Publication Society of America, 1940.

Black, Edwin. *The Transfer Agreement*. Cambridge MA: Brookline, 1999.

Black, Ian, and Benny Morris. *Israel's Secret Wars*. London: Grove Weidenfeld, 1991.

Blum, Howard. *The Eve of Destruction*. New York: HarperCollins, 2003.

Brugioni, Dino, "Overhead Imagery during the Yom Kippur War." *Studies in Intelligence* 48, no. 4 (2004).

Cohen, Avner. *Israel and the Bomb*. New York: Columbia University Press, 1998.

Cohen, Eliezer. *Israel's Best Defense*. New York: Orion, 1993.

Colby, William. *Honorable Men: My Life in the CIA*. New York: Simon and Schuster, 1978.

Collins, Larry, and Dominique Lapierre. *O Jerusalem!* New York: Simon and Schuster, 2000.

Cristol, Jay. *The Liberty Incident Revealed*. Annapolis MD: Naval Institute Press, 2013.

Dayan, Moshe. *Story of My Life*. New York: William Morrow, 1976.

Deem, James. *Kristallnacht*. Berkeley Heights NJ: Enslow, 2012.

Dupuy, Trevor. *Elusive Victory*. New York: HarperCollins, 1978.

Dwork, Deborah, and Robert Jan Van Pelt. *Flight from the Reich*. New York: W. W. North, 2009.

Eban, Abba. *My Country*. New York: Random House, 1972.

Eshel, David. *Chariots of the Desert*. London: Brassey's Defence, 1989.

Fisk, Robert. *Pity the Nation*. New York: Athenaeum, 1990.

Fromkin, David. *A Peace to End All Peace*. New York: Henry Holt, 1989.

Gervasi, Frank. *The Life and Times of Menachem Begin*. New York: G. P. Putnam and Sons, 1979.

Gilbert, Martin. *The Holocaust*. New York: Holt, Rinehart, and Winston, 1985.

———. *Israel: A History*. New York: William Morrow, 1998.

Ginor, Isabella, and Gideon Remez. *Foxbats over Dimona*. New Haven CT: Yale University Press, 2007.

Gruber, Ruth. *Exodus 1947: The Ship That Launched a Nation*. New York: Random House, 1999.

Hammes, Thomas, X. *The Sling and the Stone*. Minneapolis MN: Zenith, 2006.

Hefez, Nir, and Gadi Bloom. *Ariel Sharon: A Life*. New York: Random House, 2006.

Heikal, Mohammed. *The Road to Ramadan*. New York: Ballantine, 1975.

Herzog, Chaim. *The War of Atonement*. Boston: Little, Brown, 1975.

———. *The Arab-Israeli Wars*. New York: Random House, 1984.

Howe, Irving. *World of Our Fathers*. New York: Harcourt Brace Jovanovich, 1976.

Kahalani, Avigdor. *The Heights of Courage*. Westport, CT: Greenwood, 1984.

Karpin, Michael. *The Bomb in the Basement*. New York: Simon and Schuster, 2006.

Karsh, Efraim. *The Palestine War 1948*. Oxford: Osprey, 2002.

Kissinger, Henry. *Years of Upheaval*. Boston: Little, Brown, 1982.

———. *Diplomacy*. New York: Simon and Schuster, 1994.

Kurzman, Dan. *Genesis 1948: The First Arab-Israeli War*. Cleveland: World, 1970.

———. *Ben-Gurion: Prophet of Fire*. New York: Simon and Schuster, 1983.

———. *Soldier of Peace: The Life of Yitzhak Rabin*. New York: HarperCollins, 1998.

Josephus, Flavius. *The Destruction of the Jews*. Translated by G. A. Williamson. London: Penguin, 1959.

———. *The Works of Flavius Josephus*. Philadelphia: David McKay, 1900.

Laqueur, Walter. *A History of Zionism*. New York: Schocken, 2003.

Laqueur, Walter, and Barry Rubin, eds. *The Israel-Arab Reader*. New York: Penguin Books, 2001.

Louis, William Roger, and Robert W. Stookey, eds. *The End of the Palestine Mandate*. Austin: University of Texas Press, 1986.

Meir, Golda. *My Life*. New York: GP Putnam's Sons, 1975.

Mendes-Flohr, Paul, and Jehuda Reinharz. *The Jew in the Modern World*. New York: Oxford University Press, 1995.

Morris, Benny. *The Birth of the Palestinian Refugee Problem, 1947–1949*. Cambridge: Cambridge University Press, 1987.

Morris, Benny. *Righteous Victims*. New York: Random House, 2001.

———. *1948: The First Arab-Israeli War*. New Haven: Yale University Press, 2008.

Nordeen, Lon. *Fighters over Israel*. New York: Orion, 1990.

O'Balance, Edgar. *No Victor, No Vanquished: The Yom Kippur War*. Novato CA: Presidio, 1977.

O'Brien, Conor Cruise. *The Siege*. New York: Simon and Schuster, 1986.

Oren, Michael. *Six Days of War*. New York: Oxford University Press, 2002.

———. "The USS *Liberty*: Case Closed." Jewish Virtual Library.

Pollack, Kenneth. *Arabs at War: Military Effectiveness, 1948–1991*. London: University of Nebraska Press, 2002.

Pratt, David. *Intifada: The Long Day of Rage*. Philadelphia: Casemate, 2006.

Rabin, Yitzhak. *The Rabin Memoirs*. Berkeley: University of California Press, 1979.

Rabinovich, Abraham. *The Yom Kippur War*. New York: Schocken, 2004.

Radzinsky, Edward. *Alexander II: The Last Great Tsar*. New York: Free Press, 2005.

Reich, Bernard. *A Brief History of Israel*. New York: Checkmark, 2005.

Rose, Norman. *A Senseless Squalid War*. London: Pimlico, 2009.

Rubin, Alexis, ed. *Scattered among the Nations*. Toronto: Wall and Emerson, 1993.

Sachar, Howard. *A History of Israel*. New York: Alfred E. Knopf, 1996.

Sadat, Anwar. *In Search of Identity*. New York: Harper and Row, 1977.

———. *Those I Have Known*. New York: Continuum, 1984.

Segev, Tom. *1949: The First Israelis*. New York: Henry Holt, 1986.

———. *One Palestine Complete*. New York: Henry Holt, 2000.

Schiff, Zeev, and Ehud Yaari. *Israel's Lebanon War*. New York: Simon and Schuster, 1984.

———. *Intifada*. New York: Simon and Schuster, 1989.

Sharon, Ariel. *Warrior*. New York: Simon and Schuster, 2001.

Shavit, Ari. *My Promised Land*. New York: Random House, 2013.

Shehadeh, Raja. *Strangers in the House*. Vermont: Steerforth, 2002.

Shlaim, Avi. *The Iron Wall*. New York: W. W. Norton, 2000.

Silberman, Neil Asher. *A Prophet from Amongst You*. Reading MA: Addison-Wesley, 1993.

Smith, Charles D. *Palestine and the Arab-Israeli Conflict*. New York: St. Martin's, 1996.

Stein, Leslie. *The Hope Fulfilled*. Westport CT: Praeger, 2003.

Tessler, Mark. *A History of the Israeli-Palestinian Conflict*. Bloomington: Indiana University Press, 1994.

Tolan, Sandy. *The Lemon Tree*. NewYork: Bloomsbury 2006.

Van Crevald, Martin. *The Sword and the Olive*. New York: Public Affairs, 2002.

Von Laue, Theodore. *Why Lenin? Why Stalin? Why Gorbachev?* New York: HarperCollins, 1993.

———. *The World Revolution of Westernization*. New York: Oxford University Press, 1987.

Weizman, Ezer. *The Battle for Peace*. New York: Bantam, 1981.

Index

Ben-Gurion, David (*cont.*)
and, 76–77; Eichmann and, 166, 168;
Holocaust and, 77–78; immigrant
crisis and, 148–49; Kibbiya incident
and, 153; negotiates with Arabs, 49,
65; nuclear program and, 168; orders
attack on Latrun, 127–28, 133; at Palestine, 29; reparations and, 150–51;
Sinai Campaign and, 160, 162, 163;
and statehood, 122; Transfer Plan
and, 53; UNSCOP and, 92; vote for
statehood and, 119–21
Ben Yehuda, Eliezer, 30–31
Bethlehem, 209
Bialik, Chaim Nachman, 30, 43
Biltmore Program, 74
Bilu (writers group), 15, 16
Bint Jbail, 316–17
Bren, Adan, 158, 244–45, 248, 254–56
Britain: Arab Revolt and, 56–59;
Balfour Declaration and, 32, 40, 42,
43, 328; and end of Mandate, 92; and
establishment of Mandate, 41–43;
illegal Jewish immigration and, 66,
70–72, 79, 82, 83; Irgun and, 81, 88–
91; riots in Palestine and 47, 49; Sinai
campaign and, 155, 156, 163; White
Paper (1939), 66; World War I and,
31–33; World War II and, 74–75
Brugioni, Dino, 231
"Burma Road," 135

Cairo, Egypt, 178, 179, 184, 212, 225,
231, 248, 267
Cairo Accords, 299
Camp David Accords: importance of,
277, 323, 330; negotiations, 271–73;
signing ceremony, 273–74
Camp David MD, 271, 304
Carter, Jimmy, 271–73
Cave of the Patriarchs (Hebron), 209
Central Intelligence Agency (CIA): and
Six-Day War, 183–84; Yom Kippur
War and, 229–34
"Chinese Farm," 25–54
Churchill, Winston: as colonial secre-
tary, 41–43, 325; Jewish Brigade and, 75

Clinton, Bill: final status negotiations
and, 304, 306, 307; Oslo Accords and,
297; and Peace Treaty with Jordan,
300
Clinton, Hillary, 320
Cyprus, 66, 82–83, 128, 139
Czar Alexander II, 5–8
Czar Alexander III, 12–13

Damascus, 179, 225, 227, 233, 234
Dayan, Moshe: Camp David Accords
and, 272; intelligence estimates
and, 226, 228; Sinai Campaign and,
158; Six-Day War and, 186, 191, 192,
199–201, 208; UN partition plan and,
84; War of Independence and, 140,
144; Yom Kippur War and, 239, 240,
244, 245
Dead Sea, 1, 42, 203, 204, 300
Declaration of Independence, 122
Declaration of Principles, 296
Defense Intelligence Agency (DIA), 230
Degania, 126–27, 272
Deir Yassin, 108–10, 111, 142
Dimona, 168
displaced persons, 76–79, 82–83
Dome of the Rock, 47, 108, 266, 306
Dreyfus, Alfred, 19–21

Eban, Abba: cabinet meetings and,
179, 181; 184, 186; Holocaust and, 73;
independence and, 94; national water
carrier and, 173; Six-Day War and, 183,
184, 200, 209, 210; United Nations
and, 162
Egypt: Camp David Accords and, 273–
74; and Czech arms deal, 154; infiltrators and, 154; peace negotiations with
Israel and, 262–73; Sinai Campaign
and, 155–64; Six-Day War and, 177–
82, 185, 189–96; and surprise attack,
216–19; Yom Kippur War and, 237–
39, 244–45, 247–58; War of Attrition
and, 210–12; War of Independence
and, 125, 133–35, 39, 143
Eichmann, Adolf, 166–68
Eilat (Israel): strategic importance of, 154,
180; Sinai Campaign and, 160, 161

refugees, Jewish: *Exodus 1947* and, 83–88; Germany and, 54, 66; World War II and, 70–71, 78–79, 151

reparations, 150–51, 329

revisionists, 46, 54

Romans, 1–4, 171

Rothschild, Edmond, 17, 26

Rusk, Dean, 186

Russia: Jewish emigration from, 13, 15–16, 17, 28; pogroms in, 12–13, 26–27; shtetls and, 8–11; World War I and, 32

Sabra and Shatilla massacre, 286–89, 305

Sadat, Anwar: American intelligence estimate of, 229–30, 232, 233, 236; Camp David and, 270–73; Ezer Weizman and, 268, 269, 270; following Nasser, 212–13; Henry Kissinger and, 258; Israeli intelligence estimates of, 228; Menachem Begin and, 269, 271, 273; peace treaty with Israel and, 273–74; and preparations for Yom Kippur War, 216–19, 228; speech to Egyptian Parliament by, 263; speech to Knesset by, 266–67; and Soviets, 220; and trip to Israel, 264–66; and Yom Kippur War, 216, 228, 247–48, 258

Safed, 115

Sakakini, Hala al-, 101–2, 111

Sakakini, Khalil al-, 41, 108, 110–11, 115

Saudi Arabia, 65, 216

Scrowcroft, Brent, 232

Semiramis Hotel, 101–2

separation barrier, 313–15

settlements: at Gaza, 289; at Sinai, 270, 271, 272, 273; at West Bank, 261–62

Shamir, Yitzchak, 292, 294

Sharett, Moshe, 120

Sharm el-Sheikh, 160–64, 178, 195, 270

Sharon, Ariel: at Battle of Latrun , 128–32; at Camp David Accords, 272; Disengagement Plan and, 315; and Gaza withdrawal, 315; infiltrators and, 153–54; Kibbiya and, 152–53; during Lebanon War, 277–78, 279–80, 281,

282, 283, 284; Operation Defensive Shield and, 310; as prime minister, 309–10; Sabra and Shatilla and, 286, 288–89; Sinai Campaign and, 156–57, 327; Six-Day War and, 185, 193–95, 196, 327; Unit 101 and, 152–53; visit to Temple Mount by, 305; and water diversion plan, 174–75; Yom Kippur War and, 244–45, 248, 250, 253–55

shtetl, 8–11, 14, 16, 28

Sinai Campaign (1956): aftermath of, 161–64; fighting during, 156–61; planning for, 156

Sinai Desert: 1956 War in, 156, 165, 327; Egyptian troop movements into, 177, 178; Israeli withdrawal from, 164, 274; negotiations over, 216, 258, 260, 263, 264, 265, 269–74; Six-Day War in, 192, 193, 194, 195–97, 328; United Nations and, 164; War of Attrition and, 211, 217; Yom Kippur War in, 217–18, 220, 223, 238, 241, 244–45, 248

Six-Day War (1967): aftermath of, 209–11; capture of Jerusalem during, 200; Egyptian front during, 189–97; Jordanian front during, 197–200; prelude to, 177–87; refugees and, 202–4; Syrian front during, 207–9; uss *Liberty and*, 204–7; "the Waiting Period" of, 182–83; Western Wall and, 200–202

Soviet Union: and arming of Arabs, 211, 218, 220, 329; CIA's 1967 assessment of, 183–84; CIA's 1973 assessment of, 232–33; 1973 evacuation from Egypt and Syria by, 225, 226–28, 235, 236; false intelligence report and, 177; and 1956 nuclear threat to Israel, 163; Lebanon War and, 283; prior to Yom Kippur War, 216; and 1973 superpower crisis, 257–58

Stern Gang, 81, 108

Straits of Tiran: Egypt's 1956 blockade of, 154; Egypt's 1967 blockade of, 179; opening to Israel of, 160, 164, 165; Sinai Campaign and, 160–61, 323, 327, 329; Six-Day War and, 180, 184, 186